THE BUILD-IT-YOURSELF FURNITURE CATALOG

THE BUILD-IT-YOURSELF FURNITURE CATALOG

Franklynn Peterson

Prentice-Hall, Inc.
Englewood Cliffs, New Jersey

The Build-It-Yourself Furniture Catalog
by Franklynn Peterson

Line drawings by Jack Hearne

Printed in the United States of America

Prentice-Hall International, Inc., London
Prentice-Hall of Australia, Pty. Ltd., Sydney
Prentice-Hall of Canada, Ltd., Toronto
Prentice-Hall of India Private Ltd., New Delhi
Prentice-Hall of Japan, Inc., Tokyo
Prentice-Hall of Southeast Asia Pte. Ltd., Singapore

10 9 8 7 6 5 4 3 2 1

Library of Congress Cataloging in Publication Data

Peterson, Franklynn.
   The build-it-yourself furniture catalog.

   Includes index.
   1. Furniture making—Amateurs' manuals. I. Title.
TT195.P47   684.1'04   76-6567
ISBN 0-13-085910-9

Dedicated to the
Memory of Dan Morris

CONTENTS

II HEADBOARDS

III SMALL TABLES

IV KITCHEN AND DINING ROOM TABLES

V DESKS

VI SHELVES

VII CHAIRS

VIII THE PLAYROOM

THE BUILD-IT-YOURSELF FURNITURE CATALOG

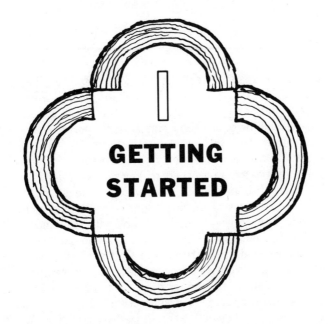

I

GETTING STARTED

1.   Who? How? Why? When? Where? How Much?

If you don't save more than the price of this book when you build your first practical piece of furniture, you ought to write me a nasty letter. This book is intended to save you money the way my furniture-building antics have saved me a bundle. And it'll help you win back some of that self-confidence which the guys on Madison Avenue have deliberately knocked out of you.

You *can* do things for yourself! And you don't need expensive tools or years of woodworking training.

The Pilgrims didn't bring a woodworking shop with them, and the Indians didn't have one waiting for them. But have you ever admired the fantastic, rugged, and beautiful Early American furniture they and their offspring turned out? They did it by hand, too, and they didn't have time to construct fancy joints and elaborate, do-nothing doodads. Neither do I.

When I move into a new home or shuffle stuff around in an old one and decide to get a new table, I want it yesterday. But I'm vain enough to want it to look like I spent plenty to buy it. So I've puttered with lots of furniture-building techniques, developed some myself, amended others. And the ones that work best I've put into this book.

I'm a firm believer in that old cliché about a picture being worth a thousand words. (With inflation, it's probably worth more.) I'll bet you could build most of the furniture shown here without knowing how to read, assuming you can "read" the pictures and sketches.

1

First of all, do read through the first four chapters. They're not long, and they do give you lots of important general information about what kind of wood to buy, how to buy it, what to do with the stuff—even how to use some simple hand tools in case nobody ever showed you before.

Chapter 4 is a real winner for you. One reason furniture projects don't always live up to their maker's expectations has to do with how the job is finished. That's also how furniture factories are able to ship a lot of shoddy items with elegant price tags —they know how to cover up their work with the kind of finish people like. Armed with Chapter 4, you can do likewise.

When you're ready to start on your first project, don't bite off more than you and your family can chew. Every project in this epic book is rated as to how easy or how hard it might be to tackle. The ratings are pretty subjective, of course, but they should help you decide what to try. If you're a novice at furniture building, start out with an easy job which can be finished in an evening or a weekend. Once you get the feel of the tools and the wood, then move on to something bigger and better.

After you've picked out a project that appeals to you (or to your spouse), read the whole chapter first. Secondly, assemble all the needed tools and materials in advance. Otherwise you might end up holding three long boards in place only to discover you need a fourth short one to complete the job.

I'm assuming you don't have a big, beautiful, well-equipped woodworking shop at home (although people who do will also find plenty in this book to intrigue them). But pick an uncluttered place to work. Chapter 3 will show you *how* to saw and nail or screw boards. *Where* to do this might be the back yard or basement. If that's out of the question, spread some old newspapers on the floor of one room and work there. But if the Smiths are coming over to play poker tomorrow night, better not start a two-night project in the living room. Each time you have to move an unfinished project somewhere else, you risk losing parts and enthusiasm.

By all means, let the kids help. We're rapidly becoming a nation of klutzes because parents want their kids to walk around looking like Mr. or Ms. Clean all day. If they get in your way while you're finishing a spanking new French Provincial table, buy them a small hammer and saw, set them in a corner with some of your scrap lumber, and let them build something on their own.

Never forget that you're the boss! *You're* the one who's going to sit on the chair you build, eat off the table you design, sleep near the headboard you build. If you think it would look better or serve you better with a longer *this* or shorter *that*, make it longer or shorter.

There just isn't any definitively "proper" way for furniture to look. Even those period pieces—French Provincial, Colonial, Early Italian, and so forth—are only figments of some furniture peddlers' imaginations. George Washington and Thomas Jefferson had differing ideas in how they wanted their homes to look, but all the furniture of their era is now labeled "Colonial."

A piece of furniture should be as personal as your watch, your hat, or your favorite slippers. Make it that way. You don't have to pay attention to the bill of goods some hotshot furniture peddler sold the Joneses next door.

Now that formalities are out of the way, let's start to build some furniture.

2. Material Wisdom

In the next few minutes you're apt to lose plenty of misconceptions and fears about lumber and lumberyards. With just a wee bit of book learning it's quite easy to make sense out of lumber sizes, grades, and descriptions.

We don't have to cover every imaginable type of wood because you're not likely to find a dealer who carries more than a couple grades of most kinds anyway. So all you have to wrestle with briefly is how that beautiful tree becomes pieces of beautiful wood for you to turn into some beautiful furniture.

§1. Lumber's Numbers

If the tree is simply sliced into 1-inch or 2-inch pieces, we call that *lumber* or *boards*. It's one of the cheapest forms of wood, but not always the strongest.

Since pine trees are tall but seldom very wide, it's hard to buy pine boards wider than 12 inches. The 2-, 4-, 6-, and 8-inch sizes are the most common and therefore the cheapest. You'll almost never find pine in odd-numbered sizes such as 5, 7, 9, or 11.

Hardwoods such as ash, walnut, oak, maple, and mahogany are cut more carefully and are more expensive. Here you do find odd-numbered sizes. And since hardwood trees are generally

4

wider than pine, you'll often be able to buy boards wider than 12 inches.

Pine or hardwood, most boards used for furniture and most other common applications are nominally 1 inch thick. For heftier jobs you can buy boards which are 2 or more inches thick.

There are also standard lengths of boards. The 8-, 10-, and 12-foot lengths are the most common. Some places handle 6-foot lengths as well as 14- or 16-footers.

There's a catch to these easy measurements, however. What lumber dealers call a 1-inch board isn't actually 1 inch thick. It's about 3/4 of an inch. Likewise, what we call a 4-inch-wide board is really closer to 3-3/4 or even 3-1/2 inches wide.

All of these measurements are based on dimensions at the sawmill, where the noble tree is sliced into long pieces. The saw that does the slicing is fast but rough. After the sawmill, rough boards go through a plane or sander which takes away the roughness, but also removes about 1/4 inch of wood in every direction.

For very accurate work, don't trust my 1/4 inch figure. Measure the real size of your boards carefully.

If you're building a set of shelves entirely from 1-by-8-inch lumber, you can overlook the 1/4 inch discrepancy. But as soon as you start to build or design wooden furniture which uses all three dimensions—width, length, and thickness—you may have to account for the missing 1/4 inch or so.

The next chapter shows how to measure accurately. Figure I-1 makes graphic sense out of the lumber-numbers game. Once you've memorized the order in which lumberyard workers are

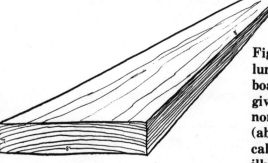

1″ × 6″ − 8′
3/4″ × 5 3/4″ − 7′ 11 3/4″

Figure I-1. When you walk into a lumberyard, here's how you call for a board of whatever size you need. First give the thickness, in this case 1 inch nominally. Second, give the width (about 6 inches in this example). Then call out the length, an 8-footer in our illustration. The real size of boards differs from what pros call trade size. The bottom line shows that this 1-by-6-inch board is actually almost a quarter inch smaller in thickness and width

used to hearing the dimensions, you can walk into their hallowed halls and sound like a pro instead of a scared novice.

First call out the thickness. Then the width. Boards 2 inches thick and 4 inches wide are usually called 2 by 4's. Same goes for lumber only an inch thick. A 1-inch board 6 inches wide would be known to lumber dealers as a 1 by 6.

When writing lumber sizes on paper, the word by becomes the symbol x. You jot down "2 × 4" although you'd *say* 2 by 4.

In case you had trouble with grade-school math, the ′ mark means *foot* or *feet* and the ″ mark means *inch* or *inches*. Therefore if you encounter 2″, that means 2 inches. And 7′ means 7 feet. Getting more complicated, 3′4″ translates into 3 feet and 4 inches.

You're now ready to call confidently for some 1 × 6's in a lumberyard, but you'll also have to specify the preferred length. If you want a board 10 feet long, say, "I need five 1 by 6's, 10 feet long." Or, "I'd like half a dozen pieces of 2 by 4's, 8 feet long."

First write down or call out the *number of pieces*. Second, give the *thickness and width*. Finally, name the *length*.

The length you buy at a lumberyard doesn't always exactly match the length you plan to use in some project. First of all, the lengths are almost always stocked by even numbers such as 6 feet, 8 feet, 10 feet, and 12 feet.

With few exceptions, there's no particular economy to buying longer or shorter lengths. A 10-foot board and a 12-footer should cost about the same per running foot. However, if you're making shelves about 5 feet wide, you'd waste 2 feet out of every 12-foot board, but zero feet out of every 10-footer. In that case you'd be wasting money if you bought 12-footers.

Most of the projects in this book are laid out so they'll fit on standard-sized boards with minimum waste. If you make sketches for your own original furniture designs, keep in mind what's available on lumberyard shelves.

You'll win few friends at lumberyards or do-it-yourself centers by asking for boards of a dozen different widths and lengths. You can buy a can of this and a box of that at supermarkets because you pick out the merchandise yourself. But at lumberyards, where someone does the picking for you, try to keep variety to a minimum.

The lumberyards you're likely to be dealing with are set up to service small builders who buy a pickup truck full of only a few sizes. The yard hand might get downright testy if you buy only one piece each of twenty-seven different kinds of lumber. When provoked, he's apt to slip you some pretty undesirable pieces of wood.

§2. Pine Boards

When most people hear you talk about lumber, they assume you mean *pine boards*. There are several different grades of lumber quality, even of pine boards. You'll find maybe two of them at most local lumber dealers.

Common pine boards are the cheapest. They're solid enough for major construction work and suitable for most shelves you plan to build. You can even use common-grade boards for projects you intend to paint.

If you plan to have a natural-wood finish on a pine desk, table, or other project, you should buy what's called *number-one* (written "#1") or *clear* grade. This product shouldn't have any loose knots or other defects found in common grade. Clear pine should be stronger and look better than common, and the grain should be finer and more regular.

Ironically, much early Colonial furniture was originally made from common pine. If you want to capture that feel, you'll be better off to specify common pine. The extra knots and coarser grain look more like real pine to the eye of the novice.

Common or clear, beware of *green lumber*. Like green apples, green lumber can make you sick. It's hard to saw and doesn't sand well. Paint, stain, and finishes don't stick well to it. As it dries, it shrinks and may pull away from other boards in a piece of furniture.

Green lumber simply hasn't been dried out properly. It's been rushed to the market too soon after cutting. You can spot green lumber by grabbing hold of it; it actually feels damp. Sawdust clings tenaciously to green lumber. You can't blow it off.

Lumberyards know the problems builders have with green lumber. If they have some, they'll shove it off on strangers and unsophisticated buyers. So when you order lumber, add these few extra words: "Please make sure it's nice and dry!"

§3. Hardwood

Not all boards are pine, which is a relatively soft wood. Large lumberyards and specialty outlets stock various hardwoods too. Most common among these are walnut, oak, maple, mahogany, and birch.

Birch wood just barely qualifies as a *hard* wood. Even though it lacks the deep tones and hard surface common to most other hardwoods, many people enjoy its soft, subtle grain.

Some yards stock *ash*. If you simply walk in any say, "Gimme some hardwood, please," the yard hand could give you ash and get away with it. Ash is plenty hard, but not considered a very pretty wood. It's reserved for use where strength is important but beauty isn't, such as on the concealed frames inside uphol-stered furniture.

Figures I-2 to I-10 will give you a rough idea what various kinds of hardwoods and pine look like. No two boards are exactly alike, so you're going to have to look at each purchase individu-ally. That's what makes buying wood so much fun.

The makers of vinyl and Formica-type plastics copy typical hardwood color and grain. The photos can also help you decide on those materials.

You can enjoy many advantages from working with genuine hardwood. It's a tougher wood in general, so you'll end up with a stronger piece of furniture if the basic design and your handi-work utilize the material's inherent strength. Once it is well

Figure I-2. Pine: soft wood but striking, obvious grain

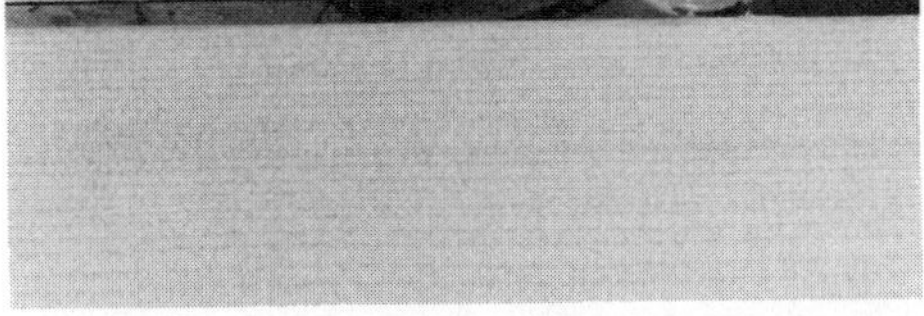

Figure I-3. Birch: somewhat hard but light, subtle grain pattern

Figure I-4. Teak: exotic, subtly grained, and expensive if you buy the real thing

Figure I-5. Mahogany: rugged-grained, the wood comes in a veritable rainbow of hues

Figure I-6. Oak: a highly distinctive grain pattern

Figure I-7. Maple: hard to find these days, but colorful and brightly grained

Figure I-8. Walnut: a rare wood native to the U.S.A. Subtle but distinctive grain and coloration

Figure I-9. Rosewood: generally imported from Brazil, has a reddish hue and a very obvious, flashy grain

Figure I-10. Fir Plywood: a soft veneer-type wood product with a wild and unruly grain pattern

sanded and finished carefully, genuine hardwood furniture looks superior to most other materials.

Hardwood does have disadvantages. It's more expensive than pine, and at times more expensive than good plywood.

Hardwood is tougher to saw and requires more time to sand. Nails will bend if you try to pound them into hardwood in the usual lackadaisical way.

Hardwood also weighs more than comparable sizes of softwood or plywood. I once bought enough mahogany boards to build a huge headboard and chest of drawers. Without thinking about the weight, I tossed the lumber on top of the old Dodge Dart, and the springs were compressed as far as they could go. That meant I had to make two trips with the lumber—but you should see how that finished mahogany looks.

Hardwood, like pine, comes in several different quality grades. You'll be lucky to find hardwood of any quality in many lumber outlets. Be thankful for what you can find.

§4. Plywood

So far we've been talking about boards, those long, thin slices of tree. If the sawmill uses a different kind of blade, it can peel off an extremely thin, continuous *veneer* of wood. Most veneers are from 1/16 to 1/8 inch thick.

Thin veneers of wood are understandably quite fragile. They're also hard to work with by themselves. However, modern science figured out how to glue several layers of veneers into a single, very solid, very strong piece of wood known as *plywood*.

Plywood is sold in standard sheets almost always 4 feet by 8 feet. Sometimes you can buy them 4 feet by 10 feet or even 4 feet by 7 feet, but don't count on finding such odd sizes.

Some lumberyards and most do-it-yourself centers will cut up the large 4-by-8-foot sheets and sell you smaller pieces. Many outlets won't sell you less than a 4-by-4-foot piece.

Materials, drawings, and lists in this book are designed to use plywood economically. For your own sketches and designs, you'd do well to follow suit or you'll end up with a big closet full of odd-sized pieces of spare plywood.

Plywood comes in four common thicknesses: 1/4, 3/8, 1/2, and 3/4 inch. Generally the 1/4 inch size is used for covering over large, well-supported areas. It is not strong enough or rigid enough to hold much of a load.

The 3/8 inch plywood starts to have some internal strength. It can be used for very small shelves, small doors, and sliding doors. You can glue two pieces together to form fancy cabinet doors.

There's plenty of strength in 1/2 inch plywood. It's suitable for most furniture applications and larger doors.

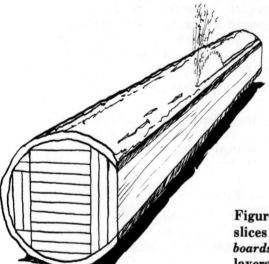

Figure I-11. If a tree is cut into long slices an inch or two thick, it becomes *boards*. But if the saw strips away thin layers of wood as the tree is spun around, the resulting veneers are glued together into *plywood* or *veneer wood*

The 1/2 inch size is substantially cheaper than 3/4 inch thick plywood, and is specified throughout most of this book. If, after you've tackled a project or two, you find that you don't have enough patience or vision to drive nails into 1/2 inch plywood without splitting it or having nails stick out in odd places, you'd better switch to 3/4 inch. That extra 1/4 inch costs more, but it's also darned near impossible to split with nails no matter how carelessly they're aimed.

You'll find 3/4 inch plywood called for in this book only where strength is very important. For example, the top of a large desk or table has to remain rigid and straight under strain and requires 3/4 inch plywood despite the higher cost. But you'll still save plenty of money building such a project yourself.

Plywood has different quality ratings: interior and exterior, smooth and rough, good 1 side and good 2 sides.

"Good 1 side" and "good 2 sides" refer to whether the surface of the plywood is unblemished on both sides or only on one. When the "Great American Plywood Machine" saws, glues, and sands thousands of sheets of plywood, knots and other surface blemishes show up on the outside of the plywood. Living, breathing, human operators go over sheets of the best plywood to look for the surface irregularities and repair them. If they fix both sides of a sheet, it's labeled good 2 sides. If only one side of the sheet gets the cosmetic treatment, it's labeled good 1 side.

Surprisingly, the good-1-side grade is adequate for most applications. As you might expect, it's less expensive. Only when both sides of your furniture project will be seen do you have to invest in the good-2-sides grade.

Regardless of side grade, the entire plywood sheet is usually sent through a sander. Unlike boards, however, plywood measurements are based on finished size. A sheet of plywood sold as 1/2 inch thick is as close to 1/2 inch as most rulers can measure.

You'll almost never find a use for rough-grade plywood unless you're really trying to save a buck and plan to cover your project with vinyl, fabric, or Formica. Most places stock only smooth grades. One or two kinds of unsanded plywood in an exterior grade used for sheathing the sides of new buildings may be available.

Unless you're building outdoor furniture or cabinets for a steamy bathroom, stick to the interior grade. The exterior grade uses waterproof glue and costs a bit more. It's also harder to buy in styles useful for furniture projects. However, if you get a good deal on some exterior grade, it'll work just dandy for interior furniture.

The plywood we've been discussing is often called fir plywood in the trade. Most of it does come from fir trees. Some common grades of plywood are made from white pine, sugar pine, or similar species; they cost about the same as fir plywood and have a similar appearance and workability. So don't worry whether you're getting fir or pine plywood. Other kinds of plywood are available, but cost substantially more than the common grades.

§5. Hardwood Plywood

Instead of making plywood out of fir or pine through and through, a softwood core can be embellished with an outer veneer of hardwood on one or both sides. This gives you the strength of plywood and the beauty of hardwood without having to work with the relatively narrow hardwood boards available.

When you're considering using expensive hardwoods, substituting veneered plywood will save you some money. Regardless of relative cost, if you want to cover a large surface with genuine hardwood, you can't do it unless you have a shop equipped with enough tools to install veneers yourself. In this case, veneered plywood is a construction aid.

Don't expect to walk into just any lumber outlet and find hardwood-veneered plywood in dozens of varieties. In fact, you'll be lucky to find any except in lumberyards catering to the furniture trade.

§6. Other Woodsy Stuff

After processing trees, lumber manufacturers end up with huge piles of chips and sawdust. The chips get squeezed together with glue to make *chipboard*. Sawdust and plastic binders get squeezed into *hardboard*, which most retailers refer to by one of its trade names—Masonite.

Both products are among the cheapest building materials available, but cause a lot of headaches for the user. First of all, they're available only in large sheets, usually 4 by 8 feet. Lumberyards aren't as willing to sell part sheets as they do with plywood.

Chipboard generally is about 5/8″ thick. Other thicknesses are hard to find.

Masonite comes in sundry sizes. The most popular, and therefore the easiest to find in most outlets, are 1/8 inch and 1/4 inch thicknesses.

Figure I-12. Chipboard, with its cool, institutional appearance, is made from wood scraps reduced to chips and then pressed, sealed, and cut. It's a cheap product, but a bit hard to work with

Chipboard has a super-clean, institutional sort of surface to it. In a few cases, that look might be just what you want. It can be cute in children's furniture. Generally, however, chipboard gets covered over with paint or vinyl.

Traditional nail or screw construction methods don't work well on chipboard. The stuff is so brittle that you have to drill holes first, and even then most builders prefer to use sheet-metal screws. The best way of working with chipboard is to hold it in place with a metal frame. Several companies offer framing materials through lumber and hardware outlets.

Hardboard has a very solid surface, but little internal strength. Its main use in and around furniture is as a backing for sets of shelves or drawers. Most hardboard is smooth on one side, textured on the other. If adjacent wooden parts are dark, then either the smooth or textured dark brown hardboard surface will blend in when used as a backing.

Figure I-13. The shiny side of pressed board or Masonite. It's hard to paint, but blends in well with some furniture

Figure I-14. The rough side of Masonite looks nice as a backing for many furniture projects finished in natural wood

Hardboard is easy to paint on its textured side—assuming you like the texture. Most painters complain that the shiny side is too shiny to paint well unless you sand it thoroughly first.

§7. Prefab Furniture Parts

A couple of slightly unorthodox materials get worked into the furniture you'll be making with the help of this book. For one, a brand new door makes a dandy, handy, and quickly made top for tables and desks. The variety known as a *hollow-core door* is both inexpensive and adaptable.

The hollow-core door is generally constructed from two layers of veneer separated by a core of plastic or wooden matrix designs. Sometimes even a cardboard matrix is used to separate the veneers. The door's edges are plugged with common wood.

Because doors made in this fashion are hollow, you can't just saw off a piece and proceed merrily with the construction. The hollow will show. If you can't find a door that fits almost exactly the dimensions you've chosen, you'll have to saw the door to size and then plug up the exposed insides with wood of your own. It's an easy enough job, but most large do-it-yourself centers will do it for you and charge only a very nominal fee. While you're at it, have them plug up the end of the "waste" piece too. That often makes a catchy top for a small coffee table.

Hollow-core doors come in so many sizes that it's foolish even to list standard dimensions here. In the end, the precise size you choose will no doubt depend upon what's on sale at special prices.

The least expensive doors are made with birch veneer. You can use the veneer that way, stain it to a richer hue, or cover it completely with Formica or other plastics. Often, however, you can find reasonably priced doors made from veneers of other hardwoods. So look around to see what turns you on.

Also in the prefab area, unfinished furniture drawers can be worked into desks, bureaus, and other elaborate furniture projects. Most towns of any size have at least one outlet that sells unfinished furniture. You don't want to buy a whole unfinished desk, chest, bureau, or anything else but a set of drawers. Only drawers! Each of the furniture projects later on discusses the ideal sizes and shapes to look for.

Basically there are three kinds of unfinished furniture construction methods in use. One employs cheap pine and cheap nails. Another uses cheap chipboard and staples. (Ironically, the staples in chipboard often hold better than nails in pine.) Unfortunately the third method, using good woods and good construction, is usually reserved for larger completed pieces of unfinished furniture.

As with most things today, you get about what you pay for. Buy the best drawers you feel you want to include in the furniture you're building. If you're a rank novice at this sort of thing, whatever kind of construction you find will be better than you could turn out, unless you have a knack for accurate measurement and patient assembly. But this book does show how to build your own drawers. As you progress at building furniture, you'll want to make your own drawers too.

§8. Spindles, Carvings, Moldings, and Such

Maybe you've been amazed at some of the elaborate carvings worked into furniture on display in the stores downtown. "How'd anybody have enough patience to do all that work by hand at that price?" you may have asked. More than likely, nobody did. Some of the same factories full of machines that spin hunks of wood into spindles or mold synthetic wood products into "carvings" offer these products in hardware and department stores to you too. Until now, maybe you just never knew the secret.

Spindles are long, skinny wood turnings used in chairs, bookcases, coffee tables, and similar wooden furniture. The few companies that retail spindles give them elaborate-sounding names. Figure I-15 shows some of the more popular styles.

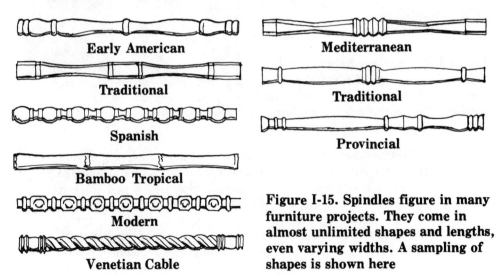

Early American

Mediterranean

Traditional

Traditional

Spanish

Provincial

Bamboo Tropical

Modern

Venetian Cable

Figure I-15. Spindles figure in many furniture projects. They come in almost unlimited shapes and lengths, even varying widths. A sampling of shapes is shown here

You may be surprised at the price of individual spindles. For a small bit of wood, the price tag seems high. But consider how few of them furniture projects require and how many dollars it would take to buy a comparable piece of furniture. In that light, they seem more reasonably priced.

Carvings are mass-produced too, but their price is admittedly dear. They're flat, ornate, thin three-dimensional devices which add richness to fronts and sides of otherwise simple furniture. Just a small sampling of the dozens of variations are shown in Figure I-16. Now that you know what they look like, you'll recognize many of these same carvings incorporated into both low-priced and expensive furniture downtown.

Figure I-16. Carvings help decorate many of our pieces of furniture. They come in dozens of varieties of sizes and patterns. Just a few are shown here

Manufacturers give exotic names to various carving styles. You don't have to worry too much whether a Spanish-named carving is really Spanish or even looks Spanish. If *you* think it goes with a French-style cocktail table you're making, use it.

There are a couple of ways to get around the cost of carvings sold as carvings. One is to go shopping in an art and novelty store. They often have plaques and wall hangings made of plastic or plaster which resemble molded wood carvings. Glue some of them onto the wood where a carving should go and you're in business, unless you expect to kick the furniture a lot.

Many hobby stores offer plastic molds in styles and shapes just like the carvings pictured here. They offer plenty of materials, generally plastics or plasters from which you can make your own molded carvings. If you want to get a wooden product that you can stain to match the natural woods in the furniture you're building, substitute plastic wood for the plaster or plastic molding compounds. Force it into the mold good and tight, give it plenty of time to dry, and you can turn out all the moldings you want for a fraction of what you'd pay for the ready-mades.

There's yet another way to avoid the high price of carvings. Novelty, department, paint, and hardware stores sell plastic wall coverings or door ornaments. They're designed to look like hand-carved wooden creations. If you or your family aren't too hard on furniture, the plastic might work for you. Styles are limited and so are sizes, but if one of them works for you, look at how much you can save without sacrificing appearance. One particularly advantageous use for plastic "carvings" is on doors for cabinets. We'll talk more about doors in later chapters.

§9. Traveling With Wood

Before dropping the subject of materials for building furniture, let's talk about how you get your purchase home. Many lumber dealers won't deliver the small quantities you'll be buying. However, even sheets of plywood can be carried safely and conveniently on top of the family car. Some station-wagon designers had the uncommon good sense to make their carrying platforms four feet wide to accommodate panels and plywood.

On short trips with narrow boards, a 30-foot length of rope is about all you need to secure your load. Spread an old blanket, sheet, or rug across the top of your car to protect the paint. Then lay the boards down as evenly as possible. Open any car doors you want to use before the lumber is unloaded again. At the very least, you have to open the driver's door. On the other doors, roll down the windows an inch or two.

Wrap your rope around the lumber and through the open back windows or doors. The rope makes a complete circle—over the top of the lumber, in the window or door, across the top of the passenger compartment inside your car, out the other window or door, and then up to the top of the lumber again. Repeat at the front seat next.

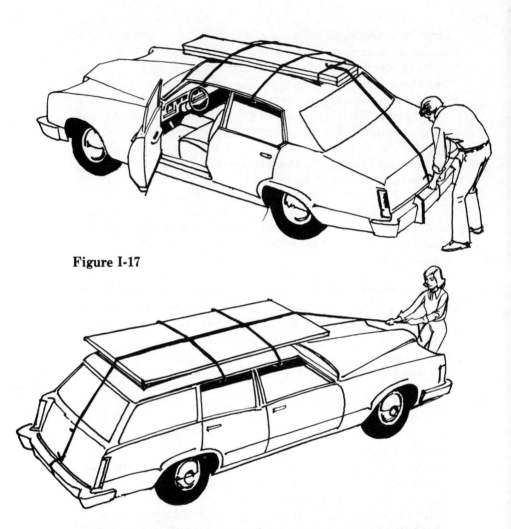

Figure I-17

If you're apt to make quick stops or if you're going a long distance, even with narrow boards you should secure the back of the lumber in addition to the double straps you already tied through the windows or doors. That will keep the lumber from sliding forward in case you hit the brakes hard. (It won't slide *backwards* unless you hit the gas pedal very hard.)

To tie down the back of your lumber, wrap a rope around it near the rear end and tie the rope in place. Run the long, loose end of your rope down below the rear bumper. You'll have to get down on your hands and knees in order to find some spot under the car where you can tie that end of the rope.

As you drive along, wind likes to lift up the front of big sheets on top of your car. When you're traveling with 4-by-8-foot sheets of plywood, hardboard, chipboard, or similar materials, your car will feel like a kite unless you add an extra rope to the front. So find a spot under your front bumper where you can tie one end of a rope. Toss the other end over the plywood sheets toward your rear bumper. Tie that end under the rear bumper, but first pull the rope as tight as you can. Thin sheets of hardboard or plywood may actually start to bend. Let them. Unless you take weeks to get home, the wood will straighten right out as soon as you untie the ropes.

When you unload full sheets of plywood or paneling on a windy day, get help. One person should hold each end of the sheet. And keep the sheet slanted so the wind blows underneath or over the top. Otherwise you'll end up blowing down Main Street like Mary Poppins.

3.   Methods Out of Madness

Nails, screws, bolts, and other handy fastening devices which will hold your furniture together are no harder to understand than lumber. All you need is a list of names, a few paragraphs about their function, and maybe a chart or two which show common sizes you'll find at hardware stores.

§10. Nails

A nail is by far the fastest way to fasten two pieces of wood together. To make a strong joint you need several nails, but nails don't always make a strong enough bond for all purposes.

There are two basic types of nails you're likely to meet: *common nails* and *finishing nails*. Sometimes the word *brad* is used instead of finishing nail. There are subtle distinctions between the brad and the finishing nail, but you don't have to worry about the difference.

The common nail has a big, common-looking head. It drives into wood easily and holds tightly once it's in place. But having all those big shiny heads poking out of soft, darkly grained wood would spoil the appearance of fine furniture.

Finishing nails are slender and have tiny heads. That makes them a bit touchier to pound. But when you're finished, the head can be camouflaged very easily.

STATISTICS FOR FINISHING NAILS

Name	Length in inches	Approx. number in one pound
16d	3-1/4	90
12d	3-1/4	113
10d	3	121
9d	2-3/4	172
8d	2-1/2	189
7d	2-1/4	238
6d	2	309
5d	1-3/4	500
4d	1-1/2	584
3d	1-1/4	807
2d	1	1,351

SMALLER NAILS ARE SOLD BY REAL SIZE AND GENERALLY IN ONE-OUNCE PACKAGES

7/8	100
3/4	135
5/8	165
1/2	250
3/8	285

The above charts show the actual size of popular finishing nails and what the trade calls them. The *penny* is the unit of size for nails, although these days manufacturers are finally adding the size in inches to many boxes.

The abbreviation for *penny* is *d*, which is the English abbreviation. If you see 8d on a box of nails, that means 8-penny nails. They're about 2-1/2 inches long. And nails are sold by the pound, not by the piece. A pound of big nails, like 8d, would represent only a few dozen, whereas a pound of small ones, like 2d, would contain over one hundred. The chart provides a rough idea of how many nails you'll get in every pound.

Select a nail about twice as long as your wood is wide. In other words, if you're working with 1/2 inch lumber, try to use 1 inch nails. Longer would be better still. If you were nailing a 1 inch board onto a 2 inch thick board, you could easily use the 2-1/2 inch long 8d nails. But if you have to nail a 1-1/2 inch board onto another 1-1/2 inch board, the 1 inch nails might go through the other side. In that case, you'd have to choose 7/8 inch nails. That's why nails are available in so many sizes.

Until now you probably thought that all you needed to hammer a nail was a hammer. Now you're going to add a *nail set* to the tool list. Here's why.

Pound a finishing nail with your hammer until its head is almost level with the wood. Then put a nail set onto the head and hit that with your hammer. There's a dent in the head of finishing nails and brads so the nail set won't slip.

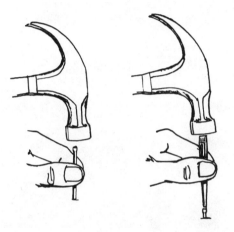

Figure I-18. How to finish off a finishing nail. First hammer it almost all the way in. Stop short of the wood, however, so your hammer doesn't damage the surface of your wood. Set a *nail set* on top of the nail head and hammer it until the head of your nail is just beneath the surface of the wood

If you plan to cover your furniture with vinyl, Formica, or any similar product, you can stop hammering when the head is exactly flush with the wood. If you plan to end up with a natural-wood finish, then pound the nail set until the nail head is 1/16 inch or even 1/8 inch below the surface of your wood.

§11. Hiding Nail Holes

There are several ways to camouflage nail holes. First, after all of your nails have been pounded into place, go back and fill each of the holes with wood dough, most often known by one of its trade names, Plastic Wood. Squeeze it into the nail hole carefully and level it off with a flat tool such as a putty knife, razor blade, jackknife, etc.

When Plastic Wood is thoroughly, *thoroughly* dry, you can start the overall sanding job on your furniture. The sanding will smooth out almost all evidence of the nails. In pine boards, properly plugged nail holes will look like no more than tiny knots in the wood.

If you're using dark-colored hardwood or hardwood plywood, the light, neutral color of ordinary Plastic Wood won't blend in so well. You can buy various brands of wood dough with color added. Theoretically these products will blend with walnut, oak, or other popular hardwoods. But before you assume that the theory works for your practical project, test it on one or two nail holes. Chances are it won't work. If it does, consider yourself lucky.

Even on dark hardwoods you will probably have to plug your nail holes with ordinary neutral wood dough. After sanding your project thoroughly, take a very tiny artist's brush and stain the plugged nail holes. If you're working on dark walnut wood, for

Figure I-19. Here's how to plug up the nail holes (or screw holes) when your furniture has been assembled. Buy one of the appropriate products

Figure I-20. Shove Plastic Wood into a nail or screw hole with your fingers or putty knife. Even a screwdriver will do.

Figure I-21. Sandpaper the dried Plastic Wood. On pine, birch, or plywood, the hole almost vanishes. On darker woods you'll have to color the Plastic Wood with a product such as a scratch remover

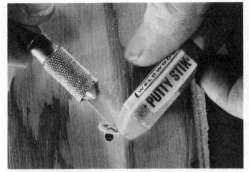 

Figure I-22. With putty sticks, peel off a bit of the product with a small knife. Shove the putty into the hole and smooth it off. . .

Figure I-23. . . . and the hole is gone, assuming you were able to select a putty color to match your wood

example, buy a tiny can of walnut oil stain. Brush it carefully onto just a few nail holes at first. Let the stain dry for fifteen minutes (or whatever time the directions call for), then rub off excess stain with a soft cloth. Rubbing also helps blend the color of the nail plug with the rest of your wood.

Assuming this technique works on your test spots, you can use it on all of the other nail holes. If not, change the technique a bit and try again.

If your nail spot comes out too dark in the test, either dilute the stain with turpentine (or any other solvent the directions mention) or let the stain dry a shorter time before you rub it. If the test proves to be too light, there are at least two solutions. You can let the stain dry for more than fifteen minutes and then rub it very gently. Or you can give the nail holes a second or a third treatment with the same oil stain.

There's yet another way to camouflage nail holes. Many paint or wallpaper stores sell what are often called *putty sticks*, although they're not really putty at all. They're sticks of waxy, plastic like stuff colored to match various types of natural hardwoods. Most of them are shaped somewhat like giant crayons.

If you find a putty stick that matches your own wood finish rather closely, let nail holes go until almost the end. Just before the final several coats of varnish or lacquer, plug the nail holes with the putty stick. Make sure the final surface is very smooth. Then add the several final layers of wood finish. The holes can't be seen unless you cheat and point them out to relatives or friends who gather around to admire your handiwork.

§12. Screws

Screws take more time to use than nails, but you generally end up with a tougher joint. You should choose a screw about twice as long as your boards are thick.

Screws have their own distinct numbering system. The diameter of a screw is indicated by a simple number such as 4, 6, or 10. The larger the number, the larger the diameter. A screw's length is signified simply by its actual length from point to head, the head itself not included.

One very common screw is known in the trade as 1-1/2 × 10. It's good for holding 1-inch pine boards together. (Boards, as you learned in Chapter 2, are closer to 3/4 inch thick than a full 1 inch thick.)

For 1/4-inch plywood, a good size is 1/2 × 4 or 1/2 × 6. Use 3/4 × 4 or 3/4 × 6 for 3/8-inch plywood. On 1/2-inch plywood, 1 × 4 or 1 × 6 screws are satisfactory.

When you use 3/4-inch plywood, something close to 1-1/2 × 10 is called for. Pine boards are best screwed into place with 1-1/2 × 10 or 1-1/2 × 12. If you have clearance for them in your work, 1-3/4 × 10 are good too.

Don't worry about remembering all of these numbers. When you want to buy screws, simply turn back to this part of the book and jot down the appropriate sizes. Then head for the hardware store.

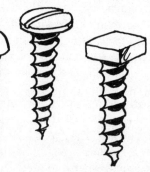

Figure I-24. Left to right: flat-head screw, round-head screw, oval-head screw, lag screw

There are several different kinds of heads on wood screws. Round, flat, oval, and lag heads are the most common. For woodwork, unless you want the screws to be big and obvious, actually a part of the furniture design, always use flat-head screws.

When using screws, it's almost imperative that you own a quarter-inch drill. They're inexpensive these days, and very handy. If you plan to build a large project which will take plenty of abuse, your investment in a reasonably priced drill should pay for itself by the time your first project is completed.

Here's how flat-head screws are used. First you should drill a pilot hole for every screw. Although some people skip this step in pine boards, it's not a good idea. Without a pilot hole you may as well use nails instead of screws. The results will be about equally strong.

In hardwood and most plywood you have little choice. You have to drill a pilot hole for screws.

The pilot hole permits the screws to twist into the wood with relative ease and without threatening to split the wood. A common wood screw exerts a tremendous mechanical force. If you simply knock it carelessly into place and twist on it, the threads can actually split some boards.

The easiest way to drill a pilot hole is with a set of drill accessories made specifically for this job. The accessory not only drills a *pilot hole* for the most popular screws in use, it also drills the *countersink hole* in the same operation.

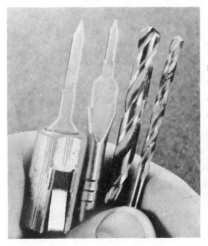

Figure I-25. When working with screws, drill a *pilot hole* so the screw turns easily into your wood. This is especially important in hardwood. To conceal the screw head a second hole, a much wider one than the pilot hole, is drilled just deeply enough to receive the screw head and a bit of Plastic Wood. You can accomplish this with drills of two different sizes, but it's easy to buy a set of countersink tools for your electric drill

The head on a flat-head screw fits neatly into a countersink hole, just as nails fit neatly into their own hole after you tap them down with a nail set. Be careful when you drill a countersink hole. Make sure the hole is wide and deep enough for the screw head to fit completely beneath the surface with a little room for plastic wood to cover the head. Don't make the countersink hole so deep that you actually weaken the piece of wood. In very narrow wood, such as 1/4- or 3/8-inch plywood, there is a very thin line between too little and too much countersink hole. And that's why nails are used almost exclusively with plywood.

Without a pilot hole-countersink accessory, here's what you do. Choose a pilot-hole drill that matches the size of the very tip of your chosen screw. Drill almost as deep a hole as your screw is long. Pick a drill for the countersink which is as big around as the head of your screw. Make the countersink hole deep enough to satisfy the requirements spelled out in the paragraph above.

Aside from the flat, oval, round, and lag screw-head types already mentioned, there are also *slotted* and *Phillips* types. The slotted screw heads take a common, straight screwdriver blade. The Phillips heads have an opening that resembles an X and requires a screwdriver blade also shaped like a three-dimensional X.

Most hardware stores stock only a limited variety of Phillips-head screws. If your store has a good selection they're worth using even if you have to buy a new screwdriver to accommodate them. With a Phillips head, your screwdriver is easier to keep under control.

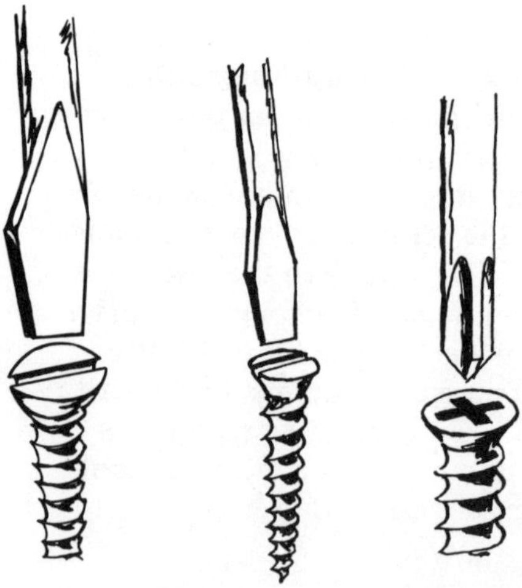

Figure I-26. The tip of your screwdriver should match closely the slot or slots in the head of your screws. Otherwise you risk damaging the slot and your project

Small screw slots require *small* slotted screwdrivers. And *large* slots require *large* slotted screwdrivers. The same goes for Phillips heads. Ideally the blade thickness on your screwdriver should match the slot thickness in your screws. Otherwise when you start twisting hard, the screwdriver will slip out of the slot and chew up the metal.

If you plan to tackle a project that involves several dozen screws, you'll probably be happy to know that for a pittance you can add an accessory to your electric drill which will twist screws into place within seconds. The variable-speed drills work best for turning in screws, but almost any electric drill will work if you're careful.

When you use a drill to turn in screws, protect the wood underneath unless you're planning to cover the project with vinyl or Formica. You're bound to slip at least once or twice, and without protection the screwdriver tip on your drill will gouge out a nasty scar.

A tin-can cover makes an adequate shield. Cut, poke, or drill a hole into the center of your cover. Then slip the hole over each screw *before* you twist it into place. That way if you slip, only the can cover gets scarred.

For screwing with an electric drill, you'll be especially happy with the Phillips-head variety. It was designed for use in automatic equipment.

After all of your screws have been turned into their countersink holes, plug the holes and camouflage them exactly as illustrated in the section on nails.

§13. Molly Screws

This peculiar bit of hardware (see Figure I-27) is like a self-contained nut and bolt with an accordion in between. A Molly Screw was designed to anchor shelves and equipment to walls and other areas where you can't reach around behind to thread a nut onto a bolt.

First you have to drill a hole just big enough for you to slip the Molly in (Figure I-28). Then shove the fastener all the way into the hole. Bang the exposed part of the Molly with a hammer or the flat of your hand so the two barbs dig into the surface of whatever material you're working with (Figure I-29).

When you start twisting the screw inside the Molly Screw, its collapsible arms are elbowed out against the inside of the wall. That anchors the device firmly in place (Figure I-30). Then you can use the screw to fasten whatever it is you want fastened.

Molly Screws have a couple of applications for furniture projects in this book. They provide a neat and solid way to hold various sets of shelves onto walls. And their big internal elbows provide a firm but gentle way of holding hollow-core doors into place when you use them on desks or tables.

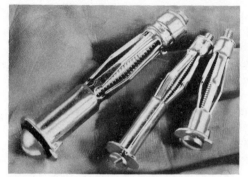

Figure I-27. Molly Screws

Figure I-28

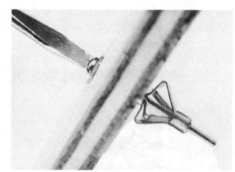

Figure I-29   Figure I-30

§14. Glue

Glue is one of the toughest wood fasteners of all. It can be more permanent and durable than nails or screws, but there's a hitch or two in that promise. Although wood glues are tough, most of them won't tolerate much motion after they've set. Glued joints aren't flexible enough to withstand a lot of bending and twisting.

When glues are first applied, they generally require a lot of pressure to create a strong, lasting joint. In other words, if you glue a table top to the table sides, you have to find some way to put a lot of weight on the top so it will bond firmly and permanently to the sides. That isn't always convenient to do.

Professional cabinetmakers have expensive sets of clamps which hold onto odd-shaped pieces of wood and squeeze them together while glue dries. It's unlikely you just happen to have such clamps in a family junk drawer, and it sure isn't economical for you to buy some. Here's a clever alternative.

We get the best of both worlds by using glue in combination with either nails or screws. The nails and screws are both easy to use, although alone neither is as tough as a well-made glued joint. But the nails and screws do serve as a clamp while the glue dries. In most cases they work every bit as well as a set of carpenter's clamps.

Screws or nails also provide a glued joint with some internal stiffness. That prevents the twisting or bending which might destroy the glue's grip on two pieces of wood. Almost every joint in this entire beautiful book relies on glue in combination with either nails or screws to make it as rugged as possible. This is a technique you'll probably want to carry over into furniture designs you'll sketch yourself.

To make a good joint, first fit the appropriate pieces of wood together so you know for sure they're cut right. Then drill one pilot hole and countersink hole, if you're using screws. After that first screw is in place you can drill the others, confident now that the wood won't slip out of place.

Squirt glue on all of the pieces of wood where they overlap. Even squirt a few drops of glue *into* the screw holes to hold more firmly onto the screws.

When you're sure everything fits well, cover the joint with glue and assemble it immediately. Then nail or screw it together firmly. Wipe away all of the excess glue which will get squeezed out of the joints. If you don't do it while the glue is wet, you'll have a heck of a mess to clean up later.

Put your work away while the glue sets. If you're continuously bending and twisting and hammering on a project while the glue is setting, the joints will never reach their full strength.

Some glues tell you on their label how much *set-up time* they can tolerate. That's simply the length of time, something like fifteen minutes or half an hour, during which you can disturb the glue after applying it. Following the set-up time, the glue starts hardening quickly.

In general, the faster the overall drying time, the less time you have to fool around during assembly. Glues strong enough to be used for furniture seldom take less than a few hours to dry.

There are three basic types of glue valuable to amateur furniture makers. Simplest of all is the white, sticky liquid glue which comes in plastic squeeze bottles. It is surprisingly tough, but some brands are tougher than others. Read the labels. Be sure you choose a glue that is specifically recommended for use on wood. Better yet, make sure the glue is *principally* for use on wood.

For projects that may get a lot of abuse, or for big projects in general, your best buy is a *powdered-resin* product. You mix it with water just before you're ready to start gluing. It takes longer to dry than the white liquids, but it also gives you more set-up time. Also, in the long run it's a bit cheaper and substantially tougher than the ready-to-squeeze brands.

The third glue suitable for home woodworking projects is *contact cement*. Many different companies market this product. Buy the best your local store has in stock.

Contact cement gets smeared onto both surfaces you want glued together. You should do the same with any other glue too, but with contact cement, the product is allowed to dry completely before you shove the two parts together.

After both surfaces of contact cement have dried, and after you shove them together, the surface areas bond together into an extremely tough glued joint. That's assuming, of course, that you bring the two surfaces together tightly enough. Like other glues, contact cement requires a certain amount of pressure before it forms a tough bond.

With flexible, thin materials, it's easy to make contact cement work well. Somehow it inevitably falls short of expectations when used on thicker pieces of wood.

Contact cement is best used on Formica and similar thin plastics. Because it grabs so well once the two glued layers are put together, you have to be very careful when contact cement is your chosen glue.

If at all possible, make one piece oversized. Then, in case the two are stuck together just a bit out of line, you can sand the oversized part to fit.

If working with oversized pieces isn't practical, line up the parts carefully while there's something between them such as waxed paper. Make sure you use several different pieces of waxed paper even if one long piece would cover the surfaces. Then when everything is in its proper place, hold one end very firmly while you slip a piece of waxed paper out from the other end. Where the waxed paper has been pulled out, a good firm push with your hand will stick the two contact-cement surfaces together permanently. Then you can pull the rest of the waxed paper out leisurely, content in the knowledge that your top and bottom are well lined up for life.

§15. Measuring Up to the Job

You'll never get pleasing results if you don't measure the parts accurately. The first secret to successful measuring is to forget

the words, ". . . and a little bit." If you haul out the old ruler, slap
it onto a piece of lumber, study the lines and sublines and sub-
sublines, then say, "*Hmmmmmm*, it's 4 inches and a little bit,"
your pieces will fit together the same way—a little bit!

The most useful single measuring device for furniture makers
like you is the combination square. It has a ruler, which should be
no shorter than 12 inches, and a handle which holds the ruler at
right angles (90 degrees) to the side of a board. Most of them can
be adjusted to produce an angle of 45 degrees too, the second-
most-useful angle in making furniture. Within reason, the bigger
the square, the more accurate your results will be.

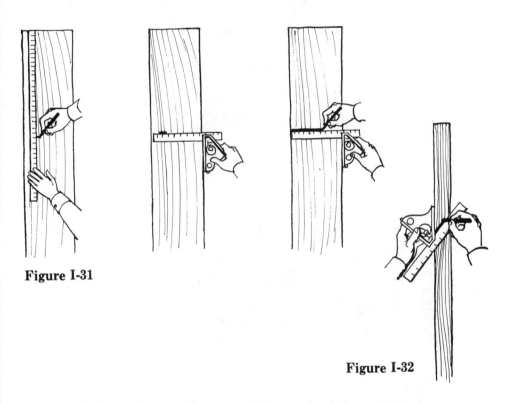

Figure I-31

Figure I-32

When working with boards which you want to measure accurately enough to insure tight-fitting joints, measure only one side
of each piece, assuming that the other edges are supposed to be
square. They are unless you've been told otherwise.

After measuring, make a single, short, clear pencil mark where
the line should go. Then lay the handle of your square along the

edge of the board so the ruler passes alongside the pencil mark. And draw the pencil line all the way across the width of your board.

Always rest your square's handle against the same edge of a board. Theoretically, both sides of a board should be parallel and therefore you should get square results by using either side. But when you're working with common lumber, never assume perfection. When you're working with plywood, however, you're safe to use any of the four factory-cut sides as a base for your square.

You're apt to forget which side of a board you used last time for the "square" side. Therefore, put an *X* mark on that side.

Aside from the square, there are plenty of other measuring devices around. Most of them work just fine for making furniture. A kid's school ruler, a dressmaker's tape measure, the carpenter's folding rule or windup steel tape, even the freebie yardstick all give accurate measurements if you use them accurately.

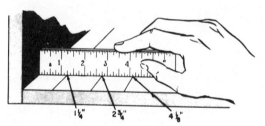

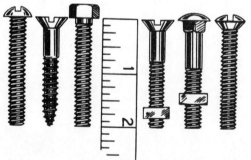

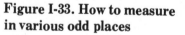

Figure I-33. How to measure in various odd places

If you're going out to buy a measuring device specifically for your furniture projects, your first purchase should be a square. But since you're asking for trouble if you try to measure 20- or 30-inch pieces with a 12-inch ruler, your next choice should be something longer. The most all-around useful long measuring tool is the windup steel tape. Figure I-33 shows how to measure in various places.

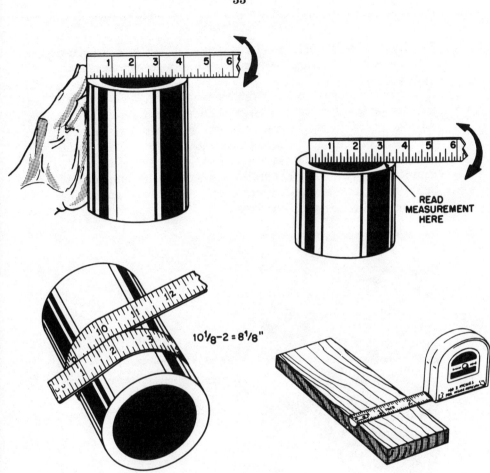

$10\tfrac{1}{8}-2=8\tfrac{1}{8}"$

READ MEASUREMENT HERE

§16. Handsaws

You don't need many tools to turn out highly functional furniture. But you should know how to use those few tools well.

The handsaw is perfectly suited to every one of the designs in this book. You can buy one for the price of a couple pounds of good steak.

Actually, there are two different kinds of saws, a crosscut saw and a ripsaw. The differences are subtle and not likely to impress you. For general use, in case your hardware store actually stocks both kinds, the crosscut saw is preferred.

Any saw has to be sharp or it's useless. When you buy it, it's sharp. And if you don't cut nails with it, don't leave it to rust in a damp basement or woodshed, and don't try to sharpen it yourself, it should remain sharp almost indefinitely. For eight years

I've been using the handsaw I own, given it plenty of use and a little bit of abuse during that time, and it still doesn't need sharpening.

You can tell that a saw needs sharpening when the wood you're working on seems to cut extra-hard and it's tough to keep the saw on your line. This can be caused by green lumber, too, so study the teeth of the saw. If their edges look more rounded than sharply squared off, your saw could stand sharpening. Take it to a pro and spend a few dollars. You'll waste more lumber and suffer more regrets than it's worth if you monkey around trying to sharpen the saw yourself.

Figure I-34. How to saw. Set your saw carefully on the line. . .

After you've drawn the line you want to saw along, put the saw teeth against the line. Set your thumb firmly against the saw to hold the teeth right on that line. Pull the saw gently back and forth just a few inches on each stroke. This will start sawing the wood exactly where you want.

When the saw cut is deep enough, the edges of the cut will act as a guide for the saw blade. Then pull your thumb away and gradually take longer and longer strokes. Ideally you should use about three quarters of the entire saw blade on each stroke.

Once your saw is able to progress steadily without your thumb to guide it, you can also push harder on the saw. Most wood saws cut only on the *push* stroke. They coast on the *pull* stroke, and so should you.

Figure I-35. Hold your thumb against
the saw to steady it while you begin
sawing with very short, light
strokes. . .

Keep your eye on the line you want to follow. Once the saw has
cut some way into the wood, you'll find that it is actually difficult
to change direction even slightly. Therefore, once you're off to a
good start, the rest is easy. If you have gone a bit off the line,
however, you can alter the direction most easily by sawing only
with the narrowest part of the saw blade while you progressively
correct your course.

Figure I-36. After your saw is deep
enough into the cut, use the full length
of the saw with vigorous strokes. . .

Don't fight the saw. If the saw doesn't go smoothly, assuming the wood is reasonably dry and your saw is reasonably sharp, it's because you're not keeping it lined up with the early part of your saw cut. If you twist the blade either from left to right or from up to down, it will bind. Then you have to tilt the blade away from you and out of the cut. Begin sawing again with the same short, smooth strokes you used at the very beginning of the cut.

Once in a great while you may saw yourself into a real jam near the center of a board. Perhaps you've strayed off the line a bit too much, and a combination of factors makes all of your efforts to get started in the right place again tough. So start over *on the other side of the board*. If you stay close to the line, your second cut will merge with what's left of your first.

Some binding and general bad sawing is caused by poorly supported boards. It's hard to saw well when you're also struggling to keep a board from sliding around or you're more worried about cutting into the family's best chair.

Lay the board you plan to saw on something solid. An old chair works very well. A Formica-covered table or chest is OK too. Wooden or heavy cardboard boxes are great.

When the end which will fall off after your cut is completed is more than just a few inches long, that part has to be supported separately. Otherwise the weight of the loose end can bend the board enough to bind against your saw. Also, when you reach the

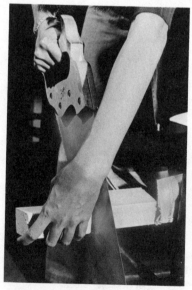

Figure I-37. Near the end, go back to the small, slow strokes and make sure the about-to-be-sawed-off portion is well supported by your hand, a box, or a friend so it is sawed off and not broken off by its own weight

Figure I-38. Saw against a chair protected with papers if you're working alone, across a table if you have a friend to steady the board for you

end of your cut, the heavy loose end will break off and you'll get a messy-looking piece of wood.

Figures I-37 and I-38 show several ways to improvise a solid cutting surface. If you're working alone, chairs or the back steps work best because you can hold the work against a support with your foot. If long boards are involved, in most other makeshift work areas you can use a little help from a friend, neighbor, or spouse.

When you get close to the end of your saw cut, switch back to those slow, short strokes you used to start the cut. You have to treat that last fraction of an inch very carefully or it'll split off unevenly.

If you find that ending a cut smoothly comes hard for you —even after some practice—try this method. When you've cut to within an inch or two of the end, stop. Turn around and start sawing from the opposite side. This takes more time than sawing straight through in a single operation, but neatness is well worth waiting for. Besides, if you get a rough cut, you'll probably spend more time sanding the rough spots away.

Ironically, almost all of this sage advice about how to saw successfully also applies to those of you with hotshot power saws. Just forget about shoving your thumb near the blade to get a cut started!

A crosscut saw is designed to cut straight lines. Don't try to make it cut curves too. There are lots of very inexpensive and efficient small saws on the market intended to make curved or wavy cuts through wood. Even powered ones are inexpensive and easy to use.

§17. Cutting Curves and Circles

For very small circles and tight curves, the coping saw is useful. Trouble is, because of the way it's built, the darned thing doesn't work much deeper than about 6 inches from the edge of a board.

The second common saw for curved cuts is the keyhole saw. This one you can use at any distance away from the edge of your piece of wood. But it can't manipulate through extremely tight curves like its coping cousin.

Figure I-40. The keyhole saw or combination saw can cut slow-changing curves easily

Figure I-39. Circles and curves are cut with these. The tools: keyhole saw (top left), combination saw (top right), coping saw (bottom), or circle cutter which fits into an electric drill (center)

When you begin cutting with either saw, put your thumb near the mark to steady it. Like the crosscut saw, begin with short, gentle strokes and then progress to more vigorous ones.

As you change direction with a coping saw, you'll probably find it convenient to change the direction of the blade too. Loosen up the wing nut which tightens the blade, twist the top and the bottom ends of the frame, and then tighten the wing nut again.

When they find out how easy the coping saw cuts curves, some people get carried away. They saw faster and faster and faster. But that heats up the blade. Heat dulls and weakens it. Pretty soon the blade snaps.

Figure I-41. In order to start a cut in the middle of a board with keyhole, combination or coping saw, you must first drill a hole. . .

Figure I-42. Then insert your saw blade through the drilled hole and proceed with your cutting. . .

Coping-saw blades aren't expensive, and they're easy to install. If one snaps on you, it's not the end of the world, but if they snap too often, it's probably a sign you're cutting too fast. And fast cuts are not clean, accurate cuts.

If the curved line you want to cut doesn't begin or end or touch the edge of your board, then you have to drill a small hole somewhere along the line. The keyhole saw will slip right into the hole. You'll have to take the coping saw apart, fit its blade through the hole, then reassemble it. When the cutting is done, you have to go through the same procedure once more.

Instead of a wiggly, squiggly line, you might want just a plain circle. If you own an electric drill, you can buy an inexpensive

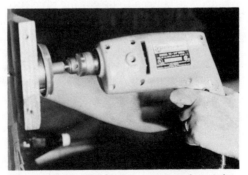

Figure I-43. Pick the appropriate size hole cutter, put it into your drill, and press firmly. . .

Figure I-44. The hole

accessory which cuts out circles neatly and fast. It's adjustable and cuts circles up to about 2-1/2 inches in diameter.

Speaking of circles, most people are let out of school never knowing how to draw one any larger than those dime-store compasses will allow. Watch a grown man or woman try to draw a big circle or curve someday. If there's no pot around the house just the right size, the circle goes undrawn.

Here's a little secret. Find yourself some string, a nail or pin, and a pencil. Tie a loop in one end of the string and then decide how big a circle you want. Stick the pin or nail through the loop and wrap the string around your pencil as far away from the loop as you want the radius of your circle to be.

Poke the pin or nail into something soft, like a piece of wood. And then, while you steady the nail with one hand, pull the string tight and carefully draw the circle. If you keep the string tight, the circle will come out almost perfect.

Whenever there are curves to be cut for furniture in this book, you can draw them two ways. First you can dig out your pin, string, and pencil. Somewhere in the project, you'll find out what the circle's radius should be. Make your string about that long and draw away. Secondly, each project will also have a drawing with lots of squares in it. The caption for the drawing will tell you how big those squares should be in real life. On your pieces of wood, make squares the same size and then carefully draw the curves onto the wood.

Using the squares method, proceed line by line. Make a small mark on your wood in the same place that the curve crosses a square in the drawing. After you've made all the marks on your piece of wood, then gently sketch a curve that links all of those marks.

Figure I-45. Before you can cut a
curve, you first have to draw one.
From this book, copy onto your board
marked with one-inch squares (or any
other given size), the place where the
curve crosses each ruled line. Then
join the marks and smooth out the
final curve by hand

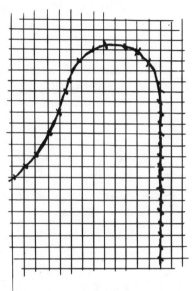

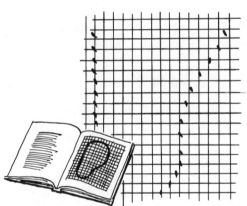

After your first curve is sketched, compare it with the one in
the drawing. If they look pretty much like each other, make your
big curve darker and smoother and then cut it out.

Don't expect the curves to come out all alike. You're not a
machine. Handmade furniture isn't supposed to look like it was
made by a machine. Small irregularities in curves and lines are
the mark of fine handmade furniture.

§18. Power Saws

Many people are buying inexpensive sabre saws and circular
saws these days. Though all the projects in this book can be made

with hand tools, there are a couple of projects which might become long and boring if you did them only by hand.

The galloping little sabre saw *can* cut straight lines if you're careful. They're especially good for doing what they're made for—cutting curves. With care, it isn't even necessary to drill a hole before using a sabre saw to cut curves or circles completely inside a board.

The instructions which come with most sabre saws are only adequate, but they'll get you into the subject deeply enough for our furniture projects. Here are a few added points to keep in mind:

- Always know where your fingers are when the sabre saw is going.

- Always know where the power cord is when your sabre saw is going.

- Always know where your family's best chair—now a sawhorse for the evening—is before you turn the saw on.

- Use the best blades you can buy for a particular job. There is no such thing as one blade for all jobs.

- The more teeth per inch on your sabre-saw blade, the smoother the cut.

For the furniture projects we're tackling, use blades with about 12 or 14 teeth per inch. Sometimes you'll have to resort to a blade with only 8 teeth per inch to start cuts in the middle of a board without drilling a hole. For cutting or trimming Formica and hardboard use a metal cutting blade with 24 teeth per inch.

§19. SurForm Tools

These gadgets are like saws in some respects. They're full of tiny points just like a saw blade. And they're used, like saws, for shaping a piece of wood. Most old-timers like to think of a SurForm tool as more of a super file. Think whatever you like. Then look at Figure I-46 if you've never seen a SurForm tool. (By the way SurForm comes from *Surface Forming*.)

Gently stroke a SurForm tool across the surface of whatever wood you want to shape. If you have a bumpy piece of wood you need flattened out, run a flat SurForm tool over it. If you have a

Figure I-46. SurForm tools in common use around the home. The flat one smooths off irregular surfaces as well as shaping the edge of flat boards. The round one fits into an electric drill. It can perform well on the edges of boards, just as the flat one does, but it is designed primarily for smoothing off or cutting curves

flat piece of wood you want rounded or cambered or beveled, run the same flat SurForm tool over its edges only.

You can also create curves with curved SurForm tools, and there are round SurForm tools which fit into electric drills. Once you get used to these funny tools, you'll probably want to design impromptu curves as you go along. At the outset, however, it'll be much safer if you draw or trace important curves onto wood and then keep stroking until your tool meets the line.

If there are children around the house, you will probably want to avoid sharp corners on the furniture you build. So you can run a SurForm tool evenly along every edge of your finished furniture. If you keep at it long enough and evenly enough, you'll get a beveled edge—the sharp corners will be flattened out, so to speak. You could get the same effect with a sanding block and sandpaper, but it would take you much longer.

You can also run a SurForm tool up and down on every corner from so many different angles that you round them all off. However, make darned sure in advance that you really like the look of rounded corners. They're nice on delicate furniture and they often blend in with projects using wood spindles, because they're round too. But round corners on a large, sharply defined piece of furniture can look out of place.

§20. Edging Tools

There are other accessories you can use with your electric drill—edging tools. They're designed to cope with those awkward edges on furniture projects of all kinds.

You can create concave curved edges, convex curved edges, wavy edges, and a few other effects depending on which tool you

Figure I-47. Edging tools which you can fit into an electric drill. Slowly move the tool along the edge of a board, and you can very soon produce a smooth, professional-looking, shaped edge on the board. The shape of each tool dictates the shape of the edge pattern

select. Put the tool into your drill tightly, and then slowly move it along the wooden edge you want to glamorize. Make sure that the top guide stays against the top of the wood and the side guide stays against the side. In a few minutes you will have transformed a common piece of wood into a proper, professional-looking table top or drawer front.

§21. Sandpaper

Sandpaper is one of the most overlooked tools in this trade. And that's why sandpaper—or more precisely, a lack of it—has been the ruin of many otherwise well-executed pieces of furniture. Like almost every other tool, sandpaper comes in a big selection of types and qualities.

First of all, sand is just about obsolete in the manufacture of what we call sandpaper. Sand, or flint as it's often called, just doesn't cut wood quickly and it doesn't hold up well, but it is inexpensive. If you're not going to do much sanding, flint paper is fine.

Garnet paper is next hardest. It costs more but it lasts longer and cuts faster.

Alumina or *carbide products* are about the best sandpaper in common use. They cost the most, but you get what you pay for. Sheets of these products last longer, if used well, and they do the sanding job substantially faster than cheaper tools.

For very fine wood finishing, you may want to wet the sandpaper between coats of paint, varnish, or lacquer. You'll need a product especially made to withstand being wet. So if you do plan to wet-sand your furniture, make sure you buy sandpaper labeled accordingly.

Now I know why a lot of my very early jobs came out kind of

second best. Nobody ever told me you could buy sandpaper finer than *fine* grade. Actually *fine* is about midway in the scale from the coarsest to the finest. Below *fine* there's *very fine, extra fine,* and *super fine*. To the heftier side you can buy *medium, coarse,* and *very coarse*.

You may encounter racks of sandpaper marked with the old identification. In case you do, here is the new classification along-side the two older nomenclature systems:

Superfine	400	10/0
Extra fine	320	9/0
	280	8/0
	240	7/0
Very fine	220	6/0
	180	5/0
Fine	150	4/0
	120	3/0
Medium	80	0
	60	1/2
Coarse	50	1
	40	1-1/2
Very coarse	36	2
	30	2-1/2
	24	3

That's enough about sandpaper for now. You'll be reading more about it as we begin making some quality furniture. As for the next chapter—how to finish the furniture—sandpaper is the star of that exciting episode.

4. The Finishing Touches

Creating a sturdy and beautiful piece of furniture will be a waste if the finishing is done haphazardly. Furniture finish doesn't have to be expensive nor consume hours and hours of time, but it does require some thought.

The finish should match the furniture's use. Softer finishes, in general, bring out the beauty of natural fine woods. If you don't have fine hardwoods to begin with, forget the soft finishes. Likewise, putting soft shellac or oil in the way of tough kids is a waste too. The following chart describes the respective virtues and demerits of most furniture finishes so you can compare them and choose the one most suitable to your needs.

FINISH	GOOD POINTS	WEAK POINTS
LIGHT-WEIGHT VINYL	Easy to apply. Resists dirt. Easy to clean. Wood and nonwood (marble, burlap, prints, etc.) easy to obtain.	Cuts easily. Won't resist many common solvents. Heat spoils it. Moisture and temperature extremes loosen adhesive. Won't fit on three-dimensional design surfaces.
HEAVY-WEIGHT VINYL	Very rugged. Wood "grain" is embossed into surface for added realism. Easy to clean. Available in prints, marble, etc.	Heat spoils it. Sensitive to a few volatile solvents.
FORMICA-TYPE PLASTICS	Extremely rugged. Very easy to clean. Resists heat and solvents. Available in wood, marble, prints, etc.	Brittle during installation. Not recommended for covering small areas.
PAINT **Enamel**	Rugged. Easy to clean. Resists many common solvents.	Looks childish or cheap in some uses. Brushes require cleaning in turpentine or benzine.
Water-based	Resists many common solvents. Brushes clean in water.	Looks childish or cheap in some uses.
Colored lacquer	Rugged. Easy to clean. Resists many solvents. Looks elegant on modern furniture.	Brushes require solvents for cleaning. Flammable until dry.

RELATIVE COST	PRELIMINARIES FOR FINISHING
Moderate	Smooth, clean surfaces with no large blemishes.
Expensive	Smooth, clean surfaces with no large blemishes.
Expensive	Smooth, clean surfaces with no large blemishes.
Inexpensive	Smooth surfaces, well sanded. Primer coat of paint is important. Sandpaper paint between successive layers.
Inexpensive	Smooth surfaces, well sanded and well cleaned.
Inexpensive	Smooth surfaces, well sanded. Sandpaper between successive layers.

FINISH	GOOD POINTS	WEAK POINTS
Antique	Rugged. Easy to clean. Resists many common solvents. Looks elegant if well applied.	Takes time to apply. Brushes require solvents to clean in most applications.
VARNISH	Protects natural appearance of real wood. Easy to clean. Relatively rugged.	Brushes require solvent to clean. Doesn't resist water or alcohol well. Dries relatively slowly. Won't stand up under heavy use.
CLEAR LACQUER	Rugged. Easy to clean. Resists many common solvents. Looks elegant where clear, shiny look is appropriate. Dries quickly.	Requires solvents to clean brush. Flammable until dry.
CLEAR WOOD SEALER	Very rugged. Easy to clean. protects wood very deeply. Resists most household hazards except cigarettes. Brings out grain well.	Requires turpentine to clean brush.
URETHANE	Very rugged. Protects against almost all household hazards. Easy to clean.	Requires solvent to clean brush.

RELATIVE COST	PRELIMINARIES FOR FINISHING
Modest	Smooth surfaces, well sanded. Primer is important on bare wood. Can be used on already-painted wood and in some cases to conceal surface defects.
Inexpensive	Smooth surfaces, well sanded. Hardwoods must be treated with filler. Fir plywood requires sealer. Sandpaper or steel wool between successive layers.
Inexpensive	Smooth surfaces, well sanded. Hardwoods must be treated with filler. Fir plywood requires sealer. Sandpaper or steel wool between successive layers.
Inexpensive	Smooth surfaces, well sanded. Hardwoods must be treated with filler. Fir plywood requires sealer. Sandpaper or steel wool between successive layers. (Often used for several first coats, and then another type of finish such as urethane or varnish is applied.)
Modest	Smooth surfaces, well sanded. Hardwoods must be treated with filler. Fir plywood requires sealer. Sandpaper or steel wool between successive layers.

FINISH	GOOD POINTS	WEAK POINTS
DÉCOUPAGE FINISH	Each coat is very, very thick and smooth. Provides a smooth covering over rough or uneven areas.	Requires solvent to clean brush. Not as rugged or easy to keep clean as more conventional finishes.
FURNITURE OIL	Beautiful grain and wood. Luxurious "unvarnished" appearance.	Gives wood very little protection against wear or solvents.
WAX	Easy to apply. Natural, "unvarnished" appearance.	Gives wood very little protection against wear or solvents.
SHELLAC	Preserves natural look of wood well. Easy to apply.	Requires alcohol to dilute shellac and clean brush. Minimum resistance to wear, abuse, and solvents or water.
ORANGE SHELLAC	Often used to provide an instant old-pine look. This effect works best on pine and on fir plywood.	Requires alcohol to dilute shellac and clean brush. Minimum resistance to wear, abuse, and solvents or water.

RELATIVE COST	PRELIMINARIES FOR FINISHING
Moderate	Surface does not have to be smooth, but natural woods should be well sanded to show off their grain. A clear wood sealer should be used for one or more preliminary coats to bring out wood grain.
Inexpensive	Smooth surfaces, well sanded. Several coats of oil are usually rubbed in with a lot of buffing.
Inexpensive	Smooth surfaces, well sanded. Several coats of oil are usually rubbed in wtih a lot of buffing.
Inexpensive	Smooth surfaces, well sanded. Hardwoods must be treated with filler. Fir plywood must be treated with sealer. Sandpaper or steel wool between coats.
Inexpensive	Smooth surfaces, well sanded. Hardwoods must be treated with filler. Fir plywood must be treated with sealer. Sandpaper or steel wool between coats.

When deciding how to finish that new piece of furniture, keep in mind the existing items in your home. If there's a rugged pine settee with dull orange shellac finish sitting on one side of the living room, you might not want to finish a coffee table for the same room with high-gloss red lacquer.

If a marble top would seem right, you can obtain it with plastics at a reasonable price. Thin self-adhesive vinyl, commonly called Con-Tact, doesn't come only in wood finishes. It is available in "marble," "burlap," "brick," "stone," and numerous prints or solid colors.

Figure I-48. Vinyl in wormy-chestnut finish

Even the old standby, Formica, comes in marble styles and other imitation materials. Remember that Formica-type plastics come in either high-gloss or dull finishes.

The type of finish should complement the kind of wood used in construction. You'd be out of your mind to buy expensive Brazilian rosewood boards and then cover them over with Con-Tact. On the other hand, if you started with common pine boards, don't expect to end up with furniture with the appearance of rosewood unless you cover it with vinyl or Formica-type plastics.

Heavy vinyl such as MacTac and Formica can hold their own even on boards which have some nicks and missing knotholes. Thin vinyl can't.

§22. Vinyl Plastic Finishes

The safest way to work with light or heavy vinyl is to begin with a bigger piece than you really need. Once the major areas are in place you can trim away the excess material.

Plastics are often used to cover only the largest parts of furniture, such as the top of a table or desk and drawer fronts. You can cover all flat and gently curved areas of furniture with vinyl, however.

Whenever you're working with vinyl plastic coverings, try to cover the largest areas first and work your way into the smaller areas. For instance, lay out the top of a desk or table first, then cut one piece which is large enough to cover not only the top but all adjoining edges and corners. Small, separately cut pieces for small areas will pull loose too easily.

Make sure the entire top is firmly and neatly in place before you tackle the corners and edges. They have to be cut to fit. In general, at corners of all sorts you want only one piece to overlap the corner. Cut the second piece so it meets the sharp edge of the corner almost exactly (see Figure I-49).

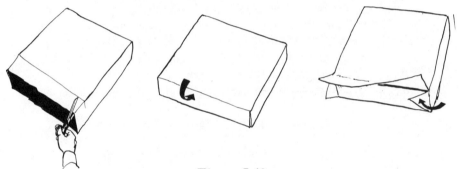

Figure I-49

Thin vinyl overlaps so easily that you can run long strips of it around something like the apron on a table. And when you reach the end of your plastic, simply lay the excess right down over the top of the beginning. Rub the edge well and the joint will become virtually invisible. This is especially true of patterns such as wood, marble, burlap and any other finely textured print. Overlapping edges of coarse prints are harder to conceal, so plan for that material to end at the least conspicuous place.

Thin self-adhesive vinyl generally comes in narrow rolls, about 18 inches wide. If you want to cover something wider than 18 inches, you must overlap two or more pieces. In that case, give yourself plenty of material to work with. Especially if you have a very stark pattern, don't try to cover a 36-inch wide table top with two pieces of 18-inch vinyl. Either use three pieces or plan ahead—make the table 34 inches wide. No matter how big and bold the pattern, at some point along the roll it must overlap inconspicuously.

Heavy vinyl such as MacTac is harder to overlap because of its thickness. Choose the areas of overlap carefully. Generally, if the wood grain moves vertically on your furniture, your line of overlap should also move vertically to get the greatest camouflage effect.

Don't try to lay either the heavy or lightweight vinyl down so that one edge lines up exactly against another edge. First of all, it's darned near humanly impossible to achieve perfect alignment between two unwieldly pieces of flexible plastic. On top of that, heat, moisture and use cause the vinyl to expand, contract or shift around just a bit. But if a dull, light piece of lumber shows through even a 1/16-inch gap between two pieces of dark, shiny vinyl, the separation looks as big as the Grand Canyon.

Don't try to lay down large areas of self-adhesive plastic all at once. Play it safe. First lay the plastic in place with the backing paper still attached. Make sure it's going to fit just the way you want it to. Then hold at least half of the sheet in place with weights such as books, bricks, bags full of sugar or flour —anything heavy enough to keep the vinyl from slipping out of place.

Now peel away backing paper from the loose portion of vinyl. Rub the sticky covering down, starting close to the unpeeled part. Make very sure that you don't let air become trapped under the vinyl, or you'll be left with big bubbles instead of a big expanse of slick plastic. Repeat the process for the remaining unpeeled half.

No matter now carefully you work, you're bound to be left with a few small air bubbles under your furniture's new vinyl skin. Jab a sharp knife point or pin into the middle of each bubble. Then squeeze all of the trapped air toward the hole. As you squeeze out the air, you're also rubbing the adhesive down. By the time you've rubbed your finger across the bubble three or four times, there won't be any bubble. And the tiny pin or knife prick will also be invisible.

A few people apply wood-grained vinyl to their furniture as if they were decorating a Christmas tree, running the vinyl in every direction imaginable. If you want vinyl to resemble real wood, you must apply the plastic so its "grain" simulates the grain direction of real wood.

Grain generally runs *the long way* through a piece of wood.

Figure I-50. With wood-grained vinyl, make sure the "grain" of the vinyl goes the same way it would if you were working with real wood. On the top, generally run it the long way. On drawers, run it from left to right. On sides, the direction is optional, although it generally runs the long way

Grain seldom goes horizontally in a vertical leg, for instance. And on a table or desk top, the grain almost never runs from front to back. You should install your vinyl the same way. (See Figure I-50.)

Marble is usually reserved for the tops of tables. When you decide to build a marble creation with the help of plastic, cover only the top with a marble design. Make sure that you fold over the vinyl so edges of the top piece become marble too. Then paint or choose a wood-grained plastic for the remaining parts.

§23. Formica

In the hands of amateurs without heavy equipment, Formica should only be used on large areas. Formica-type plastics are too tough to cut into narrow strips or odd-sized pieces.

Most lumberyards and do-it-yourself centers don't stock much Formica-type plastic. They'll order any brand cut to size for you and have it ready within a day or two. While you're waiting, read about contact cement in §14. That's about the only kind of glue used to install Formica-type plastic.

After you've glued Formica to the top of your new table or desk, there's likely to be a bit of Formica hanging over the edge of the wood, or a bit of wood sticking out from underneath.

You can trim away the wood with a SurForm tool or sandpaper. If there's a lot, use a saw. To trim excess Formica you'll need a very fine-toothed saw. A hacksaw or coping saw with a metal-cutting blade works fine. If you own an electric sander, you can buzz along the edge and smooth it with very little elbow grease. Use medium-grade or finer sandpaper on Formica since coarser grades will be chewed away by the tough Formica.

Formica doesn't have to be used only on table or desk tops. If you work accurately you can apply the tough plastic to the sides of a desk, drawer fronts, and cabinet doors.

One complaint voiced by novice furniture makers who apply Formica for the first time concerns the naked edge which remains after they have applied plastic to the top. "I don't have an accurate power saw and years of experience! I can't cut a skinny strip of Formica and stick it on that ugly edge. What do I do?"

You can paint the nude wood to blend in or to contrast with the color of your Formica. Or you can keep on reading to learn what the Pros do with embarrassing table edges. Whatever turns you on!

§24. Edges

You can buy all kinds of products designed to pretty up the exposed edges of tables and desks you've covered with Formica. Actually, you can use them with other materials too, not only Formica.

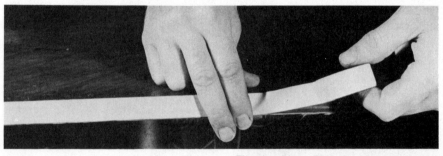

Figure I-51. Vinyl tape can cover the rough wooden edges of plywood after you've covered the top with something nice like Formica

You can simply apply a roll or two of vinyl tape to the bare edges. The tape is economical enough to cover a lot of edges. Vinyl tape, that common colorful tape sold all over town for hundreds of different uses, comes in dozens of sizes and colors.

There is a tape made especially for covering table edges. It's

Figure I-52. Wood-grained tape also covers exposed edges on furniture projects such as tables, desks, coffee tables, etc.

Figure I-53. "Metal" tape in self-adhesive rolls goes quickly over the exposed edges of plywood to give a finished, professional look to your work

generally available only in the 3/4-inch or 1-inch widths. The product comes in a limited number of wood-grained finishes. It costs more than the common vinyl tape, but looks better. You can use this woodsy tape to conceal ugly edges of plywood after finishing the flat surfaces in some natural-wood effects.

Serrated tape is also designed for table edges and is usually gold or chrome colored. It goes well with modern furniture designs and is an inexpensive, easy-to-use substitute for the real metal strips more commonly used a number of years ago. You can still buy metal strips to cover table edges, but you have to nail them in place, and they look a bit gaudy. They're strong, however, and they were good enough for Grandma, they may be good enough for you.

Figure I-54. Snap-on plastic edge strips give a rugged finish to furniture edges. Trouble is, bright kids can snap them off again

At least one manufacturer puts out plastic strips which snap over the edges you want to cover. The plastic is heavy and bright, and the strips are not inexpensive.

Wood also is available to cover embarrassing edges. There are several varieties of molded wooden strips. The designs molded into the strips range from simple cable patterns to highly ornamented flowers.

Molded strips are about 1/4 inch thick and some come in widths from an inch to two inches or more. They add a touch of elegance or charm to the otherwise bland edges of tables, desks, and other furniture. See Figure I-55 for samples.

Figure I-55. Wooden molded edge strips can finish off many otherwise unadorned pieces of furniture. This is but a small sampling of the styles available

Molded strips cost a bit, but you need only a few to cover the edges of an entire furniture project. They are available in a neutral color which can be stained to match whatever natural wood, vinyl, or Formica you've incorporated into your furniture. They're easy to paint, too.

Install molded strips with glue and tiny nails. Most of the tops you'll be putting on tables and similar household items will be no more than 3/4 inch thick. Molded strips are usually one or more inches wide. Let the extra width hang over at the bottom. This gives the effect of a wider-looking edge to your table or desk top, which in turn gives the appearance of greater elegance to most furniture.

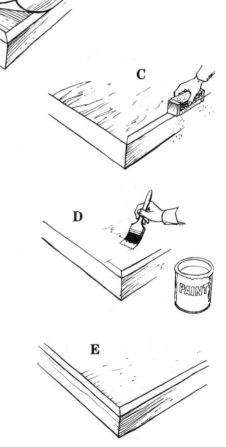

Figure I-56. Install molded wooden strips with (A) glue and a few finishing nails; (B) you can cover up the top and the telltale top edge of the molded strips with vinyl or Formica-type plastics; (C) or you can bevel the upper edge with a plane, sandpaper, or SurForm tool. Then the edge of the table top blends almost perfectly with the upper edge of the molded strip. If you sand the strip and top well, then you can (D) paint them both and conceal the fact that you tacked on a molded strip instead of having laboriously carved the design into the top by hand. (E) But you might like how the bit of difference in texture looks if you don't take care of concealing the strip.

After tacking and gluing a molded strip to your furniture project, sandpaper the upper edge until the strip blends in with the top surface. If you're painting or covering the top with Formica or vinyl, that 1/4-inch upper edge of the molded strip will never be seen. If you plan to give your project a natural-wood finish, that exposed upper edge may be a nuisance. There are two easy ways of dealing with the problem.

First, you can simply paint or stain the 1/4-inch edge to contrast with the rest of the table. Gold blends well with most old-fashioned furniture styles. The face of the molded strip (the part with decoration on it) should be stained to match the tone of the natural-wood top.

Secondly, it's simple enough to use sandpaper or a SurForm tool, preferably both, to bevel the top part of your molded strips. There's always a margin on such strips. If you strip away enough wood to make the strip pointed where it meets the table top, the union will be invisible.

§25. Corner Moldings

There are other wooden tricks for covering ugly edges. There are literally hundreds of varieties of corner moldings. They're useful for more things than covering the edge of a desk or table.

Quarter-round, half-round, three-quarter-round, outside and inside corner moldings as well as quarter- and half-circles are the basic molding designs. Within each basic type, however, there are enough variations to keep everybody happy. Many have fancy embellishments.

If you'd like to give a different look to the exposed edge of a table, desk, cocktail table, or other piece of furniture, you can glue and nail a half-round molding to the edge. If the top board is 3/4 inch thick, choose a 3/4-inch molding. As long as you work accurately, plug up any major gaps between the board and the molding with Plastic Wood, and sandpaper the project well, the molding will look like it's part of the original piece of wood you used for the top. Your friends will be impressed at how skillfully you rounded off the table edge.

When you're stuck with a Plain Jane kind of surface, maybe a cabinet door or the side of a coffee table, and want to make it look fancy, corner moldings come to your rescue at a modest price.

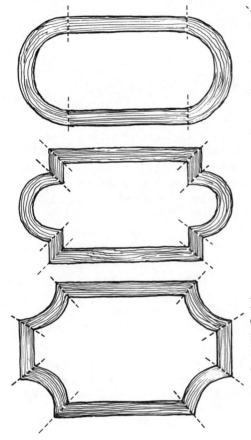

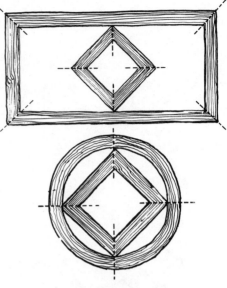

Figure I-57. These are some of the classic designs possible when you use nothing more than standard moldings. Dotted lines show where the component pieces join together

They're used on plenty of pieces of furniture in the stores. Until now you probably just never realized how easy it is to create these seemingly complicated designs.

Using from four to eight pieces of molding you can create most of the classic furniture decoration designs in use today. Figure I-57 shows some designs and how to make them in the simplest way possible. Unless you're striving for a very gaudy effect, use narrow moldings, about 1/2 inch wide.

The secret to working successfully with corner moldings is to cut them carefully after you've made careful measurement. Measure the *inside* length of all of your designs. Then mark that

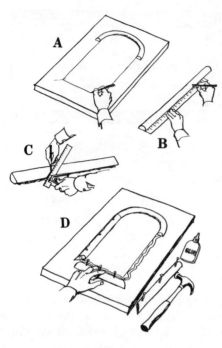

Figure I-58. Here's how you create a design with your moldings selected from earlier illustrations. (A) Sketch the design outline using the inside edge of your rounded pieces as a foundation. (B) Measure your flat pieces. (C) Draw a 45-degree line going outward from the measurement where your flat pieces join. (D) Glue and nail the design parts into place

measurement on the *inside* edge of your molding. Adjust your combination-square tool to its 45-degree setting and draw a 45-degree line from the *inside* edge toward the outside edge of the molding. As a result, the outside edge of the molding will be longer than the inside.

In those designs utilizing the ready-to-use quarter and half circles, the circular portions often have to be cut at an angle too. You can't just lay your 45-degree square on them to get a perfect angle. After the straight pieces, if any, are cut, lay out your design on any flat surface. Carefully sketch the lines onto the circular moldings, which will match the 45-degree angles on your other pieces. With a bit of Plastic Wood to plug up any mismatches once you've glued and nailed the moldings into place, you should end up with near-faultless designs every time.

When we get around to decorating some coffee tables in Chapter 15, we'll put corner moldings to even more uses. They're useful and attractive in many places on furniture which you plan to paint, cover with vinyl, or finish naturally.

§26. Sanding

The secret of fine finishes is how well the wood is sanded. Too many people have the notion that sandpaper is used only to get rid of obvious surface defects in the surface of wood, and the gentle art of sanding is rapidly becoming obsolete. Let's change that.

You have to make a tiny investment in several sheets of good sandpaper, at least medium, fine, and superfine grades. You also need a sanding block. Buy one if you like, or simply look around for a scrap of lumber about an inch thick, 5 or 6 inches long, and 3 or 4 inches wide.

Wrap sandpaper around the sanding block whenever you work on flat surfaces. That will keep them flat. Bare fingers press unevenly on sandpaper and cause problems on flat wood surfaces.

Figure I-59. When you're sandpapering a flat surface, put the sandpaper around a flat scrap of lumber or a store-bought sanding block

Even if your wood looks perfectly clean and smooth, begin sanding with medium-grade sandpaper. Any wood that lies around in a lumberyard picks up a layer of dirt on and in the grain. A gentle once-over with medium sandpaper cleans that dirt away.

Think of sandpaper as a tool. After you've kicked up a bit of dust with it, at least every minute or two stop and pound it against the palm of your hand. That'll knock the sawdust loose from your tool. If it stays there, the sandpaper grains get plugged up quickly. That means the paper will cut more slowly and have to be replaced more frequently.

Switch to the fine grade of sandpaper next. Keep sanding until the wood looks satiny smooth and the grain starts to sparkle. Periodically wipe the sawdust off the wood with a soft rag or paper towel. You can blow it away too, but if you blow, make sure your mouth is dry. Saliva or water of any sort raises the wood grain, and you'll end up with uneven spots.

Just before you're ready to apply your first coat of shellac, lacquer, filler, or paint, take out your superfine or extra-fine grade of sandpaper. You'll know when you have done the job with this subtle tool. The wood will look so soft and brilliant that you'll wonder if it needs varnish or shellac at all!

No matter what grade of sandpaper you work with, and no matter what you're trying to accomplish, always move in the same direction as the grain. If you don't, the sandpaper will etch scratches into the wood instead of removing them.

Even the edges of boards have direction to their grain. If the edges are going to show, they have to be sanded until they look just as stunning as the top surfaces. Along the long edge of a board, the grain moves the long way. On the short edge, the grain inevitably moves up and down, but not always at a perfect right angle to the surface of the board.

The short edges of most boards take more sanding than any other part of the wood. But with enough elbow grease and patience, even those pesky edges will look as handsome as the rest of the piece of wood.

Odd-shaped or curved items such as spindles and legs require sanding without a sanding block. Your fingers have to force the sandpaper into those narrow nooks and crannies. Here again, always move the sandpaper in the same direction as the grain, generally from the top to the bottom of each leg or spindle. (See Figure I-60.)

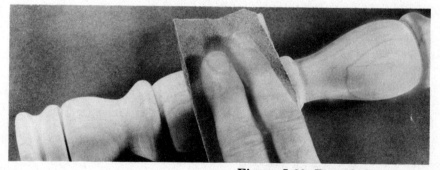

Figure I-60. Rounded surfaces, however, should be sanded with only your fingers behind the sandpaper

Makers of legs, spindles, and such enjoy advertising that their glorious product comes "ready to finish." By implication people are led to believe that means they can start slapping on layers of varnish or paint. Sorry—it really means you can start rubbing with layer after layer of sandpaper. Even "ready-to-finish" unfinished furniture needs sanding.

§27. Natural Finishes

For most hardwood projects you have to use wood filler. That includes hardwood veneer, too. The grain on woods such as maple, mahogany, walnut, oak, and other hardwoods is so coarse that you will never get it down to a smooth satiny finish which holds out dirt unless you smear on what's called *paste wood filler.* The product comes with its own directions, which you may want to alter a bit.

After you've sanded the wood with your finest sandpaper, apply wood filler. If your particular brand recommends various dilutions for different types of hardwoods, follow them.

Make sure you don't wait too long before you wipe off the excess filler. If it dries thoroughly, you'll have to start sandpapering the project over again. Too much dried paste wood filler is about as tough as lizard skin.

After you wipe away excess filler, give the filler left behind time to dry thoroughly. Then sandpaper the wood once again with extra-fine sandpaper. Each time you add something to wood, you have to sandpaper it again to bring it back to a satiny, smooth surface.

Stain comes next in my book. You'll find that most cans of wood filler recommend staining first, filling later. If you do that, however, you'll also have to color the filler. Matching colors gets to be pretty touchy. Good penetrating oil stains can penetrate the filler as well as the wood, so save yourself some headaches—fill first, stain second.

Softwoods such as pine or fir plywood don't require paste wood filler; their grain is more compact. But fir plywood does require some special treatment to tame its otherwise wild grain structure. The grain will show right through many, many layers of paint or clear finishes. Unless you want an embossed look on plywood, tame its grain.

Buy yourself a can of Firzite or a competing brand. The product is sold especially for keeping fir plywood grain in check. Stain the plywood first, if you plan to go that route, and then apply Firzite. If you feel the Firzite has dulled the effect of your stain, you can always apply a second coat of stain after the Firzite dries.

Stain is good for softwoods and hardwoods alike, although you may be wondering why somebody invests a pretty piece of change in natural walnut or oak boards if they plan to stain it later. Why not use cheap pine or plywood first and then apply expensive-looking stain? Because of the grain, for one thing.

You might be able to stain pine to match the color of dark oak, but you'll never match the distinctive grain patterns of oak. And you'll never get a hard oak surface by staining pine or plywood.

Many people have the idea that hardwood just naturally comes out looking dark and daring. Most of it doesn't. If the wood you've chosen is more light and more drab than you hoped for, don't despair just yet. Oil or stain may be called for. But let's run a test first, the sort of test you should use before slapping a lot of wood finish onto any project you hope to cherish.

Figure I-61. Sometimes furniture oil or almost any other kind of oil is all you need to turn a colorless, drab piece of hardwood into a deeply hued, rich-looking object. In this photo, oil has been rubbed only into the darker portion

Take a wooden scrap typical of the whole item you're building. Sandpaper the scrap as finely as you will sandpaper the finished wood. Surface roughness on your test piece will hang onto more of those deeper-colored solid particles in stain than will smooth wood, so your test won't be accurate.

Apply something oily to your test wood. A good rich furniture polish might do it. Any of the paint oils in a set of artist's colors will do fine, linseed oil in particular. For test purposes you can even squirt some household lubricating oil or cooking oil onto the wood and wipe it around. If oil gives your wood the richness you're looking for, then oil is your answer and not stain. Varnish and wood sealers contain enough oil that when you apply them, your wood will pick up the oil you want it to have.

If your test colors are lacking, switch to stains next. Use them only on your test pieces first. Wood and wood stains are so divergent in their qualities, there's only one way to find out how they will react with each other—try the chosen stains on your chosen wood.

Your first choice in a stain should be one with the same name as the wood you're working with or trying to duplicate. If you have oak wood but want it darker, try a dark oak stain. About the only kind of stain amateurs should try is *penetrating oil stain*. Follow the directions when you apply it to your test wood. Let it dry, cover it with an oily substance to duplicate the contribution the varnish or other finish will make, and then evaluate your test wood.

If your test piece has about the hue you're after but is too light, give it another treatment or two with the same stain. That should match your requirements.

If the hue is right but the test came out too dark, dilute your chosen stain with turpentine. Then run another test. You can also make a stain come out lighter by giving it less time to dry before wiping away excess stain with a soft cloth.

If your early choice of stain is not the right hue, you have two options. You can go out to buy an entirely new stain, this time choosing one with more red, more yellow, or perhaps more purple. Or you can simply add other stains to the can you already have.

A stain such as yellow maple will add yellowness to most stains. Red oak or medium-red mahogany stains will add redness to what you already have. For more purple coloration, choose a dark mahogany stain.

For many people the most distressing wood and stain is mahogany. Part of the problem has to do with the woods themselves. Many people remember the deep, dark, purply—almost black—Duncan Phyfe table that Grandma cherished. The wood for that table probably came up from Honduras or Brazil. Today a great deal of mahogany comes from the Philippines. The grain of Philippine—Luan—mahogany is similar to the Honduras species, but the color is not. You have to apply mahogany stain to Luan mahogany before it looks like that old, dark, Honduras kind.

When applied to plywood or pine, mahogany stains often look terrible. You're stuck with wood that looks like it has been painted with cheap purple paint. So proceed carefully with mahogany. Good results are well worth the trouble.

Some stains are easier to use and more pleasing than others. From personal experience in my own projects, as well as looking over the shoulders of others, walnut stain works well on most hardwoods, pine, or plywood. Maple and yellow maple stains soak into plywood with excellent results, although they may be too light on pine. Light oak and dark oak work well too. All light-colored stains such as ash generally prove disappointing.

Colorful stains are ideal for both showing off wood grain and adding distinctive color to furniture. Buy some flat or semigloss enamel in your chosen color, some linseed oil too, and make sure you have turpentine around the house.

Dilute the enamel half and half with linseed oil. Brush it onto your test strip sparingly and give it a chance to dry. The soft grain should soak up the color and turn quite bright. You should have more than a soft tint of color on the hard grain.

If you have trouble getting more color into one kind of grain, dilute the enamel with turpentine. Turpentine soaks in better than linseed oil, especially on pine that isn't thoroughly dry. This colorful stain idea is more useful on large areas. On small areas, the color variation looks more accidental than intentional. On fir plywood, colors come out exceptionally dramatic.

Apply sealer after the wood is colored, filled, and sanded to perfection. In many cases sealers do very little to the immediate appearance of wood grain and color. Don't skip this step unless your home is off-limits to children of all ages who spill, drop, and scratch things.

Head for your hardware or paint store and look for a can of *penetrating wood sealer*. The product will be very thin and watery looking. It soaks deeply into the surface of your wooden furniture to seal up the grain against dirt, pollution and damage.

Apply sealer evenly with a brush. It soaks in and dries quickly. One coat may not change the appearance of the wood. Apply two or three more coats. The sealer should then become apparent on the surface. As soon as the sealer produces a uniform, dry sheen, you have applied enough. Never use more than six coats of the sealer, however, no matter how much it soaks in unless you plan to use sealer as your final finishing material.

Penetrating sealer does make a fine finish. It resembles what many people call a Danish oil finish, but it's tougher. Sealer shows off the grain and color of natural wood very well. Ironically, it doesn't look finished enough for some people who want furniture to have an obvious and glossy top coat.

Finishing can never be completed with a single coat. Varnish, shellac, penetrating wood sealer, and even urethane finishes need thickness to provide glistening beauty and protection to wood.

Between applications you should sandpaper away any surface irregularities. Sand, varnish, sand, varnish, sand; varnish. . . . the procedure can *and should* go on for days. Each coat has to dry thoroughly before you sand it or add another coat. In the meantime, you can show off your new piece of furniture and even use it carefully.

Orange shellac is sometimes a favored finish to add richness and redness to dark woods such as walnut and mahogany. Personally I think it's best used to instantly age pine furniture you really want to look good and piney. When using orange shellac, however, you may reach the limit of orangeness after a few coats. If so, switch to another finish, a clear one this time such as white shellac, urethane, varnish, or lacquer.

Lacquer requires some tender loving care. Lacquer solvents are much more potent than anything you've probably worked with before. Pay close attention to the label's warnings. *Do* open enough windows so that the fumes will be dispersed, quickly. And *don't smoke.*

Lacquer dries very quickly and doesn't seal wood very well. If you plan to use lacquer as a finish be sure the wood has first been treated with penetrating wood sealer. Only after several coats of sealer should you switch to lacquer.

In addition to the high gloss and clarity it provides, lacquer is useful because it dries so fast. You can apply several coats in a day. Don't forget to sandpaper lightly between coats. If you don't sand the final coat of varnish, lacquer, shellac, or other wood-finishing product when it dries, the finish will look like it came out of a can. If you want your handmade furniture to look like it belongs in an expensive showroom, dig out the sandpaper. Wet-sanding with a superfine grade of sandpaper adds the final touch to a well-executed wood-finishing job. When you reach this stage on your project, make sure you have super-fine sandpaper approved for wet-sanding. Even glossy furniture finishes deserve a touch-up with sandpaper, except those modern pieces you feel must have a "wet look."

Wet sanding is like polishing. Use the best furniture oil or oily furniture polish around. Linseed oil works well too. In a pinch, you can even use cooking oil; it's better than no oil at all. Pour a generous amount of oil on the important surfaces of your new furniture. Wet your superfine sandpaper in the oil and very gently rub over the finish.

After you've given the furniture a thorough once-over, wipe away some of the oil to see what's left behind. If you have sanded the top or sides evenly, the finish should now have a luxurious gloss, but it won't have that "out-of-the-can" glossy look.

The more you wet-sand, the more gloss you remove. Going beyond the once-over-lightly stage, you soon approach what's known as a *satin-gloss* finish. In order to get down to a *dull satin* look, you may have to trade in your superfine sandpaper for some wet-grade extra fine. The difference between these two grades of sandpaper is pretty subtle, but so is the difference in the finishes they produce.

Dull satin, by the way, isn't an accurate description, but who am I to change a phrase that has been used for so long? There should be so much varnish, shellac or lacquer between the wood and the top layer of satiny finish that you get a "through the looking glass" effect. It really doesn't look dull at all.

I've known people who worry that they're going to sand away all the varnish from their first few furniture projects. With oil on the wood, you'd have to sandpaper a long time before wiping away any noticable amount of varnish. Besides, if you did sand away a bit more varnish than you wanted to, you'd simply have to put on some more and start the wet sanding all over again another day. By the time you reach this stage in the furniture game, a little extra work won't stop you!

§28. Paint

Paint is little more than varnish with pigments added. In fact, enamel used to be exactly that—a can of varnish into which some creative soul squirted pigment and an opaque medium.

There's no need for a lengthy discussion about how to paint. All you have to do is reread the section on how to varnish. The same rules apply, and that includes the advice on sandpapering the final coat.

Applying a single coat of paint to woodwork around doors and windows or to walls may be a good idea. Who likes the thought of messing around with five or six coats of paint on the living room walls? But if you plan to create a professional-looking piece of furniture, be prepared to overcome your brainwashing about the benefits of one-coat paint. You have to treat furniture to at least half a dozen coats, and you have to sandpaper the paint between most coats. Even then there's more to painting then meets the untrained eye!

Maybe you've stood in stores and marveled at how the painted chests and headboards looked so elegant, almost as if they were not painted at all. Aside from the final sanding, which takes off the cheap surface gloss and imperfections, there's another reason why a lot of professional furniture painting looks unpainted. *It's been painted with more than one color.*

Say you want an ivory-colored piece of furniture. That's easy—buy some ivory paint. But also invest in a small can of a color such as tan, light brown, or gold glaze.

After you apply enough ivory paint to last a lifetime, sand-paper it lightly. Then uncap your second color and dig out a soft rag or paper towel.

Dip your rag into the second paint and wipe it all over your lovely ivory paint job. With a second rag, wipe away most of the wet tan or gold paint. Wipe hardest near the middle of every large area. Wipe somewhat less vigorously near the edges and corners. In effect, you'll be leaving the most tan or gold color around the outside of doors or tops. That creates what pros call a framing effect.

It's hard to wipe away the color that sneaks into grooves and carvings on the decoration or legs. That's fine. The extra color there helps accent the decoration.

By the time you finish wiping the second color, nobody will know it's there except you and others privy to this furniture-finishing secret. The furniture will look ivory colored. But it will look elegant. The ivory won't look like somebody just opened a cheap can of paint and sloshed it into place.

Don't worry about wiping away too much of the top color. You can always apply it again. And if perchance you leave on more of the overcoat than looks good to you the next day, just apply another coat or two of the base color. Let it dry, sand it, and then tackle the overcoat again.

With a pure white base you can use ivory, tan, or beige for a wiping color. For light brown, try dark brown wipe. Dark brown paint can stand a black wipe. Light green should get a dark green overcoating.

With a dark green base, a black wipe would look rather conventional while a wipe of light green could prove to be unique. Likewise for reds, blues, oranges, and similar shades.

There are a couple of almost universal colors to use for overcoating purposes. Gold is widely used, especially over the ivory, olive, and powder blue shades popular in French Provincial, Italian and other Mediterranean furniture. Stains also work well. A maple stain can be used on lighter colors, a walnut stain on darker ones.

Thus far we've concentrated on wiping off all but a mere trace of the second color. If you wipe less vigorously all over the piece of furniture, the second color becomes an integral part of the overall coloration. The texture of your wiping strokes also becomes part of the overall appearance. Finishes like that are popularly called an antique effect.

You can buy kits which preselect the base and glaze colors for your antique effect, or you can save money by assembling your own kit from the paint shelves.

Much has been written about the pros and cons of enamel, latex, and acrylic-based paints and the flat, semigloss, and gloss varieties. Most of what's written is true, but also impractical. It's true that a high-gloss, oil-based enamel will give you the most rugged service of the popular paint varieties, assuming it's of a good quality and well applied. Many people don't like high-gloss furniture except for the use of children or in very modern styles. Many are also put off by the thought of digging out a jug of turpentine to clean brushes and hands every time they paint.

You can get fine furniture finishes with good grades of water-based paint. It's hard to recommend specific brand names or specific types because so many paints are manufactured locally. Some local factories do a splendid job. Others. . . . The best way to find a good paint is to choose a good local paint dealer.

Semi-gloss paint is the most versatile for furniture unless you want to end up with a very high gloss. If you want a very flat finish, avoid the flat paints. The formula that makes paint end up flat also makes it end up weaker than a good semigloss. With proper wet sanding after the final coat, you can reduce even gloss paints to a lustrous flat finish which is finer to look at than any flat paint.

When you paint furniture, forget about rollers. Even small rollers are harder to clean than brushes, which can get into the little nooks and crannies and corners common to almost all furniture.

Colored lacquer is ideal when you want bright, sparkling, glossy colors as well as a tough surface. It has the added advantage of drying so fast you can apply several coats in one day.

Use lacquer the same way you'd use paint. Generally you won't use a wipe of some second color over a bright, glossy finish, however. Make sure you buy *brushing* lacquer. A well-stocked paint or hardware store may have some professional-grade lacquers designed for use in spray guns. They don't brush on well at all.

If bright colors and a glossy appearance really turn you on, one place to go shopping for lacquer is your local hobby store. What they call model airplane dope is actually a fine grade of lacquer. Make sure you buy the variety designed for use on wood, not for use on plastic. There's only a limited selection of colors but they're bright!

Don't try to brush dope too much. The stuff dries so fast that if you keep brushing it back and forth, you'll be creating more brush strokes than you hope to eliminate. Dope is self-leveling. Left alone, it tends to spread itself evenly over your work.

I'm going to talk about only one more finishing method in this book—upholstery. If I told you right now how simple it is, you might not believe me, so when we reach the first furniture project that uses upholstery, I'll spring the technique on you.

Now that the preliminaries are out of the way, let's start making furniture.

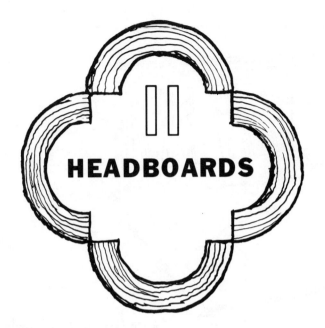

5. Traditional and Modern Headboards

SKILLS: Easy project.
TIME: Weekend.
TOOLS: Hand saw, hammer or
screwdriver, sandpaper.
For hardwood an
electric drill is helpful.
ALSO READ: Chapters 2, 3, 4.

You can build the headboards pictured in this chapter with any of the materials mentioned in Chapter 2. The modern version in particular is beautiful when done with naturally finished hardwood. All headboards are striking when finished in a mellow-colored paint or when antiqued. You can use 3/4 inch plywood or pine boards too, finishing either naturally or with paint or vinyl. Even Formica may be used if it suits your taste.

Modern

For the modern version, you need a number of 10-foot-long boards of varying widths. Hardwood is available in only a limited number of widths. Vary the widths at will if you must, but keep the combined width about 42 inches.

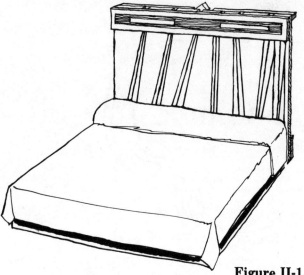

Figure II-1. Modern headboard design

Dimensions given in the drawings are ideal for a queen-or double-sized bed, allowing plenty of headboard to show off around the side of your bed. Add another 18 inches to the width for king-sized beds.

There's enough inherent strength in the design of these headboards that you can safely use chipboard without worrying that it'll break. If you use either chipboard or hardwood, you'll have to drill holes for the screws. Use wood screws on hardwood, sheet-metal screws on chipboard.

Pine and plywood can be assembled with nails if you like. No matter what materials you use, glue the parts together first, then screw or nail them on top of that.

The final piece in the assembly (#12 in the modern drawings #22 in the traditional drawings), is glued onto the top front of the headboard. It's decorative, and also conceals the screw or nail holes. You'll find a similar technique used in most furniture- —designing a decorative piece into the project to conceal some ugly construction details.

It is not necessary to countersink nails or screws which hold the bottom together because the bed conceals the construction details. And since the top piece is only glued on, not nailed or screwed, there's no need to countersink nails or screws at that end either.

Cut your wood according to the measurements shown in the materials or layout diagram for your choice of headboard. Then

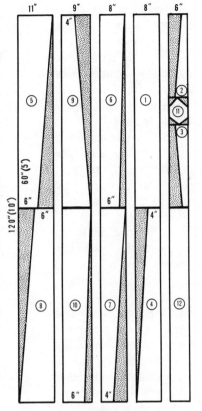

Figure II-2. Materials for modern headboard

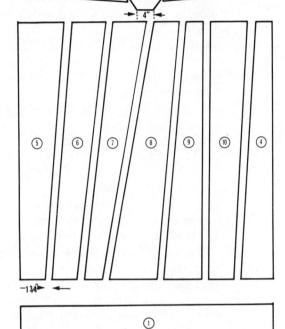

Figure II-3. Lay out your materials this way to make your assembly of modern headboard go smoothly

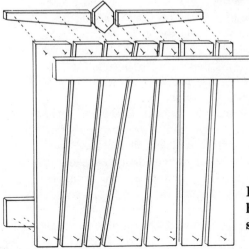

Figure II-4. Assemble your modern headboard this way, in the order shown, and you can't go wrong

lay the pieces on the floor to match the layout drawing. This gives you a chance to check your measuring and sawing before you glue them together permanently.

At this point, do almost all of the sanding which has to be done. Once the various parts are glued in place, sanding becomes more difficult. Plan to do only the extra-fine sanding after your headboard is assembled. Keep the assembly drawing close by when you screw or nail the pieces together in the order shown.

You can use a simple flat board for Piece #12, or you can fancy it up considerably before gluing the board into place. The ultimate would be an erotic carving on the board. That takes time, patience, and a certain artistic flair. I can help you become a good woodworker overnight, but don't expect me to make you into a woodcarver too.

For those not so artistically inclined who want to make an artsy-looking headboard, Figure II-5 shows several ways to use simple tools and inexpensive materials to create what will look to your friends and neighbors like a painstakingly crafted creation. You don't have to give away your secret!

The top artistry (A) is accomplished with three molded-wood "carvings." They're discussed in §8. Note that the example uses three carvings instead of only one. On any long, narrow piece, it's ideal to have a large design in the center to focus attention there. But the long board will look too empty without something to fill in the blank spaces at each end. The two end carvings should be substantially smaller or less striking than the center piece.

The middle examples B and C are assembled from molded strips. For a modest sum you can vent your artistic inclinations with the strips as shown, or you can flip back to §25 and reproduce some of the corner-molding artistry on your headboard.

The bottom bit of artwork in D is done simply with a drill. The big holes are drilled with a 1/4-inch drill bit, the smaller ones with a 1/8-inch drill bit. Don't try to sandpaper inside those holes. The rough, unfinished inside helps the decoration to show up by contrasting with the smooth, polished outside.

When you execute the drilled pattern, lay out the design on the side that is going to show. Use light pencil marks so you won't have to spend hours sanding away heavy pencil marks. Sometimes small chips of wood break out when your drill pushes out of the wood. You want those chips to be hidden. So drill from the side which will show to the side which will be glued to the rest of your headboard.

If you paint or stain the entire headboard, the decorative mold-

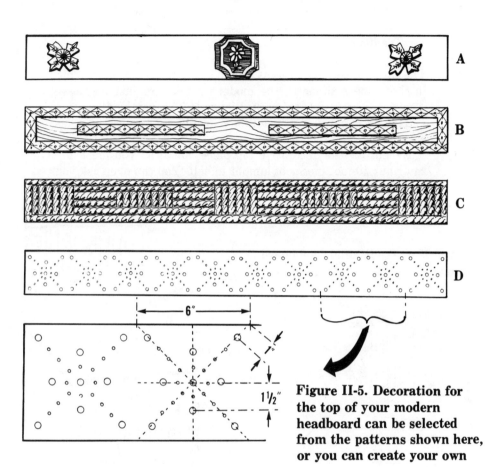

Figure II-5. Decoration for the top of your modern headboard can be selected from the patterns shown here, or you can create your own

ings should blend in with the overall coloration without extra attention. If you used hardwood, however, the moldings will need extra care.

If your wood is very dark or very light, you will have to stain the moldings or carvings carefully to blend with the color of your hardwood. Run a test with the stains you plan to use and you won't go wrong.

You can create an interesting effect if you stain the molded decoration a color or shade which contrasts with the main color of your wood. Make sure the difference is obvious enough that people know you did it on purpose.

You can even refer to Figure II-9 decorating a modern headboard. Designs for traditional headboards can work for many versions of this modern headboard.

Traditional

The three traditional designs shown in Figure II-6 are assembled in the same manner as the modern headboard just discussed. Again, any material can work. Figure II-7 shows the dimensions and layout of parts. This traditional headboard requires even less sawing than the modern one.

Except for the decorative top piece, about all you must do is saw your 10-foot pieces of lumber in half. You can even ask your lumber yard to do that for you.

Figure II-6. Traditional headboard designs

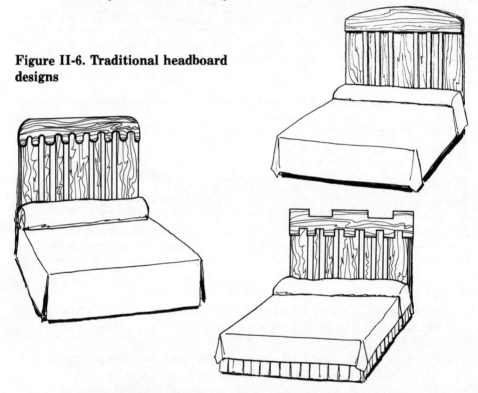

Because this elegant bit of furniture assembles exactly like the modern headboard, no extra drawing is included. Referring to Figures II-4 and II-7, you can nail or screw the headboard together in an hour or two. Don't forget the glue.

You can vary the shape of the decorative top piece to create all sorts of interesting effects that'll blend in with darned near any bedroom décor (Figure II-8). You can finish the main headboard in natural wood (or with wood grained vinyl or Formica) but

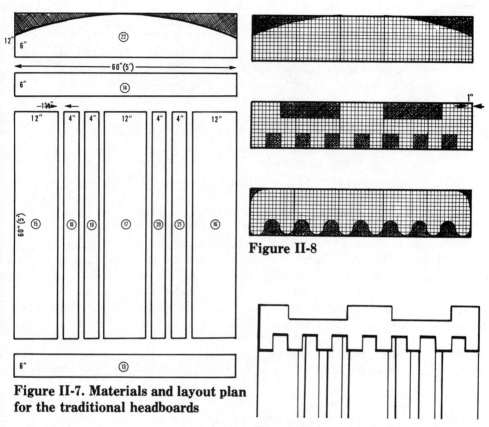

Figure II-8

Figure II-7. Materials and layout plan
for the traditional headboards

Figure II-9

finish the decorative top piece with fabric to match your draperies, walls, or bedspread.

Copy your choice of top piece design from Figure II-8 onto your wood using 1-inch squares. Or you can use one of the designs shown for the modern headboard in Figure II-5.

§29. Furniture Design

Have you noticed that we've already discussed how you can start to *design* your own furniture to fit your tastes, needs, existing furniture, or budget? In the case of this modern or traditional headboard, the design secret is based on two simple items.

The *modern* headboard incorporates irregular measurements and non-repetitive lines. Most so-called modern furniture designs simply strive to do things differently than they were done before.

If coffee tables had always been curvy, modern designers would strive for a straight, angular version. Our *traditional* headboard depends on straight lines and repeated measurements. Both designs, however, produce a symmetrical look.

In each type, the key piece of wood is the decorative top one. Because it's at the very top and physically stands out a bit from the rest of the wood, that's where the eye should look first. If you make a castle-like shape and cover that piece with tapestry, you've designed a medieval headboard. On the other hand, if you use a soft fabric done in soft colors on softly curving lines, the design is more romantic, more like Guy Lombardo than the Rolling Stones.

Here's one more design variation. You can build the traditional headboard with knotty pine or common pine. Use the simple curved decorative top piece which reflects the utter simplicity of Early American furniture. Finish the pine with orange shellac, and the design suddenly resembles an Early American or Colonial headboard. Designing furniture is just that easy.

Don't let furniture labels scare you! Because a headboard manufacturer says its product is modern, traditional, or Colonial, or Siamese doesn't mean the factory has satisfied dictates laid down by some great furniture designer in the sky. The factory has simply designed furniture which they can build easily and at a good price.

You'd probably be very unhappy with an authentic Early American chair or table. They weren't always beautiful, and the Puritan ethic made them mighty uncomfortable. Other early styles like French, Greek, or Italian likewise wouldn't do well in today's living rooms. Don't expect Colonial or French Provincial or Mediterranean styles to be exact replicas of something built in the past. The label simply means that the designer hopes to have captured the flavor and basic elements of a period piece.

Don't let arbitrary labels run or ruin your life. If a style appeals to you, use it. If you feel like changing it, change it. If you want to call one of your creations "Prudent Pompeiian" furniture, call it that and let the wags try to prove otherwise. *You* have to live with a piece of furniture 365 days a year. Label makers may never live with their creations, so concentrate on designing furniture that satisfies *you*.

6. Screwed-Together Old-Fashioned Headboard

SKILLS: Very easy. Good first project.
TIME: One to two evenings.

TOOLS: Sandpaper, drill.
Perhaps a handsaw.
ALSO READ: §'s 8, 14, 15, 21,
26, 27, 28.

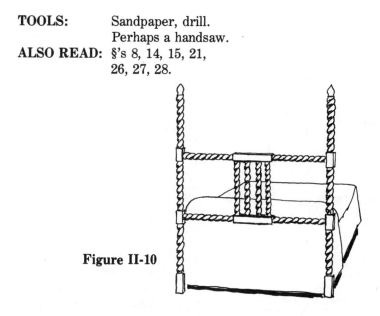

Figure II-10

The word "old-fashioned" on furniture can be mighty misleading. Because a piece of furniture is done in a style which vaguely copies old-fashioned appearances doesn't mean that it's old-fashioned in terms of utility.

From the viewpoint of design there's old-fashioned French, old-fashioned Italian, old-fashioned Spanish, old-fashioned American. . . . The last one is usually called Colonial. In general, old-fashioned designs are full of curves and twists and spirals. The lines never seem to stand still (Figure II-10).

Most old-fashioned styles have been interpreted by modern furniture designers. They all incorporate a lot of fancy carvings and wood turnings. If you tried to duplicate the curves by hand you'd still be at it next year. Fortunately, several wood and novelty manufacturers have created elaborate sets of wood turnings, carvings, moldings, and especially spindles that enable us to assemble very attractive furniture with an Italian, Spanish, or Colonial motif.

Most furniture makers vary only the style of the wood turnings and finishes when they switch from one classic old-fashioned furniture style to another. We'll do pretty much the same. The work goes quickly and the results look very professional.

The old-fashioned headboard in this chapter is made entirely from spindles. They come in various diameters, 2, and 3 inches being the most popular. They are available in varying lengths from 4 inches to over 2 feet.

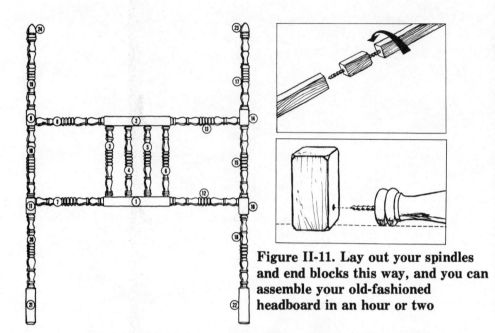

Figure II-11. Lay out your spindles and end blocks this way, and you can assemble your old-fashioned headboard in an hour or two

If you follow the design shown in Figure II-11, you can obtain the materials in the spindle section of your lumber or hardware store.

Fourteen pieces 15-inch spindles

Twelve pieces 15-inch end blocks (parts #1 and #2 in Figure II-11)

Four pieces 4-inch end blocks (parts #9, 11, 14, and 16)

Two pieces finials (parts #23, 24)

Ten pieces threaded dowels to fit your brand of spindle

Two pieces end blocks, 4 inches to 12 inches (parts #21, 22)

Sixteen pieces threaded connectors for your brand of spindles

As is, the design shown measures 49 inches wide. Using narrow spindles it isn't advisable to make the headboard much wider than the bed. With solid wooden headboards it's fun to have lots of wood showing around the covers. However, if you do want to make this design wider, you can join 2 pieces of 10-inch spindle to replace each of the 15-inch spindles shown on the crosspiece (parts #7, 8, 12, 13). That will give you a headboard 59 inches wide. Conversely, if you desire a narrower headboard for a single bed, simply reduce each 15-inch spindle on the cross-piece to 10 inches.

You can choose spindles to emulate any old-fashioned style you like—French, Italian, Spanish, Mediterranean, Colonial. . . . If you have difficulty obtaining 15-inch spindles, 14- or 16-inch work equally well. In fact you can change all of the dimensions as long as you make sure the spindles numbered 3, 4, 5, 6, 10, and 15 are the same size.

To assemble the design shown here, drill 1/4-inch holes in the 15-inch and 4-inch end blocks as shown in the insets. (Dowels for use with some brands of spindles may require a hole other than 1/4 inch.) Slip a threaded dowel into each hole after applying glue. The threaded end of each dowel couples to the threaded hole in the spindles. When a spindle meets a spindle, the threaded couplers screw into both spindles to create a perfect union. Use glue on all dowels and couplers to create a more perfect union.

Once you've drilled the 12 holes for threaded dowels, all that has to be done is simply to twist, twist, twist. Then sandpaper and stain or paint.

If you want an Early American or Colonial effect, orange shellac is a good choice for the finishing touches. A ruddy tan or brown paint, alone or antiqued, looks appropriate too.

A Spanish décor deserves a very dark stain or paint. However, if you really want to brighten up a room, you can paint the Spanish spindles a deep red, and wipe or antique them with black. The result is truly unusual.

The various French and Italian effects are usually created with a very light color such as ivory, light blue, and even olive green. The most popular overcolor for these furniture styles is gold. Make sure to let plenty of the undercolor show in the deepest parts of the spindle grooves.

You can use dark wood stains such as walnut or mahogany on the spindles. The furniture styles you'll create by doing so resemble the nineteenth-century American copies of furniture from other lands and earlier times.

Now that proper materials are so easy to obtain, what kind of furniture you make is limited only by your imagination.

7. Four-Poster Headboard

SKILLS: Easy.
TIME: Two to three evenings.

TOOLS: Coping or keyhole
saw, hammer, sandpaper.
ALSO READ: §'s 4 or 6, 8, 10,
11, 14, 15 17, 21;
Chapters 4, 6.

By using both spindles and pieces of wood, the old-fashioned style is retained but given a polished, smooth, sophisticated look. Figure II-12 shows you how to create a four-poster bed.

The "canopy" over the posts shown here is simply a 22-foot length of tasseled drapery tie. It's available at most department and sewing stores. To make the canopy more elaborate and authentic, you can stitch a top piece of muslin to the carefully measured drapery tie. With or without the top piece, slip loops in the drapery tie between the top spindle and the finial just before you twist the two pieces firmly together. Don't glue that joint so you can take the tassel off later for cleaning.

If you want to use this design without the canopy or tassel, the four posts don't look out of place at all. If you want to redesign the headboard and footboard yourself, you can simply dispense with the top two spindles altogether and eliminate the four-poster look.

Figure II-12

Since the big, solid crosspieces on the headboard and footboard support only their own weight, any rigid material can be used. If you like to lean against the headboard or footboard, however, 3/4-inch plywood (good 2 sides) is best. You can use 1/2-inch plywood if economy is important. Even chipboard is OK.

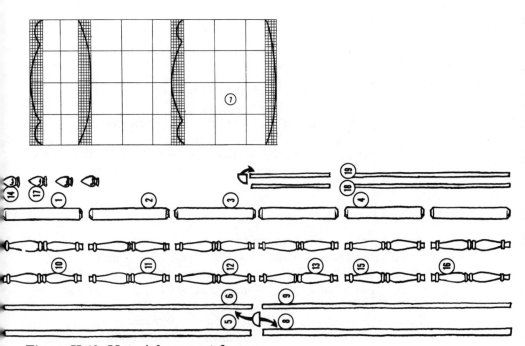

Figure II-13. Materials are cut from a single sheet of plywood and assembled with three strips of molding and a modest collection of spindles discussed in this chapter

Figure II-14. Lay out your materials this way to make assembly easy

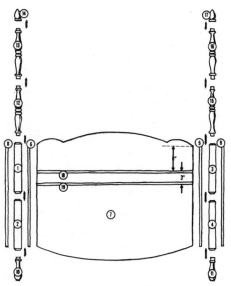

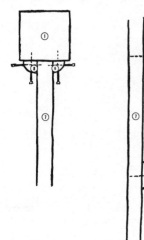

Figure II-15. Assemble the end blocks and plywood with strips of quarter-round molding in this fashion. The strips of half-round are for decorative reasons only, whereas the quarter-rounds are an important part of the construction

Draw 1-inch squares onto the top and bottom portions of your plywood or chipboard. Then copy the curves shown in Figure II-13. Cut them out with a keyhole saw, coping saw, or sabre saw. Do all of your sanding *before* you assemble the head and footboards to the spindle end blocks.

The solid boards are attached to the end blocks indirectly. You could try to nail right through the thick end blocks and conceivably land a few nails in the thin plywood, but the result could never be as strong nor look as good as that produced by the indirect method.

Figure II-15 shows how the boards are sandwiched between two pieces of quarter round corner molding. Assuming you have 3-inch wide end blocks and 3/4-inch plywood, draw a line 1-1/8-inch from the edge of your end-block assemblies. (For thicker or thinner wood and end blocks, add to or subtract from the 1-1/8-inch figure. You want the board to be centered.)

Apply glue to corner molding piece #6 and to the end blocks. Lay the molding onto the end blocks so one flat side rests on the end block and the other flat side lines up precisely along the pencil line. Nail it there carefully.

After applying more glue, lay one edge of your plywood piece (part #7) on the flat part of the corner molding (part #6) and make sure the plywood edge makes good contact with the end blocks. Drive just a few nails at an angle through the plywood and into the end block.

Then put glue on the flat sides of the remaining quarter-round molding (part #8). Position it as shown and nail it carefully to the end blocks and the plywood.

Repeat the measuring, gluing, and nailing until you secure the headboard's crosspiece to both sets of end blocks. Follow the same procedure to secure the footboard's crosspiece to its end blocks. Be sure to countersink the nails with a nail set, and fill the resulting holes with Plastic Wood. (See §11.)

Now we're ready to apply another type of molding to the headboard and footboard. This time it's 1-inch half-round molding. As you might expect by its name, it is shaped like a half circle, 1 inch in diameter. Glue and nail two strips of this molding to the headboard and two more strips to the footboard, leaving about 3 inches between the two strips. If your bed will stand away from any wall, you should also apply a set of the half-round molding to the back of your headboard.

After the sanding and other finishing is completed, glue your choice of fabric or Con-Tact vinyl onto the 3-inch space between moldings on your headboard and footboard. This is a purely decorative feature, but important for design purposes. This 3-inch strip of decorative fabric between moldings, serves as a focal point. Instead of using moldings and fabric, you can choose one of the molded carvings discussed in §8. They'll cost you more and unless they really appeal to you, probably won't look as nice.

Ideally, you should wait until you've finished the staining or painting on this project before deciding on the decorative touches. The tasseled drapery tie should be as similar as possible to your fabric or Con-Tact, or you'll risk getting a mish-mash effect. One decoration is important to the good looks of this bed project, but two are too much.

8. Colonial Headboard

SKILLS: Easy.
TIME: Weekend.
TOOLS: Saw, hammer, coping or keyhole saw, sandpaper.
ALSO READ: Chapters 2, 3, 4.

You can just about picture Betsy Ross laying thirteen stars on her sewing table before crawling under the quilts beneath an all-American-style headboard like this. If you finished some of the earlier styles appropriately, you have a Colonial look too. You used Colonial-style spindles and either maple- or pine-wood finish or antique. Those are the two wood types which seem to say "Early American" to most people.

Walnut was a favorite wood in Colonial days, as well as cherry and birch. But if you used those woods or stains on other designs, people wouldn't immediately get the Colonial impact unless your headboard sat in a room full of other Colonial furniture.

The very shape and configurations of this headboard are so Colonial that even if you painted it firehouse red (please don't), people would say, "My, that sure is a bright Colonial-style headboard."

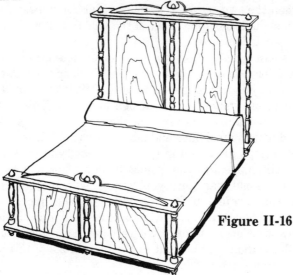

Figure II-16

The headboard shown in Figure II-16 was designed to be built from plywood. They didn't have plywood back in 1776, of course, so if you want to do this one up with utter authenticity, use two pieces of 12-inch-wide pine board in place of the large piece of plywood shown. Of course you can use cherry, walnut, maple, or birch boards too, assuming you can find any.

Crosspieces for the design shown here should be made of 4 inch boards. Use pine to go with plywood or match your hardwood if that's what you've chosen.

Figure II-18 shows how to lay out your materials. Trace part #25 by drawing 1-inch squares onto the bottom of your plywood sheet. There is enough plywood to build the footboard shown in sketch Figure II-16.

For a footboard, use two pieces of 10-inch spindles for each upright column. Make the two upright boards 20 inches long. Other than those changes, everything else stays the same.

Nail or screw and glue the wooden pieces together in the order shown in Figure II-18. Essentially what you're doing is assem-

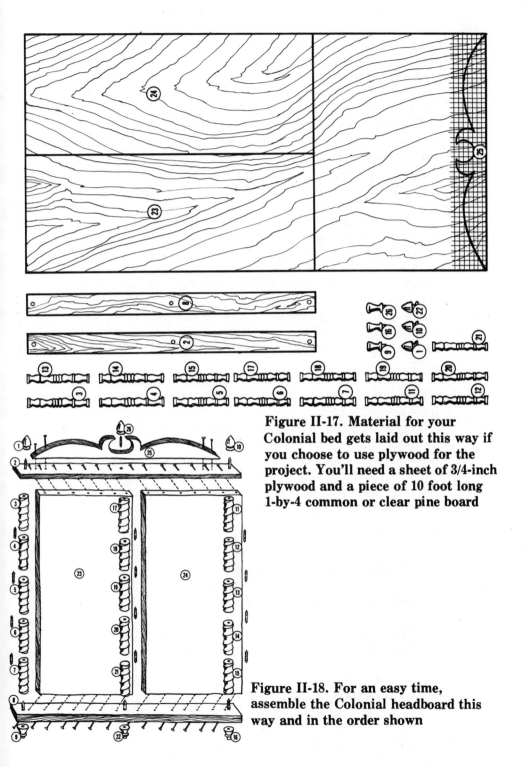

Figure II-17. Material for your Colonial bed gets laid out this way if you choose to use plywood for the project. You'll need a sheet of 3/4-inch plywood and a piece of 10 foot long 1-by-4 common or clear pine board

Figure II-18. For an easy time, assemble the Colonial headboard this way and in the order shown

bling three columns of spindles between the top crosspiece and the bottom crosspiece. Then you nail the two big pieces of plywood to the crosspieces. There's no need to countersink nails or screws. The ones on the bottom won't be seen. And ones on the top will be covered by the fancy top cutout, part #25.

The decorative top piece doesn't get much structural support except for glue, the middle finial, and just a few nails. This seems like a design weakness of this headboard, but the piece doesn't support any weight. It's unlikely somebody is going to bang the decoration with their foot since it's five feet off the ground.

If you build the footboard of this project, however, you should pay more attention to that curved top piece. Don't put it in the center of the crosspiece. Fasten it about 1/4-inch in from the outside edge. It doesn't look out of place there and gives you a chance to put plenty of nails or screws into it from the bottom of the crosspiece. And finally, by keeping away from the very edge of the crosspiece, you don't have to make everything fit perfectly.

There are all kinds of ways to finish this headboard. An all-pine-and-plywood version should have orange shellac as part of its finishing treatment. Alternately, you can use maple or walnut stain.

Plastic finishes will work too. Stain or antique all of the spindles and small wooden parts. Then apply vinyl or Formica to the large upright pieces.

In most furniture designs you can choose finish for the painted or stained portions to match or to contrast with the plastic covered areas. With a Colonial design like this one, however, you stand to lose the authentic look by using two different colors. But it's your furniture, your bedroom, and your project. If mixing colors looks good to you, go to it!

9.   Upholstered Headboards

SKILLS:	Easy but requires some patience.
TIME:	A weekend.
TOOLS:	Hammer, saw, coping or keyhole saw, scissors.
ALSO READ:	§'s 4, 15, 16, 17; Chapter 36. ·

I defy you to put upholstered headboards into any of those overly neat categories such as old-fashioned, modern, traditional, and so on. They're not Colonial or Spanish, for sure. Even if an upholstered headboard does not exactly match the style of furniture you already own, you can make it blend in nicely.

The very idea of trying to upholster something sounds out of the ballpark to most people who've never tried it. But it's so simple! And inexpensive to boot. All you need to make your own smashing, different, and soft upholstered headboard is a board, some foam rubber to give the creation a three-dimensional effect, fancy upholstery tacks, and a large piece of cloth. The board and foam will be hidden from view so buy the cheapest that's on the market.

Plywood sheathing is rough on both sides, and lumberyards sell it for closing up broken windows or putting rough exteriors on buildings under construction. It's very cheap, and it'll work dandy inside your new headboard.

Figure II-19 shows what a finished upholstered headboard looks like. Figures II-20 to 24 show variations of the same design.

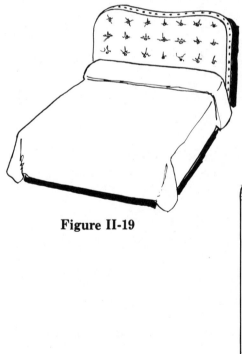

Figure II-19

Figure II-20. Materials for your upholstered headboard, aside from fabric, consist of a sheet of plywood which you'll cut into one of the following shapes (1-inch squares)

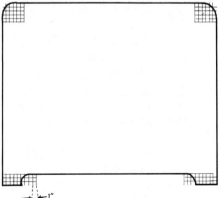

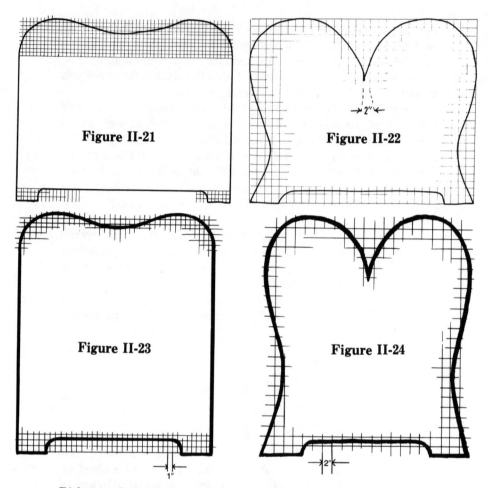

Figure II-21

Figure II-22

Figure II-23

Figure II-24

Pick one that suits your taste and draw the diagram for it onto your plywood form. (These plans take into account the fact that plywood is 48 inches wide. Therefore, these headboards are no higher than 48 inches.)

You can vary the width of these designs simply by adding or subtracting from the center of any of the drawings. That means you'll also have to redraw the curves just a bit. But even that goes smoothly if you work with 1- or 2-inch squares as in the drawings. First redraw the right side to fit your preferred dimensions. Then use the squares to trace the redrawn curve onto the left side.

You need about 10 linear feet of 4-foot-wide foam rubber to cover your plywood base. If you can't find a store that stocks the product that wide, invest in 20 feet of 2-foot-wide foam rubber.

Most upholstered headboards you can buy downtown are made

with a 1-inch-thick foam padding underneath. You too can use 1-inch padding, but if you really yearn for a plush feel and appearance, use 2-inch-thick foam rubber. Your new headboard will be the softest thing on the block.

Almost any fabric will work well on an upholstered headboard, but stiff, heavy fabrics are harder to work with, and frilly, light ones are not as durable. But spend more time considering the colors and patterns than the actual fibers used in weaving the cloth. Since the headboard is often the focal point of a bedroom, your choice in cloth should stand out a bit from the rest of the items in the room. But don't pick out something that screams whenever you walk into the bedroom. If you're handy with a needle or sewing machine, you might want to use the same cloth for a bedspread as well as your headboard. Even if you buy a new bedspread, you should be able to find a bolt of cloth which complements the pattern and color very closely.

Perhaps you want your headboard to match or contrast with your bedroom paint or wallpaper. If all else fails, stick to some universal color such as gold or shades of white. Under very carefully weighed conditions, black can be very striking.

Buy 4 yards of material. While you're shopping, pick up about 250 upholstery nails. They come in so many colors that you should be able to find some that will go with the cloth you are using.

Now let's start building this headboard. Lay your plywood on a floor and mark off 1- or 2-inch squares along the top and bottom. Then draw the necessary curves and lines onto your board.

Cut out the pattern with coping saw, keyhole saw or sabre saw. If there are any rough edges left when you're done sanding, get rid of them before they tear your foam rubber or fabric. There's no need to sandpaper the rough flat surfaces before you cover them.

Lay the curved board on top of the foam rubber. Line up the edges. Use a Magic Marker to trace the shape of your wooden frame onto the foam. Move the board to the unused area of foam and trace again. Cut the foam with scissors or a razor blade. You should end up with two pieces of foam shaped like the plywood frame.

Cut off a piece of cloth about 66 inches long. Mark a grid on the fabric so you can tack it and the foam into the plywood every 6 inches. You can use a Magic Marker to put a dot every 6 inches, but that's hard to clean off if you make a mistake. Chalk is much safer.

Set one piece of foam onto your plywood frame and line up the edges. Then center your marked piece of cloth on top of the foam.

Start at a mark near the very center of the headboard-to-be. Push one of your fancy upholstery tacks through the fabric and through the foam. Shove it into the plywood so the tack will stay put while you reach for your hammer. Pound the first tack firmly into the wood.

Move to the mark just to the right of your first tack and repeat the shoving and pounding. Move leftward and do the same. Then tack the spots just above and just below your center mark.

By the time you've hammered the first five tacks into place, you should start to see the ridges and valleys forming. The tacks pull your foam-backed fabric into three-dimensional patterns. If your cloth is flexible like vinyl, the process only stretches it. On a rigid weave, small wrinkles may form. Don't let small wrinkles worry you. They fit into the effect. Just keep the wrinkles near the tacks and not in areas between tacks. Keep smoothing out the loose fabric as you go along.

Work in an ever-widening pattern around the center tack. That keeps the cloth from bunching up excessively in any one part of the headboard. Shove and tack, shove and tack. . . .

After all of your tacks are in place on the front, you should have a couple inches of cloth hanging loose around the edges. Leave that for now. Flip the headboard over, lay the second foam pad carefully into position, spread the marked cloth on top, then go through the entire shoving and tacking process again. You should be pretty good at it by now.

The edges on your almost-finished headboard can be worked on more easily if you'll stand the headboard upright. Lean it against the bed, against some chairs, against a chest. Even standing it against the wall is easier than trying to work with the thing flat on the floor.

Depending on what tools you have and what kind of fabric you selected, choose a way to finish off the edges. The easiest method, though not the most attractive, is to cover the edges with tape. Either fabric or plastic tape will work depending on the kind of cloth you selected.

The alternative is to use the leftover fabric. You should have about 1 foot of it left. Cut that into 2-inch-wide strips. Fold over both edges into a deep hem, leaving you with a finished strip about an inch wide. The precise width isn't important. It can even vary a bit. After you've folded the edges, iron them so they won't flop loose while you're working.

Before you can apply the edge tape or edge fabric, you still have a few preliminaries to attend to. At this point, life may be a bit simpler if you own or can borrow a staple gun. But if not, don't worry. You'll get the job done just as well.

With a staple gun, gently pull the loose ends of cloth down to the edge of the plywood and staple them into place every few inches. Pull just hard enough to round off the edges of the foam padding. Don't pull so hard that the edge of your foam rubber is compressed right down to the surface of the plywood base. Staple a foot or two of cloth from the front, then do likewise with cloth from the back.

You may have a considerable amount of excess cloth hanging loose around the legs and rounded corners. Trim it off with scissors or a razor blade. In general, the cloth from the front side of your headboard should easily reach the plywood core, but not extend beyond the back edge of the wood. And the back's fabric should not extend beyond the front edge of wood. If they do, start trimming with your scissors.

After all of the edges are secured with staples, you can start covering the unflattering edges with tape or fabric strips. The best place to start is at the bottom.

Lay your tape or folded cloth over the plywood core so it covers up all of the stapled edges of cloth from the front and back. If you're working with plastic or cloth tape, the adhesive will hold it temporarily in place as you move along. With fabric strips, you have to hammer in an upholstery tack every foot or so. Go back with more tacks later.

Hammer your fancy upholstery tacks into the edge strip about every 6 inches to match the tack pattern on front and back. When you've finished that, go back and add a couple more tacks between the 6-inch spacing. You want to end up with tacks about every 2 inches along the edge.

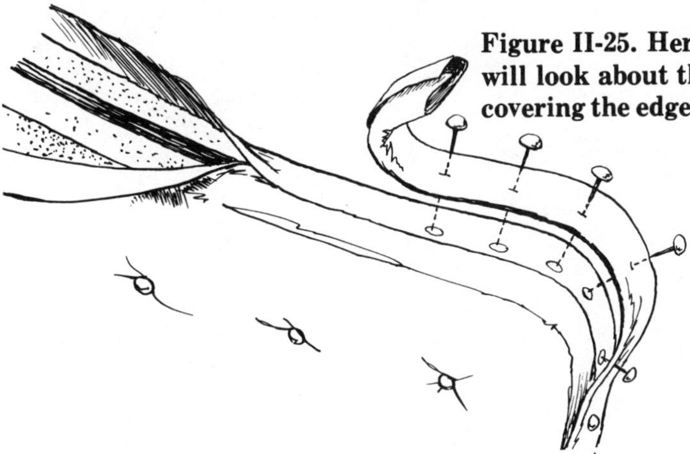

Figure II-25. Here's how your project will look about the time you're covering the edge of the upholstery job

If you're not using a staple gun, invest in a tube of silicone adhesive. Apply it along the edge of the plywood core. Then pull the loose ends of fabric from the front and back into the adhesive, trimming away excess cloth first. The adhesive will hold the fabric ends in place while you're working as well as after the project is finished.

Go through the trim-and-glue routine for several feet. Then stop and tack your decorative tape or fabric strips to the edge. Glue and trim some more, then tack, and so on.

As you're working, check periodically to see that none of the silicone adhesive is oozing out from beneath the strips. If it is, wipe the excess away before it sets.

Before plunging into the actual upholstering, drill holes near the bottom of the plywood frame for mounting the headboard to your bed's frame. After all of the padding and fabric are tacked into place, locate the holes again. Use scissors or a knife to poke through the pad and fabric so you can slip mounting bolts through the opening. Once your headboard is mounted firmly against the bed frame, the fabric shouldn't fray. If you're worried about that happening, apply a bit of silicone adhesive or polyvinyl glue around the hole. *That* will definitely keep loose threads from unraveling.

If you chose a light-colored fabric, use stainless steel bolts and nuts. For a dark fabric, buy black iron hardware. If you are a perfectionist, paint the heads of your bolts to match the upholstery.

Tighten the bolts and crawl between the covers to enjoy your new headboard. You deserve a break today!

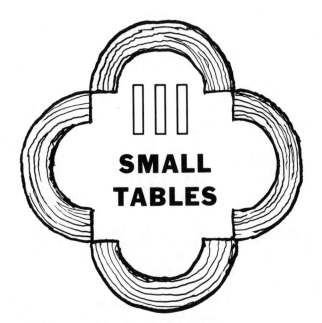

10. Square Tables Not for Squares

SKILLS: Easy.
TIME: One to two evenings.
TOOLS: Handsaw, keyhole saw, hammer, sandpaper.
ALSO READ: §'s 4, 10, 11, 14, 15, 16, 26, 28.

Coffee table, cocktail table, end table, vanity table, night stand, hall table. . . The variations in names for small tables go on and on and on. You might have trouble telling the difference between a coffee table and a cocktail table if some eager table peddler didn't tack on a label. Other than the label, there *isn't* any difference.

The major difference between various tables is in the length of their legs. Coffee and cocktail tables are about 16 to 18 inches high. End tables are in the 18-to-30-inch bracket. Night stand and hall tables come close to 36 inches. Just for the record, dining room and kitchen tables stand about 28 or 30 inches high.

You can often take plans for a small coffee table, lengthen the legs a bit, and end up with a dandy large end table. We're going to make all kinds of variations of the squared little table. Originals and duplicates like it were the rage of modern decorators for years. For a very modest price, you can make one or a dozen. Let them stand by themselves or stack several of them together in a corner until they're needed.

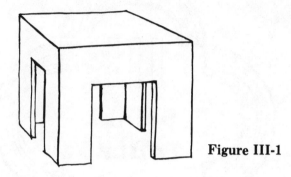

Figure III-1

The table sketched in Figure III-1 was laid out so its size won't be evident. That way you can get an idea what one of them will look like in your living room. You decide how big you want the top to be—12, 16, 24 or 32 inches.

Figure III-2 shows how to make the legs. You'll need four of them. Since you're working with 1/2-inch plywood, trim 1/2 inch off the left side and 1/2 inch off the right side of two legs. That way, the four legs will form a perfect square when nailed together. The top that will go on next, is a perfect square too. The caption for Figure III-2 gives the dimensions for the legs to match the top of your choice.

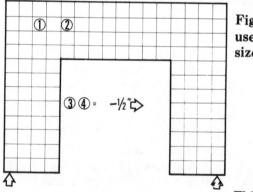

Figure III-2. Leg pattern which can be used for a square table of almost any size

This chart shows how to adapt the leg pattern to match various top sizes.

TOP WIDTH	LEG WIDTH	LEG HEIGHT	SIZE OF SQUARES ON PATTERN
12″	3″	9″	3/4″
16″	4″	12″	1″
24″	6″	18″	1-1/2″
32″	8″	24″	2″

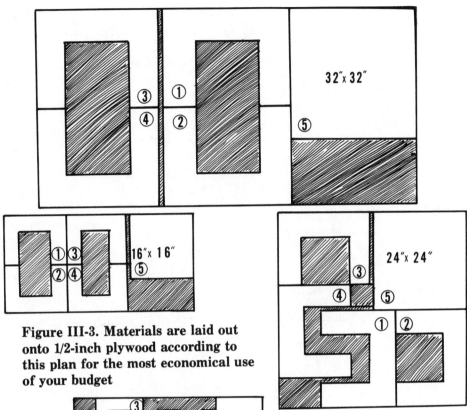

Figure III-3. Materials are laid out onto 1/2-inch plywood according to this plan for the most economical use of your budget

Lay out the legs and top on 1/2-inch plywood (good 1 side) according to Figure III-3. This way you have to spend the least possible amount of your budget on lumber. Economy is also why the largest table is 32 inches square instead of 36 inches. It would take one and a half sheets of plywood to fit in all the parts for the 36-inch model. If you give up those 4 inches, the whole thing fits neatly on only one sheet of plywood.

Saw the parts carefully. When you're ready to cut out the inner piece from the legs, saw one of the easy, vertical lines first. Use a regular handsaw (or power saw) for that. Then use your keyhole saw and carefully cut away some of the waste lumber along the cut you've just completed. Gradually expand the size of the hole you're cutting near that inside corner until you can fit at least the narrow part of your handsaw into the hole. Then make the horizontal saw cut.

There's a reason why I didn't recommend that you start cutting the horizontal part of each leg with a keyhole saw. The blade on most ordinary handsaws is about twice as thick as most keyhole-saw blades. Even if you cut for 6 or 8 inches along the horizontal portion with the keyhole saw, you probably wouldn't be able to slip your handsaw blade into the cut made.

You can hammer this project together with 1-inch nails. Don't forget the glue. Make sure that the two narrow leg pieces go *inside of* the two bigger ones. The base will then be perfectly square, and the square top will fit perfectly.

On smaller tables, space the nails about 2 or 3 inches apart. Leave 3 or 4 inches between nails on larger versions.

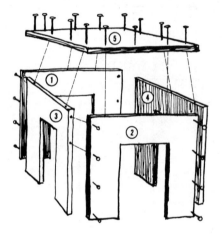

Figure III-4. Assemble parts of your square table this way and in the order shown

When you sandpaper this project, concentrate on more than just smoothing out surface irregularities in the wood. No matter how carefully you cut and assemble, there will be some uneven corners and rough joints. Tackle the rough corners and joints with coarse or medium-grade sandpaper on a good sanding block. Be careful that you don't round off the corners. This is supposed to be a square project.

After the shape of the table is taken care of, switch to finer and finer grades of sandpaper. Although you can give this table a natural-wood finish, most people prefer the brightest, glossiest paint or lacquer they can find. Vinyl plastics or even Formica also work well.

You're not through with this design yet, however. It comes back to haunt you as an elongated night stand and a grown-up kitchen or dinette table.

11.   Square but Shining Night Table

SKILLS:	Easy.
TIME:	One to two evenings.
TOOLS:	Handsaw, keyhole saw, hammer, sandpaper.
ALSO READ:	§'s 4, 10, 11, 14, 15, 16, 26, 28; Chapter 10.

Figure III-5

All you have to do is stretch the legs on the squared 16-inch table in the last chapter, add a shelf or two, and you end up with a very functional, stylish nightstand to complement your modern bedroom (Figure III-5). You'll be surprised how little of the squared off, symmetrical look is lost in the process.

Figure III-6 shows two ways to lay out the parts on 1/2-inch plywood to get the most table out of the least lumber.

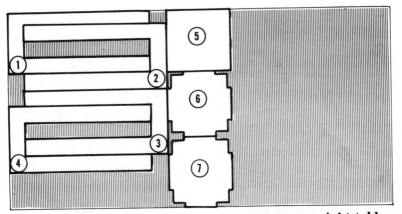

Figure III-6. Materials for your square night table can be laid out in one of two ways. The above method saves space, but requires more careful work with a saw. Sketch on next page is easier, but makes less efficient use of the plywood unless you can find a use for the odd-shaped pieces left over

OR

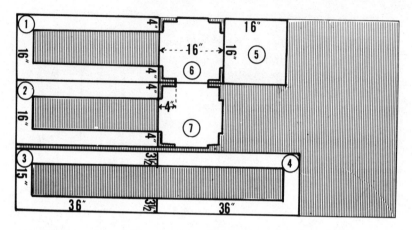

Follow Figure III-4 for basic assembly directions. Then nail the two shelves into place, also with 1-inch finishing nails. Put the first shelf 6 inches from the bottom. Position the second shelf 24 inches from the bottom. Sandpaper it well and add the finish which goes best, with the décor of your bedroom.

See you in the morning.

12. Natural-Wood Night Stand

SKILLS:	Easy.
TIME:	Weekend or one to two evenings.
TOOLS:	Handsaw, keyhole or coping saw, hammer, sandpaper.
ALSO READ:	§'s 3, 27; Chapters 3, 5.

This stand is designed to fit into your bedroom next to the modern headboard featured in Chapter 5. Natural wood is ideal, but if you finished the headboard with paint, antiquing, lacquer, or plastic, use the same finish on this night stand (Figure III-7).

You need 12 feet of whatever kind of 12-inch-wide lumber you plan to use. It's possible to save a bit of cash by buying only 9 feet of hardwood and making the back, part #1, out of something cheaper.

Make 1-inch squares where you plan to cut the curved shelf pieces. Trace the curves and cut all the pieces out carefully.

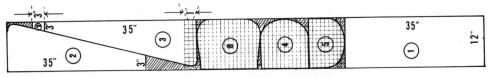

Figure III-8. Lay out your parts onto the 10-foot-long hardwood board this way

Figure III-7

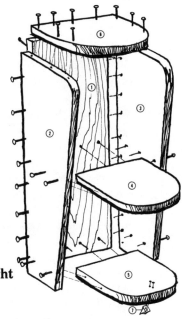

Figure III-9. Assemble your night stand in the order shown

Sandpaper all of the edges. When that's done, you can assemble this project in less than half an hour.

I haven't given measurements for exactly where the shelves should go. The bottom shelf must rest on the leg, part #7, which is 3 inches high.

Curved shelf #4 may be slightly larger or smaller than it appears in Figure III-7. This will depend on how you draw the curve, saw the board, and sandpaper the edges. It's more important that the shelf's edges be hidden within the sides than that it be pounded into place in some pre-determined spot. When you're ready to put the center shelf in, lay the night stand on its side, slide the shelf up and down until it fits just right, and *then* fasten it into place.

My personal preference is to leave this night table as simple as possible, but you can adapt it to your taste. If you finished the modern headboard with molded strips, you might want to carry that design through on the sides of this nightstand. If you used the drilled decoration on the headboard, you can transfer the design on the back of this night table. Make the drilled design four times on top, four on the bottom.

Without a lot of advanced training, you may have started to think like a home furniture *designer* and not just a follow-the-leader builder. Didn't hurt a bit, did it?

13. Glass-Topped Coffee Table

Glass coffee-table tops have been the rage for years. They fit in with most decoration styles and are easy to maintain. But the thought of working with glass probably scares you.

In some ways, working with glass is easier than with wood. It can even be cheaper than hardwood or plywood.

Glass used for the top of a coffee table must be many times thicker than the glass in your windows. If you tried to buy new glass for a table top, your budget might be strained for a couple of months. But in the case of glass, somebody else's misfortune can be your good fortune.

Those huge department store plate glass windows are just thick enough to make nice coffee table tops. Most glass companies save the bigger pieces whenever such a window breaks, and they'll sell nice-sized pieces at bargain prices.

You may have to shop around or make some phone calls to find a glass shop with plate glass scrap, but the savings are well worth the bother. Don't tell the glass shop you want a coffee-table top exactly 3 feet by 4 feet. Say, "About 3 feet by 4 feet." Glaziers are nice people. As a rule, they'll cut a jagged piece of glass into a nice looking rectangle or square without jacking up the bargain price. But don't ask for precise measurements as part of the deal.

Another way to save cash on a coffee-table top is to make sure the glazier understands that you plan to polish the edges yourself. On your way home with the piece of glass, stop at the hardware store and buy a sharpening stone. It doesn't have to be longer than 4 or 5 inches.

Run the sharpening stone smoothly over each of the corners of the glass. Polish away the top and bottom edges as well as the four corners. Lubricate the stone periodically with light oil or kerosene. Synthetic stone is ordinarily used to put a sharp edge on metal tools. Here you're using it to take a sharp edge off glass.

In about an hour, you should be able to polish all the sharp edges off a large coffee table top. If you want to make the corners and edges obviously rounded as well, you'll have to polish for several hours. When the polishing is all over, you'll be ready to set the glass onto its base, producing a beautiful table at half the going price.

To avoid the risk of injury, follow these guidelines to determine what thickness of glass to use. The longer the table top, the thicker the glass:

Up to 2 feet long, 1/4-inch-thick glass.

Up to 3 feet long, 3/8-inch-thick glass.

Up to 4 feet long, 1/2-inch-thick glass.

These size requirements assume that the glass top will be well supported by a sturdy base or set of legs. If you tip the glass onto a hard floor, it's apt to chip or break no matter how thick it is. If one of your high friends does a high dive onto the glass top, thick as it may be, you may still have to call your lawyer and insurance agent.

If you have lingering doubts about glass tops, use plastic. Ordinary acrylic plastics, known commonly as Lucite or Plexiglas, have always been as clear and as beautiful as glass. And they don't break unless you really try, but unfortunately, sharp pins, nail files, stones, clay flower pots, and scouring pads can scratch acrylic plastic.

You can buy an inexpensive kit at hardware or hobby stores which gives you all the materials you need to polish away the scratches that eventually accumulate on plastic coffee-table tops. You shouldn't have to go through that act more often than every couple of years unless your living room is a stable for a half dozen untamed tigers.

There's an uncommon plastic on the market that rivals the scratchproof qualities of glass. *Coated acrylic plastic*, marketed under trade names such as Lexan, is used for shatterproof windows in schools, buses and trains. It costs more to start with, but requires less care than common acrylic plastic. You're paying the bill. And you're going to care for the coffee table top. So you have to decide whether it'll be glass or plastic, common acrylic plastic or coated.

Plastic table tops require about the same kind of care you'd give fine natural-wood tops. They'll withstand some heat, but if you plunk a pot fresh from the oven on plastic, you'll be shopping for a new top by sundown. If you put a hot pad down first, you can take a pot of beans out of the oven and set it on the coffee table for your bridge club.

Don't use abrasive cleansers on plastic. You shouldn't even use them on Formica!

The recommended thickness for glass given earlier should be followed for plastic tops as well. With glass, thickness is needed for safety. Plastics need thickness mainly to remain rigid. If you plan to use a plastic table top with longer unsupported lengths than the designs included here, you should buy a thicker piece. You usually can't return a piece of plastic once the shop has cut it for you. You'd better ask for that extra 1/8 inch in advance if you have a hunch your project may need it.

Plastic has some advantages also. You can cut it with hand tools and put holes in it with an inexpensive electric drill.

Some spindle manufacturers discovered that people really like the looks of a glass top supported by nothing but four individual legs. They tell you to buy four of their legs and just screw them into place with a piece of glass that has four holes in it.

Cutting holes in glass isn't tough if you have the right tools. But not many glass cutters have them, so the price of a glass coffee-table top soars drastically the minute you mention those four little holes.

You can pick up the cheapest electric drill and put four holes into a plastic table top in four minutes. Add up the cost of the premium price for coated acrylic plastic plus the cost of buying an electric drill, and you'll still probably save money over the bill for a piece of glass with four holes in it.

Cost comparison favors plastic even more if you want a round top or a fancier curved shape. You can cut the plastic curve or circle of your choice with any fine-toothed saw such as a sabre saw, coping saw, hacksaw, or keyhole saw with fine blade.

When the sawing is done, sandpaper the edges as if they were wood. Start with medium grade. If you want the edge to look glassy and transparent, continue down through extra-fine and then switch to a plastic polishing powder or stone. The store that sold you the piece of plastic will also sell you the buffing material.

If you'd like a translucent, ground-glass effect on the edge of your coffee table top, don't use anything beyond fine-grade sandpaper. Sand away the gloss evenly all around the edge and you'll end up with a white edge to contrast with the clear top.

When in doubt, experiment. You can always change from translucent to clear again or vice versa. But now let's get down to work and actually build something.

A. Glass Top Suspended-In-Air (Figure III-10)

SKILLS: Very Easy. Good
               first project.
TIME: One evening.
TOOLS: Saw, drill, sandpaper.
ALSO READ: §'s 8, 21, 26, 27, 28.

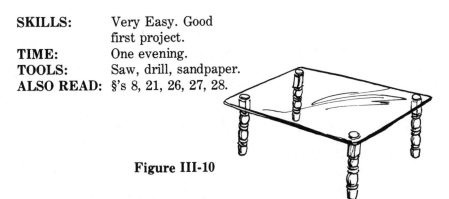

Figure III-10

Materials for this clever-looking project consist of four legs or spindles and a glass or plastic top. Size isn't critical, but when it starts getting longer than 2 or 3 feet, you can start expecting troubles.

If you happen to find a bargain in glass tops with holes already drilled, use one for this table. Otherwise you're money ahead to buy a plastic top and drill your own holes. Makers of the legs or spindles you choose, also make screw-in caps or finials. Set the top onto the legs, one at a time please, and slip the finial or cap into the hole. Screw the leg and cap together tightly before going on to the next leg.

You can tackle the same project with an even wilder approach. Silicone and epoxy glues stick to glass and plastic as well as they do to wood. You can glue the top to the legs and create something that looks like glass sitting on top of four skinny legs with no apparent connection.

Epoxy glues are a bit tougher than silicones, but less flexible. The silicones come in colors. For legs finished in a light, natural-wood tone, choose a tan colored silicone adhesive. For very dark paints or stains, choose a black silicone product.

There are only two major warnings to go with this glued-on-top idea. First, make sure the areas where the top and legs meet are cleaned very thoroughly before you apply glue. Secondly, when the project is finished, don't slide the table around too much. Pick it up to move it. The glues are tough, but they won't resist a lot of sliding or twisting.

This suspended top doesn't have to be square or rectangular or even round. You can support any shape with four legs. And in the next few pages you'll find plans for less-orthodox tops.

B. and C. Pedestal Coffee Tables (Figures III-11 and -12)

SKILLS:	Easy, but requires some patience.
TOOLS:	Keyhole or coping saw (sabre saw makes life easier), hammer or screwdriver, sandpaper.
TIME:	Weekend.
ALSO READ:	§'s 1, 2; Chapters 3, 4.

Figure III-11

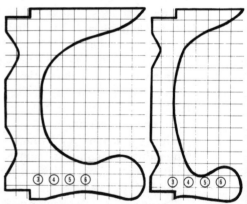

Figure III-12

Figure III-13. Lay out four leg patterns like these onto either 1-by-8 or 1-by-12-inch common or clear pine. The 8-inch model will support tops up to about 3 feet across. For bigger tops, switch to the 12-inch version. Each square is 1 inch wide in this sketch

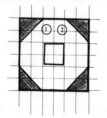

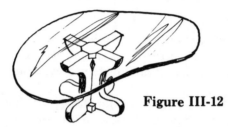

A curvy "tree" cut from four pieces of wood makes a quietly elegant support for a glass or plastic coffee-table top. In general, round or curved tops look best with this support.

Figure III-13 shows how to lay out the parts for this "tree" on your lumber. You need four uprights and two caps. Since you'll see one of the caps through the transparent table top, give it the more elegant shape by cutting off all four corners as shown.

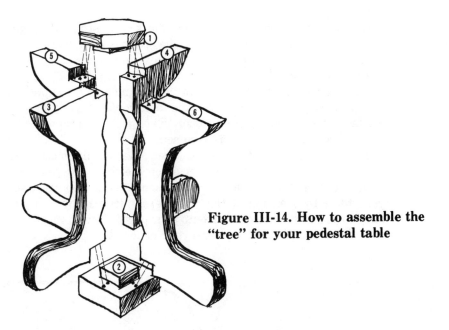

Figure III-14. How to assemble the "tree" for your pedestal table

Figure III-14 gives a bird's-eye view of how the four parts and the two caps fit together into one tree. The two caps are all that hold the four legs together—and that's all that will support your table top. So make sure that the caps fit snugly. Nail or screw them into place carefully. And use plenty of glue on all surfaces where the legs and caps meet.

One version of this tree is made from 2-by-8-inch lumber. That model can support tops up to about 3 feet in diameter. For bigger tables, switch to the bigger tree.

With 2-by-12-inch lumber, the resulting tree spreads its limbs to almost 26 inches. It will support tops up to 4 feet wide if you place them well. When in doubt, be conservative. This table doesn't depend on massive size to achieve its impact.

Buy the best grade of pine lumber you can find for the tree. If you really want to do the project up proud, hardwood will look superb, but it promises to be hard to find. No matter what kind of wood you settle on, plan to spend many hours cutting it out slowly. By machine or by hand, you can't rush through the curves in a 2-inch-thick piece of wood.

This base presents a splendid example of how the finish on your furniture projects influences the overall style. If you keep all of the edges very sharp when you sand them, and if you paint the base, the resulting table will fit nicely into a modern décor.

Given a natural-wood finish, regardless of whether the edges are kept sharp or rounded off, and the effect is more likely to be called traditional or contemporary. Those terms are as ambiguous as this pedestal.

Now, if you round off all parts of the leg and give the support a rich, probably dark, wood finish, the table could fit nicely into an old-fashioned living room or parlor. Even a dark antique finish could make the grade as old-fashioned.

You're going to meet up with this set of legs again in chapters to come. But now you have to decide on the shape for your top. That becomes strictly a matter of personal taste. You can whet your taste by glancing at the curvy examples nearby. All you have to do is trace one of them onto your plastic, saw it out, finish the edges, and plop the top onto your pedestal.

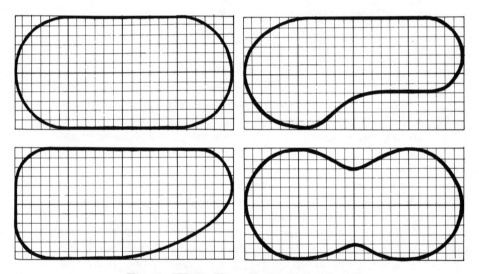

Figure III-15. Top shapes for pedestal tables. Each square is 2 inches big. Tops from these patterns will be 2 feet by 4 feet

D. Hand-Carved Table Base (Figure III-16)

SKILLS: Easy.
TIME: Two evenings or a weekend.

TOOLS: Saw, drill, sandpaper.
ALSO READ: §'s 4, 8, 14, 21, 26, 27.

The "hand carving" for this hand-carved table base is not done by you but by a machine. A trip to your favorite building or craft outlet will reward you with four pieces of molded carvings. All you need is money. But let's try to save some of that.

Figure III-16.

Figure III-17. Alternate shapes for the end pieces. If you cut the outside piece like one of these, you can dispense with the somewhat costly carvings shown in the original model of this table

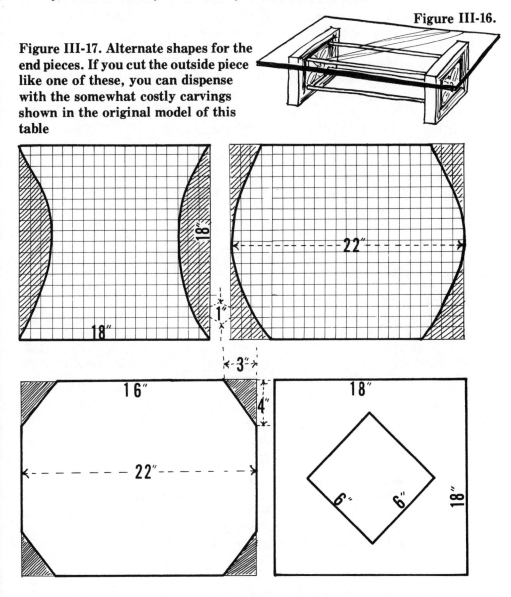

The carvings come in sizes up to 24 inches square, but something that size runs into a lot of money. Plastic carvings don't look as luxurious as the "genuine" wooden ones. So the table base shown here is built with 14-inch-square moldings. We make it appear larger than 14 inches by surrounding it with a molding, just like you surround a picture with a molded picture frame. You can buy these moldings precut to size and with corners already cut at 45 degrees so all you have to do is tack them into place. You can see plenty of carving designs in §8.

How much of a top you can mount on this hand-carved base depends on how big a base you decide to build. Length is very flexible up to about 40 inches. On a base that long you can safely put a glass or plastic top 54 inches (4-1/2 feet) long.

With 14-inch carvings enclosed in moldings, a 24-inch-wide (2 feet) top is OK. If you want a top 30 inches wide, you can use 20-inch carvings by themselves. Enclose the 20-inch carvings in molding and you can use a 36-inch-wide (3 feet) top. Same goes for the 24-inch carvings. This base is at its best with rectangular-shaped tops.

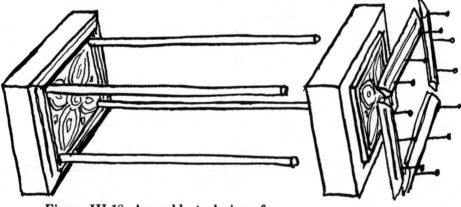

Figure III-18. Assembly technique for the "hand-carved" table base

Figure III-18 shows about all there is to know on the subject of assembling a hand-carved coffee-table base. Make the core from 3/4-inch plywood cut to the exact dimensions of your carved panels or carved panels plus molding. If you want to play it safe, leave the core piece a bit too big and later pare it down to size with a saw, sandpaper, or SurForm tool. If you go the coward's route, however, you still have to get at least two sides of the front and back lined up precisely.

It isn't easy to nail most molded panels. So, this is a good place to use epoxy glue, which can grab firmly onto wooden surfaces without the clamping effect you get from nails or screws with traditional glues. Lay plenty of books or other weights carefully on top of the glued pieces until the epoxy has had plenty of time to set.

First glue only one carving to each base. Then pick a spot near each corner where you can drill a 1-inch hole without totally destroying the beauty of your carving. Since the wood and plastic carvings are sometimes hard to drill, the easiest way to make the 1-inch hole is with a hole-cutting tool in a 1/4-inch electric drill. Cut all the way through the carving and through the 3/4-inch plywood. Make sure that the 1-inch dowel sticks fit snugly into your holes. Then glue the remaining carvings to the other side of your base piece.

After the glue has had plenty of time to set, measure how deep the holes go. That will be 3/4 inches for the plywood plus the thickness of your carving at the point you drilled the hole. For example, let's say it's 1-1/8 inches.

Draw a line around each dowel stick exactly 1-1/8 inch from its end. You want to push each dowel as far into its hole as possible when you glue your table base together. But if you shove it *too* far, you risk knocking the outside panel loose. That's why you draw the 1-1/8 inch line.

Glue all four dowels to one base first. Before that glue sets, apply more glue to the other base piece and to the other end of your dowels. Fit each dowel stick into its appropriate hole in the second base piece and firmly force them together until your lines show that each dowel is in as deeply as it can go. Use the pencil lines on the dowels to make sure the four dowels are inserted into the bases evenly. Otherwise the bases will not come out even.

When all the glue has set, sandpaper the edges of your bases thoroughly. Even before gluing the dowels into place, you should have taken care of major roughness with a SurForm tool or heavy sandpaper. The base edges have to be so smooth that the core and the two panels seem to be made from a single piece of material.

With a bit of extra puttering you can stain the dowels, the edges of your plywood plus carvings, and the face of your carved panels so they all take on the same hue. Or, after proper coats of primer, you can paint and then wipe or antique the whole base.

The length of your dowels determines how long a piece of glass you can put onto this base. The width is governed by the width of the base, of course. On smaller tables, you can allow about 4 inches of glass to hang beyond the base on all sides. You can have 7 or 8 inches hanging over on the largest table tops.

You can double the usefulness of this coffee table if you lay a glass or plastic shelf across the bottom two dowels to supplement the top shelf. You can use a shelf 4 to 6 inches wider than the dowels. If you get a piece about exactly the full length of the dowels, the bottom shelf will be protected from being shoved off. A bump toward one side will twist the shelf just a bit, but the end will bump against the other base and keep the shelf from tumbling off.

E. Floating-Glass Coffee Table (Figure III-19)

SKILLS:	Very easy. Good first project.
TIME:	One to two evenings or weekend.
TOOLS:	Saw, drill, sandpaper.
ALSO READ:	§'s 4, 10, 11, 14, 21, 26, 28

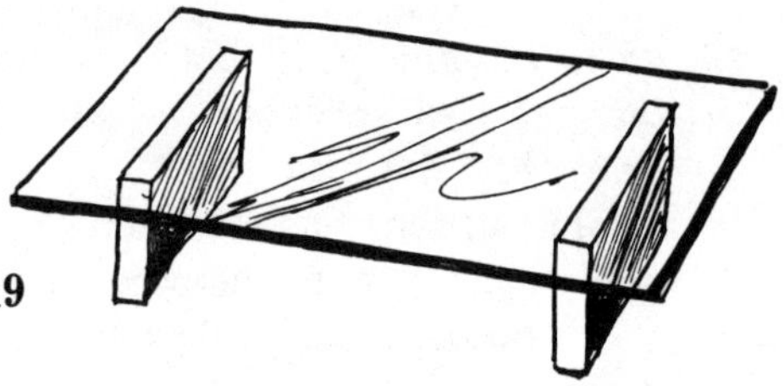

Figure III-19

Actually this coffee-table base is little more than a simplified, modernized version of the "hand-carved" model IV above. Instead of gluing a carved panel onto a piece of plywood, glue two pieces of plywood together for each base. Use a good wood glue and 1-1/4-inch nails.

Use the same criteria as for the table shown in Figure III-16 to decide how big a base you need. A base about 18 inches square works out nicely.

Drill your four holes 3 inches from each corner. You can use 1-inch wooden dowels as in the earlier "hand-carved" table. But if you want to create a very unusual effect, buy four lengths of half-inch acrylic plastic rods instead of dowels. If you use plastic rods you'll have to glue them into place with an epoxy glue instead of wood glue.

Although I personally prefer a square shape to the base of a table like this, Figure III-17 gives some alternates you might prefer. Likewise, painting the base black (and the dowels too if you use them instead of plastic rods) gives the most striking, floating effect. But white or any other color can sustain the impact too.

14. Inlaid-Wood Coffee Table (Figure III-20)

SKILLS:	Pretty demanding.
TIME:	Several weekends, depending upon the finish.
TOOLS:	Saw, hammer or screwdriver, sandpaper. Possibly drill, electric sander.
ALSO READ:	§'s 24, 26, 27, 29; Chapters 2, 3.

Stock up on plenty of sandpaper. You're about to make an eye-stopping traditional coffee table out of untraditional materials and methods.

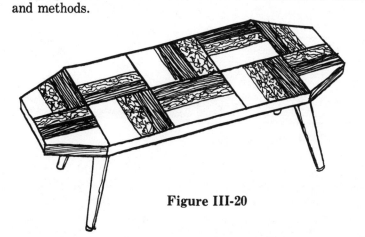

Figure III-20

The most beautiful way to execute this inlaid-wood coffee table is with real hardwood from three different kinds of trees. My own table was built with practically white ash, very ruddy red oak, and deep brown Philippine mahogany. Those three woods provide about the greatest contrast possible. You can be more subtle by using woods obviously different in grain and hue but not so far apart as mahogany and ash.

Your basic table shape is a squared-off oval, or an ovaled-off rectangle, whichever way you want to look at it. The one illustrated in nearby drawings is 5 feet long and 2 feet wide. You can add or subtract a foot without sacrificing the streamlined look.

For the genuine hardwood version you need a stock of 4-inch-wide hardwood boards. For the 5-foot table, buy 10-foot-long 1 by 4's in each of the three hardwood species.

Saw the boards into 12-inch lengths. The more accurately you measure and saw, the less sanding you'll have to do later.

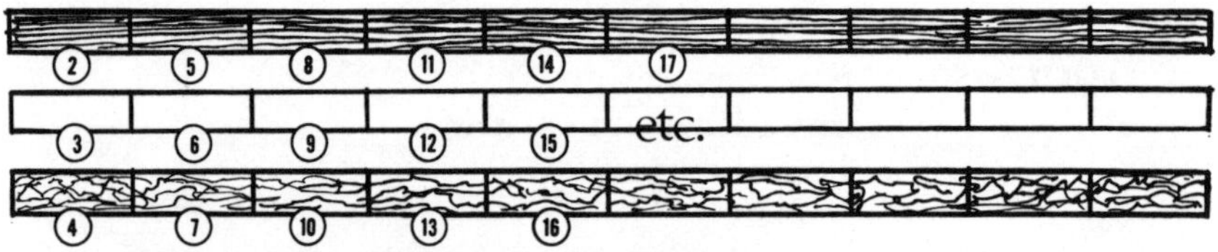

Figure III-21. Materials are laid out and cut in this manner. Each 10-foot-by-4-inch piece of hardwood is cut into 10 pieces, each a foot long

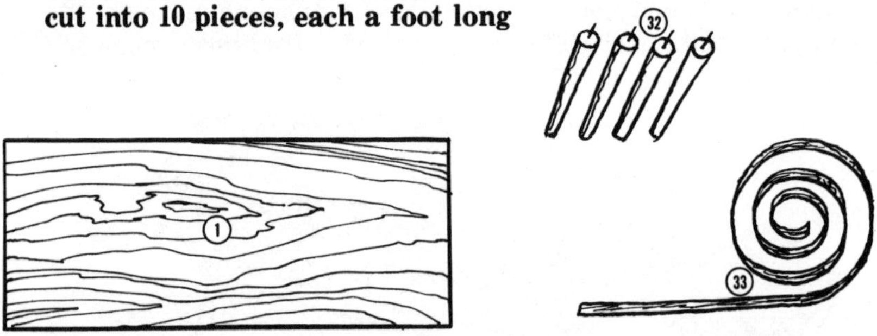

It's unlikely your lumber dealer will have 1 by 4 hardwood boards sitting on a shelf. They'll have to cut some for you. Specify that you want *full 4 inch* so the yard hand will take the saw cut into account. Otherwise you'll end up with boards which are maybe 3-7/8 inches or less. If that should happen to you, just reduce the length of each board.

You want the *width* of three glued-together boards to equal the *length* of one. So if your own boards are 1/8 inch shy of 4 inches, take 3/8 off the 12-inch dimension.

After all of your sawing, lay the pieces tentatively on your

5-foot-by-2-foot slab of 3/4-inch plywood. Make sure that they fit together snugly. If not, sand until they do. (Figure III-21)

There are thirty individual pieces of wood which have to be fastened firmly into place. The strongest method of all would be to peg them, glue them, and clamp them all. Unfortunately, that takes precision equipment and precision technique, clamps, and extraordinary patience. But there is a practical alternative. (Figure III-22)

The most practical way for amateurs to install thirty pieces of hardwood on top of plywood is with a glue called *panel cement*. It comes in a caulking tube and was designed for fastening wood panels to walls. It's a pretty good wood glue, sticky enough and fast-drying enough that you can safely use it to fabricate an inlaid wooden table like this. Make sure you buy the best brand your store stocks.

Don't be put off that you have to buy panel cement in a caulking tube. In the long run, buying the very inexpensive caulking gun *plus* a tube of the panel cement should be cheaper than buying the cement in smaller tubes. Besides, you'll end up owning a reusable caulking gun.

You need some glue on the narrow edges of the boards, but keep it to a minimum. Panel cement is thick and sticky. If you squeeze too much into the spaces between boards, the boards won't fit together tightly. You can put plenty on the bottom of every board.

Before you glue your boards down, draw lines across both the top and bottom of your plywood base to guide you in positioning the pieces. Then glue the bottom of your first piece of wood to the plywood base. Flip the base over and screw or nail the board (part #2) firmly into place. You have to drill pilot holes and countersink holes for screws. Depending upon how hard your particular hardwoods are, you may also have to drill small pilot holes for the nails. Use 1-1/4 × 6 screws or 1-1/4-inch finishing nails. Put about four of either wood fastener through the base and into the hardwood piece.

You are securing this first hardwood board to the base extra firmly because it will be used to align many of the other hardwood boards which follow. When part #2 is all glued and screwed, then glue parts #3 and #4 to the base.

Always align the edges closest to the center. If there is a discrepancy in the length, fit, or position of some boards, always make sure that the board in question lines up with the center line. You can always sandpaper away mistakes along the table's outside edges, but you can't sandpaper down the middle!

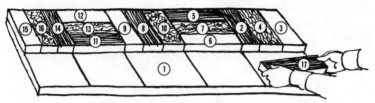

Figure III-22. Hardwood blocks are glued onto the plywood base in this order

Parts #5 and #6 go down next. After you've glued down #7, nail or screw it too. Then continue to glue hardwood pieces into place until you reach part #13. Screw or nail that one too; likewise for the last part in your first row, part #16.

In the second row of hardwood parts, #19 gets nailed or screwed in addition to its dose of glue. Likewise for the outside piece, #25. The last hardwood board, #31, also gets the double fastening.

Give your glue plenty of time to dry before you plunge into the next step. While the glue is setting, you can decide how to finish the wooden surface.

More than likely the various hardwood boards were not precisely the same thickness. The hardest woods tend to be a bit thicker, the softest a bit thinner. If you own, can borrow, or feel like renting an electric sander you can sand the surface for a couple of hours to even out all the wood. But who ever said a wooden table top has to be perfectly smooth? It's kind of chic to own a rough, natural-wood table. You can sand individual wooden blocks but ignore the overall up-and-down surface. The top won't be satiny smooth, but it will be beautiful. You can use almost any traditional wood-finishing material. Wood sealers are especially well suited to this type of job, keeping the beauty of the wood intact but protecting it well too.

Here's how to avoid the arduous sanding required for a perfectly smooth surface, yet leaving you with a smooth surface. After you sandpaper individual blocks, apply wood filler and some sealer. Then apply some instant découpage finish, made for those people who like to paste paper pictures onto things and then cover the picture with so much glue or varnish that nobody can tell where the paper ends and the other item begins.

With a single coat the découpage finish can build up a glossy layer so thick that it will obliterate most or all of the unevenness

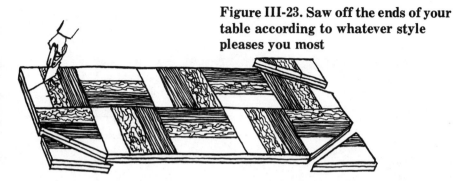

Figure III-23. Saw off the ends of your table according to whatever style pleases you most

in your wooden blocks. If need be, you can apply several coats of the découpage finish.

Better cover up the découpage coat with several coats of something like urethane or a good varnish. And then sandpaper the final coat down to a satin or other traditional furniture finish. (See §'s 26 and 27.)

Before you completely finish the top, however, don't forget the sides. First, assuming you've opted for the elongated shape shown in most of the drawings nearby, saw off the corners. Then sandpaper the edges as much as you have to. (Figure III-23)

If you plan to leave the edges uncovered, thereby showing off the natural wood, you have to do a lot of sanding to smooth down the wood. You might prefer an alternative way of finishing the sides. Cover the edges with a roll of thin tape which looks like natural wood. You may find it only in 3/4-inch widths. If so, you have to make two applications to cover the 1-1/2-inch side.

There are plenty of variations you can give to this basic table size and shape. Figure III-24 shows a 4-foot-round table made with the hardwood. For that project, buy 16 feet of the three different types of hardwood. That same sketch shows different oblong shapes as well as two different materials you can use instead of hardwood boards.

Your local lumberyard may have wooden parquet flooring. The price is kind of steep if you plan to create an entire wooden parquet floor, but if the dealer will sell you the few pieces needed for a table, the cost won't break your budget.

Wooden parquets are generally 9 inches square, so you'll need twenty-one pieces for the 2-by-5-foot table. Most parquets are assembled from woods of only one color. A few, however, can give you the multicolored effect.

Tile dealers can also help you attain instant success with an "inlaid-wood" table top. Higher-priced floor tiles have wood grains embossed into their vinyl surface. Use the cement recommended for whatever type of tile you choose. If you cement ten of the 12-inch squares onto a plywood base, you'll be able to floor your friends with the overnight appearance of an "inlaid-wood" table. Of course the tiles don't have to be wood grained. There are some colorful and different patterns you might like better.

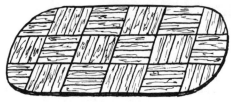

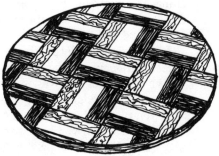

Figure III-24. Variations on this basic table theme. Also note how the edges are covered with wood-grained tape

Legs for this coffee table come right off the shelf at your local hardware or lumber store. Pick the height that fits into your room best; something about 16 or 18 inches is normal. You can choose 14 or 20 too, even 24 inches.

As a rule, stock legs come with metal plates which you screw to the bottom of your new table. Then you simply screw the legs into the metal plate. Some can be varied from slanted to straight depending upon which of two holes you decide to screw the legs into. Although some fancy legs are available, the smooth hardwood design of this table is best matched by the simplest, straightest legs in town. Stain them to match one of your wood colors, then call the neighbors over to see what you've created.

Figure III-25. Legs go onto this table last of all

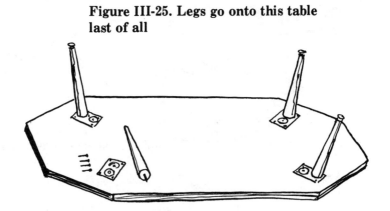

15. World's Most Flexible Table Design (Figure III-26)

SKILLS:	Easy.
TIME:	An evening or a weekend.
TOOLS:	Handsaw, coping or keyhole saw (sabre saw if you already own one), hammer, sandpaper.
ALSO READ:	§4; Chapters 3, 4.

Maybe the headline for this chapter is an overstatement, maybe not. Judge for yourself.

With a sheet of 1/2-inch plywood (good 1 side) plus Figures III-26 and III-27 you've got the start of a table you can use for a super-simple shiny colorful modern cocktail table. Or a warm, traditional, natural-wood coffee table. Or a really heavy-looking, richly grained, dark, gaudy parlor table.

Basic construction is extremely simple. The rounded cutouts can be done with a coping saw, keyhole saw, or sabre saw. The smoother your cut, the less sanding you'll have to do later.

After you've nailed the two ends to the two sides, fit the bottom into the bottom's space and nail it there. Then give the top a little thought.

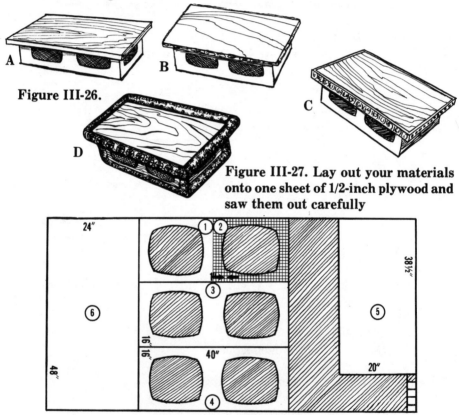

Figure III-26.

Figure III-27. Lay out your materials onto one sheet of 1/2-inch plywood and saw them out carefully

The four blocks, one for each corner of the top, are there to hold the top onto the base without nails. The nails that go through the sides and ends into the blocks are so close to the top that they get lost in the shadows. But nail and glue those blocks carefully into place. You want the top to fit snugly even before you nail the blocks from the outside.

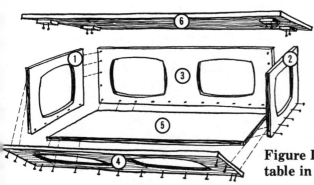

Figure III-28. Assemble your versatile
table in the order shown here

Since the top will shut out almost all light underneath your
table, the cutout portions should look black from the shadows. If
you find more light is showing up inside the cutouts than you
want, simply buy a small can of flat black paint. You can reach
through the cutouts to paint the insides black, and those stray
bits of light will never bother you again. (At the end of this
flexible chapter, there's even another way you can deal with the
cutouts.)

Figure III-26 shows four typical styles you can make from this
base. Table A, the modern one, is simply sanded and finished.
You can give the plywood a natural-wood finish, generally kept
very light-colored. For a bit more money you can use a hardwood
veneer instead of plywood. Formica is OK too. Even vinyl plastics can be used if nobody slams a hot pot onto the top.

The most modernistic effects of all come from shiny paints or
lacquer. Black or white seem to be the favorite modern colors.
You can even do it up in black *and* white. Paint one side and one
end black. Do their opposite numbers in white. Then divide the
top diagonally, one side white and the other black.

About all you need for a table to fit in a traditionally outfitted
living room is some end molding. You can buy plenty of varieties
of 3/4-inch and 1-inch moldings. Tack and glue them to all four
edges around the top. Antiqued, painted, stained, and varnished,
covered with Formica or vinyl, your basic traditional table is
ready for use in an evening or two.

Tables B and C in Figure III-26 show two different kinds of
moldings in use. The upper version is simple and flat. It's available as edge molding. Simply cut it to the proper length and put it
into place with glue and nails.

The molding on table C is called *outside-corner molding*,
among other names. Since it's so wide, you have to cut it rather

carefully. You're going to have to do a bit of shopping around to find ornate moldings like the ones pictured here, so you'll be well motivated to install it with loving care.

You'll find moldings like this explained in §25. The more carefully you measure, the better they'll fit. If there's too much molding when you test it for fit, sandpaper away the excess. If there's a gap, plug it with plastic wood.

When you get ready to pull out all the stops and build a big-looking, gaudy, and elegant old-fashioned table like D in Figure III-26, you may have to shop for molding in a picture-frame store. They generally offer a wide selection of elaborate moldings, some 3 and 4 inches wide. You have to be careful to select the rounder picture-frame moldings. The flat ones will look out of place on the edge of your table instead of up against a wall.

When you get ready to install the four vertical moldings for table D in Figure III-26, you'll have to putter a bit. The upper edges are cut off straight, at a right angle. They rest flush against the bottom of your table top. But the bottom edges have to be trimmed by hand until they fit the approximate shape of the moldings you've already tacked onto the bottom of your table base. Cut them a bit oversized and then trim each one to shape with a SurForm tool or sandpaper. It'll take time, but will look it when the work is done.

There's another refinement on table D: Cover the cutouts with fabric before you nail the top finally into place. Actually you can put fabric over the cutouts in any of the styles you want, but most folks find it most pleasing in conjunction with big, bold, brassy corner moldings.

All you need to know about finishing this flexible table design in the style of your choice is covered in Chapter 4. Pick a finish that goes with the furniture scheme you prefer.

16. Quiet Elegance (Figure III-29)

SKILLS: Easy. A good first
project if you're confident
or already know
how handy you can be.

TIME: A weekend.

TOOLS: Saw, hammer,
                square, sandpaper.
ALSO READ: Chapters 1, 2, 3.

This table is every bit as elegant as the more gaudy versions in Chapter 15. But this is a quiet work of furniture design. It just *looks* too elaborate for an amateur to make.

You can adapt the basic design of this table to your own preference in furniture styles. The three sets of decorative features worked into this design—spindles, moldings, and carvings —should match each other. But you can select matched sets to create the various classic, traditional, and old-fashioned styles —Italian, Venetian, Roman, Grecian, Spanish, French. . . .

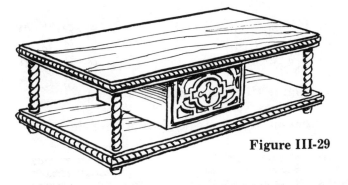

Figure III-29

Colonial styles will work on this basic design too. For the classical carvings, substitute some American symbols—eagles, acorns, shields, and sundry other carved or molded decorations.

Some spindle makers, aside from peddling spindles, moldings, edge strips, and carvings, also sell precut tops for tables like these. The precut materials have two advantages which will save you some time. The grooves routed into their edge will save you from putting on edge decorations of your own—but also *prevent* you from putting on edge decorations of your own. The ready-to-use tops also have holes drilled in them for fastening on the spindles. Trouble is, their holes go all the way through and require a cap or finial interrupting the smooth top to cover up the hole.

A finial or other doodad in the corner of a table looks OK on a Colonial style, but is definitely out of place in French Provincial and other old-world furniture schemes. Besides, the precut tops are much more expensive than even the best grades of plywood.

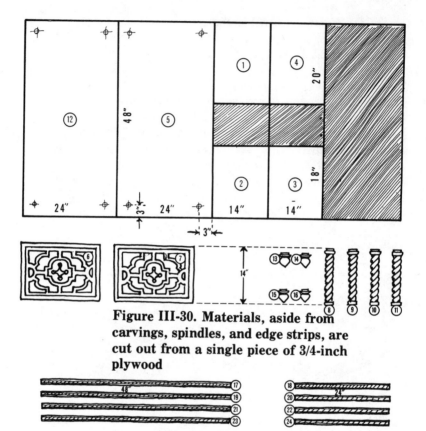

Figure III-30. Materials, aside from carvings, spindles, and edge strips, are cut out from a single piece of 3/4-inch plywood

Figure III-30 shows how to lay your parts out on a sheet of 3/4-inch plywood (good 1 side). Before you do any cutting, however, shop for all the carvings and spindles you plan to use. The size of the box portion of your new table depends upon the size of your chosen carvings and spindles.

The dimensions in III-30 result in a box portion about 14 inches high and 20 inches long. That's just about right for the major carvings on sale. If yours are smaller, you can either center them on the bigger box or reduce the size of your own box.

With even an inch or so of space all around the sides of a carving, the table loses none of its gracefulness. But if you do decide to alter the height of your box, don't use fractions of an inch. Spindles come in standard sizes such as 12, 14, 15, 16, or 18 inches. Your box height has to match your spindle length.

In case you can't find a spindle you like which matches the size of the desired box, don't overlook *extenders*, which slip onto the top or bottom of a spindle to increase its length by 1 inch. You can find out more about the gadget in §8.

Legs for this table can be finials from the set of spindles you've chosen. Or you can buy legs to match the spindles. In general, this design does best with short legs. About 2, 3, or 4 inches is plenty. Legs 6 inches high may already be too much.

After you've accumulated all the legs, spindles, and carvings, cut out the plywood. Assemble the various parts according to Figure III-31. Make the box first. Then fasten it to the bottom of your new table. Glue on the carvings next, then put the spindles into place.

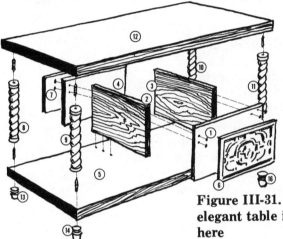

Figure III-31. Assemble your quietly elegant table in the order presented here

The bottom of each spindle fastens to a threaded connector. The connector goes through the hole in the bottom and screws into the finial or leg. Spindle tops connect to the top via threaded dowels. Glue the plain part of each dowel into holes in the top (not *all the way through* the top).

Your last step is to install the edge molding. Most of it comes in 6-foot lengths, which is one reason why this table top is 4 feet by 2 feet. A strip of edge molding covers one long side and one short side with no waste. You can read more about edge strips in §24.

Spanish- and Colonial-style tables like this are best given a natural-wood finish—stain and then varnish. You can use that approach for other furniture patterns too. Since there are so many different types of wood involved in this project—spindles, edge moldings, carvings, and plywood—plan to spend a lot of time doing the staining. Each of the four types of wood products may need special treatment to end up with a table that looks carved from the same kind of wood.

The fastest way to finish this table is with antiquing (covered in

§28). Regardless of whether you stain or antique this quietly elegant table, make sure that plenty of contrasting pigment stays deep in the grooves of all the spindles, edge moldings, and carvings.

Only you and I know that this complicated-looking piece of furniture was assembled from very simple parts. But life is that way too.

17. French Provincial Coffee Table (Figure III-32)

SKILLS:	Complicated as a whole, but individual steps are easy.
TIME:	A month of Sundays.
TOOLS:	Hammer, screwdriver, saws. Although you *can* make this table with a handsaw, a sabre saw is recommended.
ALSO READ:	§'s 4, 26, 28; Chapters 3, 23, 27.

Figure III-32

A delicate table for a delicate setting—I call it French Provincial, since the lines are inspired by furniture of that era. But you don't have to use delicate chisels to carve the delicate edges by hand. You don't even need the mighty machines which today's furniture copiers use to get the grooves and feathers and flutes in their versions. All you need is three sheets of 1/4-inch plywood (good 1 side), plenty of sandpaper and patience, plus time to read other parts of this book.

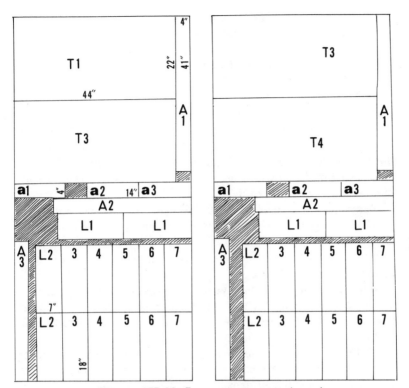

**Figure III-33. Lay out your parts onto
1/4-inch plywood according to this
diagram for utmost economy**

Chapter 27 is about the desk version of this table. Make the top and apron according to hints given there. A pattern for the legs, plus all the practical and theoretical information you should need, are in the chapter on French Provincial style tables, Chapter 23.

Figure III-33 shows how to lay out the 24-by-50-inch top and the 18-inch legs most efficiently on your sheets of plywood. Change the size of your coffee-table top at will, finish it to your own specifications or mine given in Chapter 23.

18. Baker's Dozen of One- and Two-Evening Projects—Coffee Tables, End Tables, Hall Tables, and Night Stands

SKILLS: Very easy. Good first
projects.

TIME:	One or two evenings.
TOOLS:	Handsaw, screw-driver, hammer for some, drill for some, sandpaper.
ALSO READ:	§29; Chapters 1, 2, 3.

Tables in this roundup section are a real switch from the heavy, ornate, elaborate ones in the last chapter or two. But these tables don't look cheap, even though their price tag is. Impressive and well styled in their own right, they fit into furniture styles where simpler lines are called for.

Nearly every one of these tables can be built without even picking up a saw, assembled from precut parts available at stores that stock spindles. That way, you don't need even a drill or a hammer. But don't overlook the sandpaper. It's vital to a professional-looking job.

Most of the precut tops have a grooved edge, lending a professional, finished look. But you can put such an edge on tops you cut out of plywood (see §20). The grooves fit in best with traditional and most old-fashioned furniture styles.

Modern tops should not be grooved, as a rule. Colonial table tops were generally rounded off, but you can use a grooved edge too. Spanish is grooved or rounded.

Precut tops require a finial or cap on top of your table. If you cut the top and drill holes partway through the top yourself, you can avoid cluttering up your top piece.

You can switch around the shape from one of these designs to another; stack two parts on top of each other; buy the carvings, moldings, spindles, and edge strips of your choice; plus more. Just for a start, however, here are some of the more common ways to work with this baker's dozen of designs.

Figure III-34: A great way to use up a leftover piece of flush door. You can also cut the top from 3/4-inch plywood. *With* edge molding, it can be Italian, French, Mediterranean, Venetian, etc. With no edge molding or a simple rounded one, it's useful as a modern table.

Wrought iron legs are best. Attach them to a flush door with Molly Screws (§13). Wood screws hold the legs to a plywood top.

Typical size, 2 feet by 4 feet, may be varied so you can take advantage of bargains at your lumberyard. Some 16-inch legs are ideal.

Figure III-35: As shown, this table comes right off the assemble-it-yourself shelf of a spindle supplier. Use 14-, 16-, or

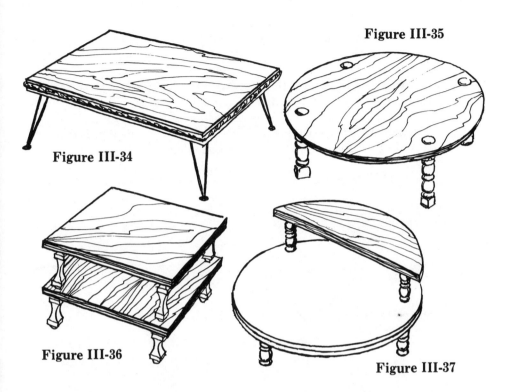

Figure III-35

Figure III-34

Figure III-36

Figure III-37

18-inch legs and a 2-foot or 3-foot diameter top. If you cut and drill the top yourself, you won't need the finials sticking into the top surface. But then you won't get the grooved edges unless you cut them with your own drill (§20). It's tough to bend most edge strips around into a circle, but tapes will do that.

This table doesn't have to be round. You can buy ovals, squares, or any other shape that appeals to you.

If you stack two top pieces together, you have style III-36 instead of style III-35. Again, it can be round, oval, half circle, or—as shown in Figure #17A—square. A 2-foot or 3-foot top works well for a coffee table; smaller sizes are best for most end tables.

For a coffee table, use 8- or 10-inch spindles for legs and dividers. To turn this design into an end table, switch to 12-, 14-, or 15-inch spindles for legs and dividers.

Figure III-37: Actually this is little more than a variation of style III-36. Build it entirely with precut parts from your favorite store's spindle department, cut the tops and groove or strip them yourself—at a substantial savings.

Depending on your choice of spindles and edge finishes, styles III-36 and 37 can fit into almost any furniture décor.

Figures III-38 and 39 are other variations of the basic 2-tier table shown in style III-36. And style III-36 was little more than two tables of style III-35 piled one on top of the other.

Buy precut or build with your own cuts. Typical sizes are 24 inches square or round for the bottom piece and 12 or 16 inches for the top. You can use a 12-by-24-inch rectangle or oval for the bottom and a 12-by-12 square or 12-inch circle for the top. Look back to style III-36's write-up for recommended leg and divider sizes.

Figure III-38

Figure III-39

Figure III-40 is a fine representation of a Colonial coffee table. The edges are nicely rounded, the shape curved from hand-drawn figures, and the legs are carved. Somehow the legs on this type of table look their best when mounted at an angle, as shown. A Colonial table such as this just cries for maple or pine finish, although walnut works well too.

If you fancy up the edges with molded strips or embossed metallic tapes, switch to wrought iron legs, mount the legs straight up and down instead of at an angle, you've simply created an oval-shaped version of the table shown in style III-34.

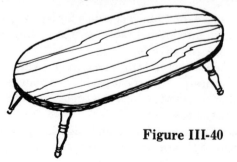

Figure III-40

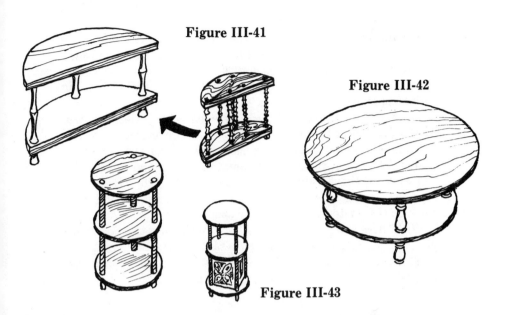

Figure III-41

Figure III-42

Figure III-43

Figures III-41 and 42 are continuations of the 2-tier tables discussed in styles III-36, 37, 38, and 39 above. The big innovation here is in III-42, where the bottom is smaller than the top. (In the other designs, the top comes out bigger than the bottom.)

Use semicircles of 16 to 36 inches for end tables done in style III-41. If you put about 4-inch legs on the bottom, try for upright spindles in the 16- to 20-inch range. Making the semicircles bigger, up to maybe 4 feet in diameter, you can create a fine hallway table as the little extra sketch alongside style III-41 shows. Twist on legs that are close to 4 inches, but use 28-inch spindles for uprights.

If III-42 is to be a coffee table, try for 4-inch legs and 12- or 14-inch upright spindles. The bottom piece can be 1 to 2 feet in diameter while the top may be 2 to 3 feet. Use the same top- and bottom-piece size but longer legs on an end table. By expanding the top up to 4 feet in diameter and the bottom to 3 feet, you can make a dandy hallway or library table with 4- or 6-inch legs and 24- or 28-inch upright spindles. You can finish it to go with almost any basic furniture style by selecting compatible-style edges and spindles.

Style III-43, as you can see, is just a three-tier version of all the styles discussed already. You can leave the openings open, or work carved panels into the space. Left open, it's a telephone stand, hallway table, end table. Closed, it works as a night stand or end table.

You don't have to use only circular components. And they don't all have to be the same size. Choose precut parts or cut your own.

For night stands, 16-inch circles, squares, or other shapes work well. Use 2- or 4-inch legs or finials at the very bottom. Put 14-inch spindles up and down.

To create end tables, 14-, 16-, or even 36-inch tiers are OK. Stick closer to 12-inch spindles for the upright parts.

Figures III-44, 45, and 46 are just variations on the same table theme. They're at their best as night stands or end tables. You can look at these table designs simply as style III-43 with plywood having replaced two or three of the spindle uprights. Look to the write-up of III-43 for choice dimensions.

With these few pages of sage advice and a quick trip downtown you can become a table maker literally overnight. And if you don't have room for another small table around your house, maybe you could build one as a gift for a friend.

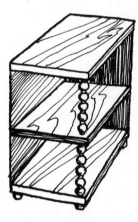

Figure III-44

Figure III-45

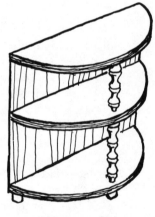

Figure III-46

19. Upholstered Coffee Tables

SKILLS:	Easy.
TIME:	Weekend.
TOOLS:	Saw, hammer or screwdriver, square.
ALSO READ:	§'s 4, 10, 14, 15, 16, 25, 27, 28.

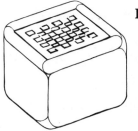

Figure III-47

Figure III-48. Lay out your coffee-table parts onto a sheet of plywood in this fashion

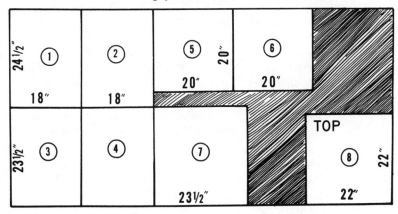

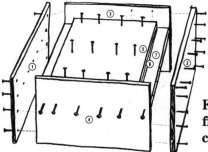

Figure III-49. Assemble the wooden frame for your upholstered square coffee table in the order shown here

An upholstered coffee table or end table is so unique that you may not find any in some downtown department stores. They're reserved mostly for plush, jet-set furniture stores.

There's a wooden frame under this gem in Figure III-47. Make yours out of 1/2-inch plywood of the roughest sort. Figure III-48 shows how to lay out your sheet of plywood most economically, and III-49 illustrates how to nail it all together. Although the finished table will be bigger than 2 feet square, the useable top space will be 22 inches square.

There's a good reason for what looks at first like a wacky way of putting this table's frame together. Part #7 is nailed onto all four of the side pieces to make the frame strong. Parts #5 and #6 fit on top of part #7 to support the finished coffee-table top, part #8. The top doesn't have to be nailed or glued down because it rests on the flat surface of part #5.

The padding, which goes around the entire outside of this table, gets tucked in at the top to form a gently curved edge. Without the space between the edges of parts #5 and #6 and the inside of the frame, there'd be no room left for tucking the padding.

You need 2-foot-wide foam rubber padding for this table. Three yards is enough. At a minimum, you need 1-inch-thick foam padding, but 2 inches gives even more of a padded appearance.

At one time society required you to cover a table such as this with black vinyl or genuine leather. That looks nice, but if you prefer green print corduroy, it's your table.

To put it all together, first assemble the frame. Wrap your foam rubber padding around the outside of the frame (Figure III-50). Start about in the middle of one side by tacking or gluing the beginning to the wood. Silicone adhesive will help hold the foam onto the wood all the way around and make your job easier. But you can spare that expense if you want to.

As you wrap the foam rubber around the wooden frame, pull it firmly around all of the corners. You want the corners to be nicely rounded and not square. When you've reached the start, trim off the excess so the beginning and end meet squarely.

You'll need 3 yards of fabric to cover this coffee table in the easiest fashion. You could get by with 1-1/2 yards by covering only half of the object at a time. Your fabric would have to overlap twice instead of only once, but it's harder to install that way. By buying a piece 3 yards long, you wrap the one piece all the way around.

Actually, you can cut the 54-inch-wide fabric in half. Then you could upholster two coffee tables from the same piece of cloth.

Start wrapping cloth around the outside of the foam somewhere other than the side where the foam rubber is joined together. Put on a piece of tape to hold the cloth in place. Wrap the cloth tightly enough around the foam and frame that it will cling to the sides of the foam rubber. When you've made a full circle, tape the two ends of fabric temporarily together (Figure III-51).

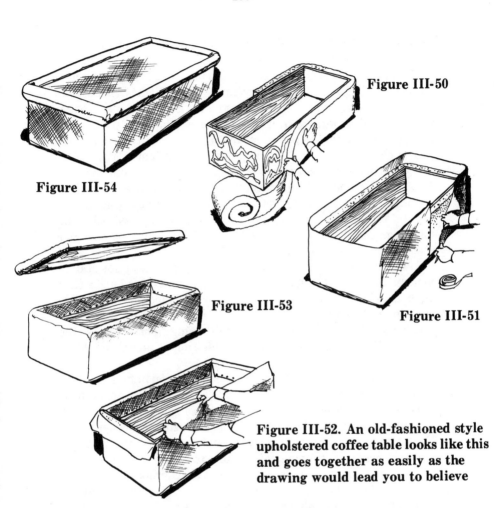

Figure III-50

Figure III-54

Figure III-53

Figure III-51

Figure III-52. An old-fashioned style upholstered coffee table looks like this and goes together as easily as the drawing would lead you to believe

When you've finished wrapping the foam and then the fabric around your table frame, there should be 2 or 3 inches of foam rubber sticking out from both the top and bottom of the frame. And 6 or 8 inches of fabric should extend beyond the top and the bottom of your frame.

The entire upholstering job is held together by bending the fabric over (which bends the foam too) and tacking the cloth to the inside of the wooden frame. Work on the bottom first. Any mistakes you make won't show there as much as they will on top. Start from the point where the beginning and end of the cloth come together. Stretch the bottom as tightly as you can without pulling the outside skin of cloth out of shape.

Finish up the upholstering by bending the fabric over on top (Figure III-52). Don't pull as hard on top as on the bottom. If you let the foam bend over as gently as possible, you get more of a plush, cushiony look.

When you approach each corner during the bending-over process, you will have to snip away some of the foam. Otherwise it will bunch up right at the corner and form a lump. Cut a triangle right at the corner; make it 2 or 3 inches wide at top and stop cutting about 2 inches before your scissors reach the frame.

The cloth is more flexible. You don't have to cut it at corners, but you must fold over enough to keep big wrinkles from forming. What you're doing, in essence, is creating one big, controlled wrinkle instead of taking your chances on what forms naturally. Figure III-52 gives you an idea of what the process looks like (although the sketch for that table doesn't have any foam rubber sticking over the top or bottom of the frame).

Make sure that the upholstery tacks, carpet tacks, or staples you use to fasten the cloth down to the frame are not longer than 1/2 inch. When the last tack is in place you should be able to slide the top on. Even though the sides will never be seen, make sure they're smooth. The foam and fabric shoving tightly against the top is all that keeps it down. Rough sides might tear through the fabric.

You may have to trim a bit of wood off the top before it will fit into place (Figure III-53). When you're ready, the top can be finished in dozens of striking ways. You can glue Formica or vinyl in any color onto the plywood top. You can paint or lacquer it too. Even thin copper or stainless steel sheet contact-cemented to the plywood makes a stunning coffee-table top. In Figure III-47 the top was done up with a black and white checkerboard painted or lacquered onto the plywood. If you like the idea, you can glue a piece of leftover upholstery fabric to the top.

Now the most versatile coffee table gets a coat. Back in Chapter 15 we looked into what was billed as "the world's most flexible table." Turn back there and build the whole thing, but this time eliminate the cutouts in the sides.

With that wooden coffee table as a base, wrap 4 yards of 2-foot-wide foam rubber around the project. You can tack or tape the foam temporarily into place until it's covered with fabric. But the sturdiest way is to glue it into place with silicone adhesive.

Wrap your chosen cloth around the foam next. You'll need 4-1/2 yards of fabric if you get enough of a bargain that you can waste some. If not, buy 2-1/2 yards of fabric, cut it in half into two narrow pieces, and wrap the cloth around the foam in two operations.

Excess foam has to be trimmed away from the table top. You can leave it at the bottom. As with the earlier table job, stretch the cloth over to the bottom so it gently rolls the excess foam rubber. Tack or staple the cloth to the wooden bottom. Be sure to snip the foam rubber at corners and fold over the fabric there.

When you're ready to do the top, pull the cloth over toward the inside just hard enough to keep it tight against the foam. You don't want to roll the foam over very much. The previous illustrations show how this operation goes and what your completed effort can look like.

If you tack some heavy molding to the edge, as in Chapter 15, then one good finish for the top is to glue a strip of your upholstery fabric over the plywood. Unless the fabric is particularly resistant to water and stains, give it a good dose with several coats of wood finish at the same time you finish the molding.

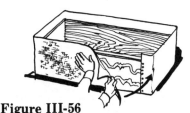

Figure III-55. Carpet can upholster one heck of a nice coffee table, as this sketch shows

Figure III-56

Figure III-57

There's another way to upholster the base of the flexible coffee table. Buy a small bit of carpet remnant, or use a remnant of the carpet installed on your own living room floor. With a base done up with carpet matching what's on the floor, the top of this coffee table seems to float in air (Figure III-55).

Figure III-56 shows the simple way to glue your strip of carpeting to the wooden base with silicone adhesive. When you're working with carpeting, start and stop at a corner to camouflage the seam. Don't trim away the excess carpet until after the adhesive has dried (Figure III-57).

You can hold the top in place by gluing its blocks to the inside of the frame. It's possible to hammer long finishing nails through the carpet to hold the top even more firmly in place, but that's seldom necessary.

A shiny finish with Formica, lacquer, or paint is the catchiest way to finish the top of this upholstered coffee table. But from now on, this is your table. Finish it to your specifications.

KITCHEN AND DINING ROOM TABLES

20. Modern Pedestal Table

SKILLS:	Very easy. A good first project.
TIME:	An evening or a weekend.
TOOLS:	Saw, screwdriver, sandpaper.
ALSO READ:	§'s 4, 14, 15, 16; Chapter 4.

Figure IV-1

Fortunately, kitchen and dining room tables—among the most important pieces of furniture in your whole house—are also among the easiest furniture projects to do. The job is quick, clean, and straightforward.

Dining tables are so much larger than most other home items that materials cost more than for a small chair or end table. But the price of a table you build in an evening or two still falls way below what you would have to pay for anything of comparable size, appearance, and durability. Delivery schedules being what they are, you can probably build a table long before a store-bought one could be dropped off in your front yard.

The fastest of all to build is the pedestal table (Figure IV-1). A modern style as a rule, it blends in well with traditional furniture too. With some ingenuity you can even make some pedestal tables fit into Colonial or other old-fashioned furniture schemes.

Pedestals generally can support a top up to 4 feet square, or any shape that doesn't go beyond 4 feet in any direction. Ready-to-use pedestals are sold at many do-it-yourself centers, hardware stores, lumberyards, and most of the big mail-order-catalog department stores. Generally your choice is limited to black, white, gold, or—at an extra price—chrome. If you're diligent, you'll find a couple of wooden styles too.

There are four holes in the tops of ready-to-use pedestals. Put four 3/4 × 10 flat-head wood screws through the holes and your table top is fastened down and ready to use. If the table gets a lot of abuse or gets moved around a lot, you might want to fasten the top down in more rugged fashion.

Since kitchen tables deserve Formica-type plastic tops anyway, why not bolt the top to the pedestal? Drill holes through the plywood top and into the pedestal top. Countersink them so the heads on your 1-1/2 × 1/4-inch carriage or machine bolts end up flush with the wooden surface.

Set the top onto your pedestal, slip the bolts through their four holes, put nuts and washers onto the bolts from below, and then tighten up the whole thing securely. After you add Formica to the wooden top, the bolt heads will be covered forever.

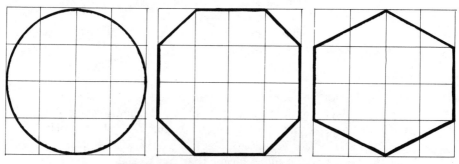

Figure IV-2. Lay out your table top according to the diagrams shown here. Each square is 1-foot big

Squares are pretty uninteresting to look at unless your kitchen or dining area incorporates that shape into its décor. Figure IV-2 shows several alternatives to a perfectly square table. You can knock off the corners, ending up with an irregular 8-sided top, or go on to round the whole thing off into a circle. Or you can lop off a bit more to create a stylish, irregular, 6-sided top.

There's a reason, though, why regular 6-sided and 8-sided tops aren't recommended. Their sides are too short, for one thing. If you drew a regular octagon for your top, none of the eight sides would be longer than 1 foot, 8 inches. The irregular version shown in Figure IV-2 has four sides that stretch out to 2 feet and another four sides that are 1 foot, 5 inches long.

If you really want a regular octagon top, draw a line 1 foot, 8 inches long in the very middle of each of the top's four sides. Then connect those four lines. You should have an almost perfect octagon.

After you've cut out an octagon from a 4-by-4-foot piece of plywood, you have a top with 8-1/3 square feet of eating space. A regular 6-sided top would have even less. The *ir*regular 6-sided top shown in Figure IV-2 has 12 square feet. A perfect 4-foot-wide circle has 12-1/2 square feet, and the irregular 8-sided top ends up with 14 square feet of eating area.

Use 3/4-inch plywood for your table top. Assuming you plan to make the final cover Formica or heavy vinyl, you can buy rough-2-sides-grade plywood to save a few dollars.

All of the traditional ways for finishing off table edges work here. In fact, the photos in §24 were taken of the edges of the pedestal table I built seven or eight years ago. It's survived three kids and a moving van without a whimper.

21.   Old Pedestal Table (Figure IV-3)

SKILLS:	Somewhat demanding.
TIME:	Evenings for a week.
TOOLS:	Screwdriver; drill is very helpful. Handsaws can be used, but a sabre saw is plenty useful.
ALSO READ:	§'s 26, 27; Chapters 2, 3.

Figure IV-3

For a pedestal table, you can build your own pedestal, a favorite device of many Early American furniture builders.

Invest in a 10-foot length of 2-by-12-inch pine, buy half a sheet of 3/4-inch plywood (good one side), and you're in business. Trace the pattern for a pedestal leg, Figure IV-4, onto cardboard or directly onto your lumber. Then cut out four pieces just like it. (If the leg looks sort òf familiar, you may have noticed it in the coffee-table Chapter 13.)

Figure IV-5 reviews how to assemble the pedestal leg. Use plenty of wood glue and 4-inch-long nails or screws.

Like most store-bought pedestals, this one will support a table top up to 4 feet across. Most old American families used a roughly cut round top, an effect you can duplicate by drawing a circle onto your half sheet of 3/4-inch plywood. Other Colonials used a square top with well rounded corners. You, of course, decide what Colonial shape to put in your Colonial dining area.

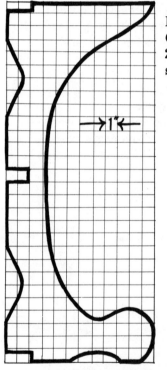

Figure IV-4. Leg pattern for this Colonial pedestal table. Lay it out onto 2-by-12-inch pine boards (1-inch squares)

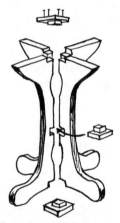

Figure IV-5. Assemble your pedestal this way, using both glue and nails or screws, preferably screws

However you decide to shape the top, you can add a note of authenticity when you fasten it on the pedestal. Use 2×12 or 2×10 screws. Countersink them. But when you finish the top, try to accent the Plastic Wood plugs in your screw holes. Ordinarily you should try to camouflage them, but since early tables were assembled with wooden pegs, and since your Plastic Wood plugs look like pegs, why not take advantage of them?

Instead of using the traditional ways to finish off the exposed edges of plywood, you can just round off the edges wtih a Sur-Form tool. Use the same wood finish on the edges that you plan to use on top. Make the finish a tough one such as urethane.

You can use Formica or vinyl finishes if you really want to. Stick to maple, knotty pine, or walnut if you crave authenticity.

Speaking of authenticity, plywood wasn't exactly common back in Colonial times. Tables like this were often cut from a set of rough-hewn timbers. Your "rough-hewn" planks can be pieces of 2 by 12 pine boards.

Buy two pieces of 8-foot-long 2 by 12's and one piece of 8-foot-long 2 by 4. Saw the boards in half and use the 2 by 4's to hold the 2 by 12's together into a 4-foot-by-4-foot-square table top.

You can round off the corners if you wish, or even cut off the corners to form the irregular 8-sided top shown in Chapter 20. Or you can saw the fool thing into a 4-foot-wide circle. The 2 by 4's will hold the top together no matter what shape you choose.

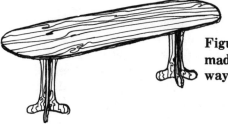

Figure IV-6. Finished Colonial table made from rough boards and left that way

If you really want to do this table up big, make two pedestals and shoot for an 8-foot-long table. For just a few nights of labor, you'll end up with a very impressive piece of furniture.

The table in Figure IV-6 is 3 feet wide and 8 feet long. You get that size by using three pieces of 8-foot-long 2 by 12's. Lay the three boards together, line up their ends, then nail them together with 2 by 4's. A single 8-foot-long 2 by 4 yields 4 pieces, each 2 feet long.

If you own an electric drill, use it for this project. Screws 3 × 12 help this table withstand moving and twisting much better than nails will. Drill pilot holes through the 2 by 4's and screw them into the bottom of your table top. Then drill pilot holes and countersink holes through the table top into the pedestals.

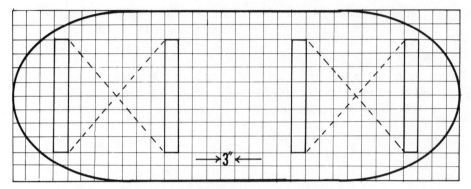

**Figure IV-7. Pattern for a 2-legged
Colonial pedestal table. This diagram
works for both the plywood and the
rough-plank version**

Figure IV-7 shows where to locate the pedestals for greatest
stability. Notice that the 2 by 4's aren't spaced at random, but are
located specifically to reinforce where the pedestals meet the top.

After your three planks are screwed into one massive table
top, you can saw it into the final shape you've chosen. The one
shown above is the best all-around. If you leave this particular
top too squared, some people may think it's a picnic table at first
glance. You want it to look like an Early American table
deliberately left in the rough. Smooth off corners and rough
edges with SurForm tools. But don't do any more sanding than
your family and personal tastes require.

For homes with smaller dining areas, Figure IV-7 shows how to
create a smaller top to fit over the two pedestals. By shrinking
the midsection you can end up with a curved top measuring 7
feet, 6 feet, or even 5 feet.

Finish the top with wood sealer, orange shellac, and then
urethane. Or stain it maple or walnut protected by penetrating
wood sealer. Or leave the boards unfinished except for a generous soaking in linseed oil. The rougher the better.

If you want to copy this old American top onto 3/4-inch
plywood, you can stain it maple or walnut or leave it natural. Add
knotty pine, maple, or walnut Formica if you want. Don't forget
to finish the pedestals to match. Even if you use such genteel
materials, you'll end up with a fine table looking sort of Early
American.

22. Traditional Tables (Figure IV-8)

SKILLS: Easy. OK as a first
project for well-
motivated people.
TIME: A weekend.
TOOLS: Saw, hammer or
screwdriver, sandpaper.
ALSO READ: §'s 2, 4, 8, 29;
Chapters 3, 4.

Figure IV-8

There's nothing very exciting about an ordinary table unless you don't have one. If you don't, here's how to build one in quick time.

A table consists only of three basic elements: a top, some legs to keep the top off your lap when you're eating, and an apron skirting around the bottom of the top to hide the clumsy-looking tops of the legs. In good table designs, the apron also lends additional strength to the legs. We'll only build good ones.

The top is nothing but a slab of wood. Some 3/4-inch plywood is just great. After you cut the top from a full sheet of plywood, you can cut a skirt to match with what's left over.

However, most lumberyards will cheerfully cut a sheet of 3/4-inch plywood into the specific size you request. And if you don't feel like dragging the remainder home, some common pine 1-by-4-inch boards will make a dandy skirt.

You can buy all kinds of legs at hardware and lumber stores. They come mainly in 28-inch lengths, which is about how far off the floor Western civilization expects us to eat.

Don't be in a hurry to cut out your pieces for the apron. You want the device to fit snugly alongside all four legs. So make the final measurements *after* the legs are fastened to the table top.

Nail or screw the four apron pieces together. Then set the apron over the legs and put one or two screws through the apron into the two sides where the apron and the leg meet. Use 1-1/2 × 10 screws and countersink them. (If you don't own a drill, use 2-inch finishing nails.) If the legs you choose are drastically tapered, you may have to glue a tiny piece of wood between the bottom of the apron and the leg so the screws don't pull the legs out of line. But this isn't often necessary.

At last you can screw or nail the top onto the apron. In general, in case you want to use your own measurements instead of mine, the apron is made from wood about 4 inches wide, and sets back under the edge approximately 3 inches.

Here's a set of recommended table sizes:

TABLE I: Top, 36 by 60 inches (3 by 5 feet). Apron, 30 by 54 inches. Assembled from 1-by-4-inch pine boards or plywood. Make two pieces 54 inches long and two pieces 28-1/2 inches long.

TABLE II: Top, 40 by 72 inches (6 feet) from 3/4-inch plywood. Apron, 34 by 66 inches. Assembled from 1-by-4-inch pine boards or plywood. Make two pieces 66 inches long and two pieces 32-1/2 inches long.

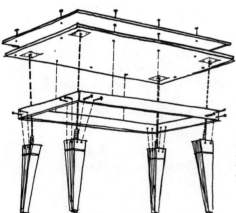

Figure IV-9. Assemble a traditional table this way

Figure IV-9 shows how to assemble the materials for a typical traditional table. Since the legs you buy are usually designed to screw into a metal plate which you screw onto your table top, draw some lines about 4 inches from the edge near every corner. Where the lines intersect is where you put the outside corner of each metal leg plate. Screw them down securely with 3/4 × 8 screws or whatever free hardware the manufacturer provides.

For finishing off the edges of this table, you can get plenty of ideas from §24. Installing Formica tops is covered in §23 and §14. Make sure you install the Formica before you round off or bevel any corners. Once upon a time even an oval-shaped table top had a rectangular apron under it. It was set way back from the edge so the shape of the rectangle didn't conflict badly with the oval shape. Today, however, aprons are set close to the table edge. Therefore if the top is oval, so is the apron. The technology needed to build a curved apron is beyond most amateurs. So if the Joneses buy a nice 5 foot long oval shaped table, instead of keeping up with them by trying to build your own 5-foot-long oval table, build a 6-foot-long rectangular one.

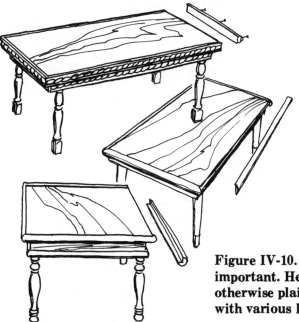

Figure IV-10. Decoration can be important. Here's how to embellish an otherwise plain, traditional-style table with various kinds of moldings

Figure IV-10 shows a few ways you can work with simple materials to turn an otherwise common table into an elaborate creation.

For a table longer than 6 feet, four legs no longer are adequate.

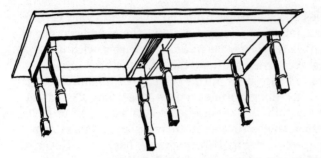

**Figure IV-11. For tables longer than
six feet, you'll need six legs. Here's
how to accomplish that so you'll get
the least wobble possible**

You need six. Figure IV-11 offers graphic advice about what to
do with those extra two legs. They get fastened on after the four
corner legs are in place, after the apron has been measured and
fastened together, but *before* you screw or nail the apron permanently to the legs and top.

Six legs should prove adequate for a top up to about 10 feet
long. And if you want to go longer than that, it's probably best to
simply build two separate four-legged tables and set them side by
side.

23. Elaborate, Old-Fashioned Table Simply Built (Figure IV-12)

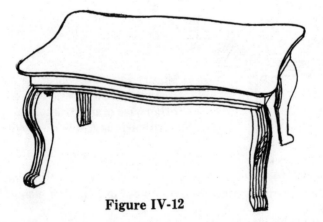

Figure IV-12

SKILLS:	Complicated as a whole, but individual steps are easy.
TIME:	A month of Sundays.
TOOLS:	Hammer, screwdriver, saws. Although you *can* make this table with handsaw, a sabre saw is recommended.
ALSO READ:	§'s 4, 26, 28; Chapter 3.

This is about the most complicated-looking table you're likely to encounter. Basically it's inspired by French Provincial lines, as mellowed by furniture makers down the years. It will fit into rooms decorated with an Italian or Mediterranean style too. How you finish this table has a lot to do with where it will fit.

Even after close inspection, furniture builders might swear that you used a powerful, expensive router to cut all the grooves lining the edges, sides, and legs on this table. But they just *look* like grooves cut into a big piece of solid wood.

Actually you don't cut grooves at all. You assemble the various big pieces from smaller pieces. Industrial designers and engineers call such a process *laminating*. Each "groove" in this table is actually the space between the rounded edges of two pieces of thin plywood. We laminate every thick piece of wood from shaped pieces of 1/4-inch plywood.

Once you get the idea, this becomes a rather simple although time-consuming project. It would take you a while to cut out by hand all of the curved pieces you need to laminate legs and tops and aprons, so it's recommended for families with a sabre saw. Even a very small one will do, since 1/4-inch plywood cuts very easily.

Materials

You need five sheets of 1/4-inch plywood (good 1 side) for this project, as well as lots of glue and 1/2-inch brads. The best glue for this table is a big can of the powdered synthetic-resin product. It's very tough and reasonably priced. And it dries slowly enough that you can move pieces around long after you've smeared glue onto your wood.

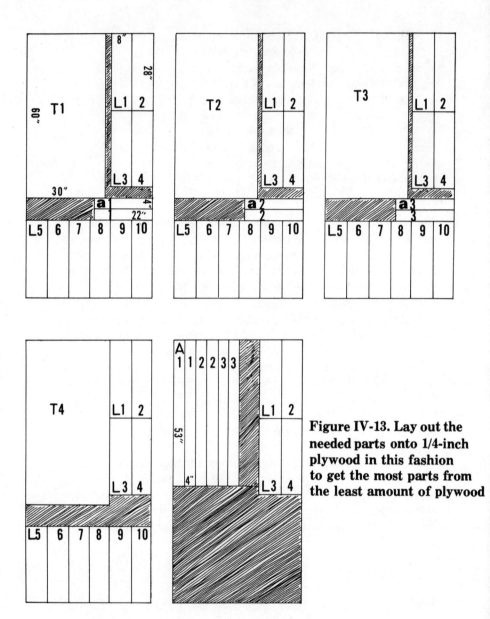

Figure IV-13. Lay out the needed parts onto 1/4-inch plywood in this fashion to get the most parts from the least amount of plywood

Figure IV-13 shows how to lay out the various pieces to get the best use of your plywood. In all there are sixty small pieces of wood in this project. They all fit together into one top, four legs, and the four sides of an apron which fits around the top.

Top

Start with the top. It's the biggest single piece, but also the simplest. Figure IV-14 shows the shape you can use in this table as well as in several other pieces of furniture all in this same style. The pattern is universal for all sizes and all shapes. To make the 30-inch-by-60-inch top for this table, get yourself a piece of cardboard or heavy paper at least 15 by 30 inches big and turn it into a pattern.

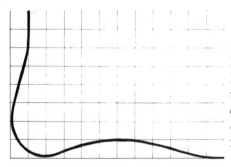

Figure IV-14. Universal top pattern for French provincial furniture. It can be used for desks, coffee tables, and dining room tables by varying the size of your squares according to requirements given in text

Mark 2-1/2-inch lines the long way on your pattern. Then make lines every 2 inches the short way. The "squares" which result will actually be 2-1/2 inches by 2. But when you draw a curve, you concentrate on where the curve crosses your guidelines, so the oblong "squares" shouldn't bother you. If they do, take a look at Figure IV-15.

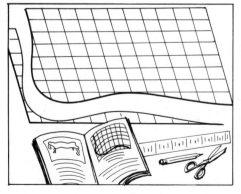

Figure IV-15. How to use the universal pattern for creating a top or apron for your French Provincial tables.

(A)
Find in the text how big to make your squares on a pattern. Mark them onto cardboard. Then trace the curved-top pattern onto the squared cardboard. Cut out the pattern. You'll have a pattern for one fourth of the top.

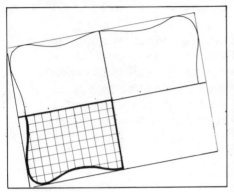

(B)
On your plywood for T1 draw horizontal and vertical lines at the exact center. Line up your pattern on those center lines and trace the curved edge onto the plywood. Repeat until you've traced all four quarters of the top.

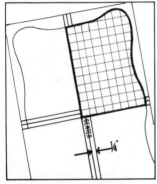

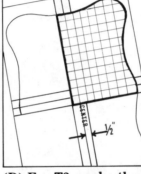

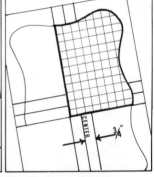

(C) For top piece T2, draw a second set of lines 1/4 inch on both sides of the center lines. Line up the pattern on the off-centered lines farther away from the corner on the quarter you plan to trace.

(D) For T3, make the off-centered lines 1/2 inch away from the center line and do the same as Step C.

(E) Repeat the two operations, only make the off-centered lines 3/4 inch away from the center lines.

Top piece T1 goes on the bottom of the pile. It's the biggest. Part T2 will go on top of T1. You want its curve to be the same, but it should be 1/4 inch smaller all the way around. That's why you set up the pattern 1/4 inch away from the center when you draw T2 (see Figure IV-15). The edges for parts T3 and T4 should each be still farther away. Figure IV-16 shows what the table edge will look like after the top is finished.

Before the four top pieces are laminated together, resulting in a top about 1 inch thick, let's fancy up their edges a bit. The finished top will then look like a wood carver spent hours on the edge with an expensive router or shaper.

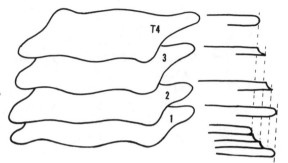

Figure IV-16. Laminate your
top pieces into a single, curvy,
groovy top in this way. At the
right is a profile view of how
the edge of this top should
look

Round the edges of T1 with a SurForm tool followed by medium-grade sandpaper. When you're finished the edges should be smooth and circular like the T1 edge in Figure IV-16.

Parts T2 and T3 get a different edge treatment. Eventually you will give them a slanted, concave shape.

If your sabre saw lets you adjust the blade or the platform so you can cut at an angle, set it to 45 degrees when you saw off pieces T2 and T3. Make sure to keep the top of your sabre-saw blade *on the line* and the angled bottom part of the blade always pointed toward the center of the board.

Without an angled saw cut, you can roughly trim the edges of T2 and T3 to shape with a SurForm tool. After T2 and T3 are slanted, go to work with sandpaper. As your fingers force the medium-grade sandpaper against the edge, they'll generate the concave curve shown in Figure IV-16.

Top piece T4 is rounded the same way as T1. Before you decide which piece will become T1, T2, T3, or T4, consider that the top of T4 will become the table top. Make it a good one.

There's no need to sandpaper the big, flat surfaces of the four sheets of 1/4-inch plywood you plan to laminate into a 1-inch-thick top. Except for the top of T4, nobody's going to see them again.

Find yourself a big, uncluttered place to work where you're not afraid to slop a little glue. Lay several thicknesses of newspaper on a tile or wooden floor.

Before you mix up some glue, be sure the four pieces for your table top actually do fit together properly. Lay T1 down first, then put T2, T3, and T4 on top. When you spread them out evenly, the resulting edge should resemble the laminated cross section in Figure IV-16. Don't expect perfection. It's possible but not necessary. *This is handmade furniture.* The edges and curves won't be machine-made perfect, which is what gives this project its charm.

Lay part T1 flat on the floor by itself. Lay T2 upside down nearby. Apply a generous coating of glue to the top of T1 and the bottom of T2. Then lay T2 on top of T1. Slide it around until all of the edges look evenly spaced out. The outside of T2 should be 1/4 inch from the outside of T1.

After T2 is accurately in place, tack it down with a couple of dozen 1/2-inch brads. Put a few nails near the middle, then work toward the outside. Put most of your nails near the outside, but stay more than 1/4 inch away from the very edge. That bit of wood will be seen after your next layer of wood goes on.

Now lay piece T3 upside down. Apply glue to the top of T2 and the bottom of T3. Lay T3 accurately into position and nail it down.

The top piece, T4, is laminated to the others just as you did with T2 and T3. This time, however, hammer very carefully. A bit later you are going to have to sand away every gouge and scrape.

After piece T4 is in place, flip the whole laminated table top upside down so the bottom of T1 points up. With a couple of boxes of 1-inch brads or finishing nails, nail the four pieces together, spacing the nails only 3 or 4 inches apart.

There's about 1 inch of wood for your 1-inch nails to penetrate. If the nails were a bit too long, they'd penetrate the surface of the table top and make a terrible mess. The three thicknesses of glue add just enough margin for safety. Do check once in a while, however, to make sure the points are not going all the way through T4.

Wipe away all the gobs of glue your nailing squeezes out. Then lay your laminated top aside to dry.

Legs

The legs are the most time-consuming because there are four of them to make. Convert the leg shape in Figure IV-17 to a cardboard pattern just as you did when you made the top. The dotted lines at the top of the leg pattern are 1/4 inch apart.

Make a separate cardboard pattern for the L10 and L11 shape. You're going to make eight pieces like that anyway, and you'll have trouble trying to duplicate the rear curve if you don't use a cardboard pattern.

The 28-inch leg is used for this table. It's also designed for use on a similar desk you'll meet up with later. The smaller leg is only 18 inches high and fits into a coffee-table project. There are only

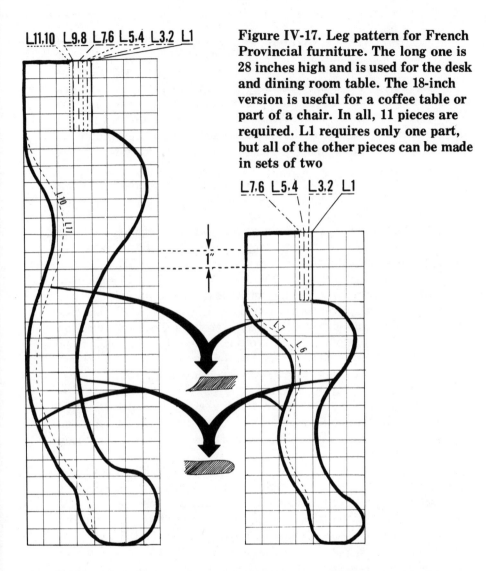

L11.10 L9.8 L7.6 L5.4 L3.2 L1

L7.6 L5.4 L3.2 L1

1"

Figure IV-17. Leg pattern for French Provincial furniture. The long one is 28 inches high and is used for the desk and dining room table. The 18-inch version is useful for a coffee table or part of a chair. In all, 11 pieces are required. L1 requires only one part, but all of the other pieces can be made in sets of two

seven pieces of laminates in each of the 18-inch legs. Our 28-inch version, being much wider, requires eleven pieces for each leg.

There is an efficient way to cut those forty-four pieces of wood without making forty-four separate cuts. That could be brutal as well as inaccurate.

Trace the pattern for leg L1 into one piece of plywood. Then carefully lay three other pieces of wood underneath. Line up the four edges. Then put several 1-inch nails through the four pieces of wood. Put only two nails into the wood that actually will go into the leg, one near the top and one near the bottom. Put the rest of the nails into parts that will be discarded.

Now you can make a single curvy cut and end up with all of the L1 pieces you need. Assuming your sabre saw can cut through 2 inches of wood—most can—you can nail eight pieces of 1/4-inch plywood together next. That way you can make a single saw cut and end up with all of the L2 and L3 pieces your table requires.

Keep drawing, nailing, and sawing until all forty-four pieces are cut.

For fine woodwork, you would ordinarily use a sabre-saw blade with a fine set of teeth, something like 14 teeth per inch. That way you'll have less sanding to do later on.

Since every piece will be sanded anyway, you can use a coarser blade which cuts faster and may be more accurate for this kind of job. A long blade with 4, 6, or 8 teeth per inch is OK.

You must be careful that your saw cuts straight up and down. Otherwise pieces on the bottom of the pile will come out bigger or smaller than pieces at the top. To help you hold the saw vertically, first cut off the back portion of the legs. Then go to work on the front. Most of the excess wood surface is cut off with the front of the legs. By saving that until the end, you can keep the biggest flat surface to guide your saw in a true up-and-down path.

Aside from parts L10 and L11, every edge is rounded off except for the squared-off top, which is concealed in the finished piece of furniture, and the flat bottom of each leg, which rests on the floor. Figure IV-18 shows what the sanded edges should look like.

Figure IV-18 also shows how to laminate each pile of eleven pieces of wood into one "groovy" leg 2-3/4 inches thick. (Shorter legs for use on coffee tables are 1-3/4 inches thick.)

Line up individual leg pieces by comparing their flat tops and flat bottoms. Starting with part L1, work out to L10 and L11. Put plenty of glue between each layer, but just a few 1/2-inch nails.

After part L7 is in place, pick up your box of 1-inch finishing nails. Drive fifteen or twenty nails through L7 toward L1, and another fifteen or twenty nails through L6 toward L1. Then put L8 and the other pieces into place using glue and 1/2-inch brads.

When L11 is glued and nailed down, then use 1-inch finishing nails again. Use fifteen or twenty on a side, as you did earlier, but this time hammer them into place very carefully. You'll be working on what is now the outside of your new leg.

The right side of Figure IV-18 shows an X-ray view of a com-

Figure IV-18. Laminate your leg parts this way. At the right, a profile view of what a laminated leg should look like. There are only seven pieces in the 18-inch leg, but other details are similar

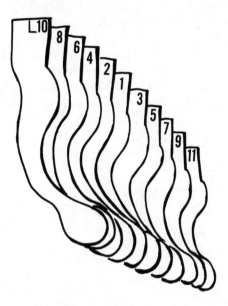

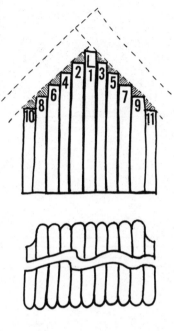

pleted leg. The top front portion of each leg is V shaped so it will fit snugly into the square corner of the apron. These legs don't stick out to the front or to one side, but project outwards at a 45-degree angle.

While the glue is drying you can fill in the canyons of your leg with Plastic Wood. The shaded areas in Figure IV-18 represent Plastic Wood. You don't have to smooth and sand the Plastic Wood filler carefully. It's there just to give some surface to glue against the inside of your furniture's apron.

Apron

Now cut out and assemble the apron. If you want, you can trace the shape from Figure IV-19 directly onto plywood since there are relatively few parts to make. Or you can cut out a cardboard pattern first.

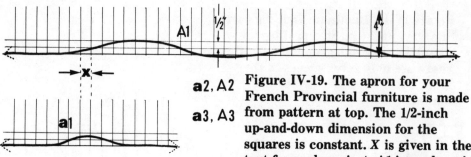

a2, A2
a3, A3

Figure IV-19. The apron for your French Provincial furniture is made from pattern at top. The 1/2-inch up-and-down dimension for the squares is constant. X is given in the text for each project. A1 is made as is. A2 is 1/4-inch narrower than the pattern. And A3 is 1/2-inch narrower. Assemble the pieces according to the bottom sketch

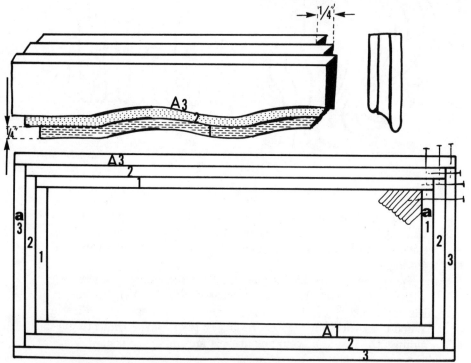

Figure IV-19 is another universal pattern for tables, desks, or other projects no matter how big or how small. Since the top-to-bottom size of aprons remains about 4 inches, the horizontal lines remain 1/2 inch apart.

Going vertically (the long dimension of each apron piece), make your lines 1-1/4 inches apart for this table. That will give you a pattern only 51-1/4 inches long. You want the long apron piece to be 53 inches long, however. So simply lengthen the straight end line by 7/8 inch on both ends. The ends of both apron patterns are deliberately long and straight so you have the kind of flexibility you want when you build bigger or smaller projects.

To make the shorter apron pieces you could use 1-1/4-inch spacing between the vertical lines, the same as you'll use for the long apron piece on this basic table project. However, if you make the squares 1-1/2 inch, you can shorten the end lines until your apron is the prescribed 22 inches long.

In general, here's how to design an apron to match your own choice of table or desk size. Figure out how big you want the table top. Then subtract 7 inches from the length, 8 inches from the width. those two numbers are the length and width of your apron parts.

There are forty-one squares in the long apron pattern, so divide the length of your apron's long piece by forty-one. Round the answer off to some convenient number such as 1 inch, 1-1/4, 1/2, etc. Either lengthen or shorten the end lines so your pattern matches the desired apron length.

Do likewise for the short apron piece. There are only fifteen squares in that pattern, however, so divide the width by fifteen and round off to the nearest convenient size for your vertical lines.

After you've drawn the curved pattern onto cardboard or your 1/4-inch plywood, here's how to make the edges come out right. Pieces A1 and a1 are cut the full 4 inches wide at their biggest part. A2 and a2 are drawn 1/4 inch back from the edge, just as you did with the top pieces. But the overall length of the apron parts A2 and a2 is stretched by 1/2 inch.

Parts A3 and a3 follow suit. They're 1/4 inch narrower than A2 and a2 but 1/2 inch longer.

For the 30-by-60-inch table, here are the dimensions of the apron pieces:

A1: 4″ × 52″   a1: 4″ × 21″
A2: 3-3/4″ × 52-1/2″   a2: 3-3/4″ × 21-1/2″
A3: 3-1/2″ × 53″   a3: 3-1/2″ × 22″

With those individual parts, the finished apron will be 53 inches long and 22-1/2 inches wide. That should result in a margin between the edge of the table top and the outside of the apron of 3-1/2 inches along the side, 3-3/4 inches at the ends. Figure IV-19 goes into this graphically.

After all of the apron parts are cut, you have to sandpaper

their edges. The inner and outer pieces, A1 and A3, a1 and a3, are rounded off. The middle pieces, A2 and a2, have to end up with that slanted, concave curved shape you saw on the middle parts of the table edge.

When all of the shaping is done you can glue apron pieces together. Start with the two long segments first. The three upper edges should line up well and the spacing at their ends should be precisely 1/4 inch, for reasons you'll soon discover.

Start with part A3, attach A2 to it, then A1. Use 1/2-inch brads and plenty of glue. After you've laminated the two long apron components, then you can work with the short pieces. You don't even have to wait for the glue to dry.

Lay the long components on their flat edges. That will leave the rounded, fancy parts pointing up. With a friend, spouse, or heavy books supporting the two long laminates, make sure that the sets of three shorter laminates fit snugly into their appropriate slots. Assuming they do, mark their precise locations before you remove them. If they don't fit well, saw or sandpaper them until you get a good fit.

While you're testing for fit, make sure that the long and short apron segments are square with each other. Use your square as shown in §15.

Glue and nail (with 1/2-inch brads) both short apron components together. Then apply a generous amount of glue to all of the connecting apron ends. And fit them all together as shown in the bottom sketch of Figure IV-19. Make sure they're square. Then use 1-inch nails to fasten the apron together.

Set the entire completed apron aside so the glue can dry. But make sure it's square one more time.

Put It All Together

Maybe people will want to finish a table like this with paint or antique finishes. If that's your choice, you can attach the apron to the table top simply by nailing right through the top into the apron. That's how Figure IV-20 shows to do it. (Don't forget to use glue when you attach the apron to the top.) Space the nails about 4 or 5 inches apart. Use a nail set and fill the resulting holes with Plastic Wood. The sanding, plus many layers of paint you'll apply in a little while, will make the construction marks absolutely invisible.

If you have a yen for natural-wood finishes, especially a light-colored finish, you'd best attach the top to the apron indirectly.

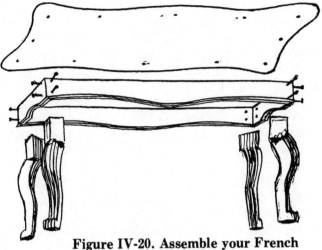

Figure IV-20. Assemble your French
Provincial table this way

The number of nails you need to bond the top and apron securely
demands a terrible amount of later puttering to match the color of
all those Plastic Wood plugs to the main body of wood.

To attach your apron indirectly, invest in some 3/4-inch, quarter round molding. If you buy two pieces, each 4 feet long, you
can cut it into two pieces of 3-foot-long molding and two pieces of
1-foot-long molding.

Lay your table top on the floor, top down. Then set your apron
in place carefully. Nail one of the short strips of molding to the
table top so one of its flat sides is against the table top and the
other rests against the inside of your apron. Use glue plus 1-inch
finishing nails. Then do the same with the other short strip at the
other end of the apron.

After you make sure that the apron is still correctly centered,
lay one of the long strips of molding along the long side of your
apron. Nail and glue it to the table top. Then do the same for the
other long side.

Once all four molding strips have been nailed down, and after
you're satisfied that the apron is in the right place, you can go
back and nail the molding to the apron too. Again, use 1-inch nails
spaced about 6 inches apart.

As you nail the molding to the inside of your apron, keep a foot
or a knee against the outside of the apron. Otherwise the force
from your hammering might shove the apron or molding out of
line.

There should be large gaps in the molding at all four corners. That leaves space for your table legs.

After you test the legs for snug fits in their appropriate corners, drill pilot holes through the apron and into the legs. You should make two holes in each of the slanted sides of your leg. Make countersink holes too.

Apply glue to the top as well as the sides of your legs. Put a leg into place, and then carefully start all four of the 2 × 12 or 2 × 10 screws into place. Don't tighten one down and then another. Make two or three turns on one screw, then move to another for two or three turns. That will help to hold the leg in good alignment as it's being installed. (See §12.)

After all four legs are glued and screwed into place, make two holes through the table top into each leg. Use 2 × 10 or 2 × 12 screws. Countersink them carefully. These extra screws are to help stabilize the apron and legs so you won't end up with a wobbly table after a couple of years. They're important enough that you should be willing to go through the extra bit of work to fill the screw holes with Plastic Wood, sand them smooth, and match the color of the plugs to the main wood in the top if you plan to give a natural-wood finish to the completed spectacle.

In case you don't own an electric drill for making pilot holes and countersinks for the screws, you *can* use 2-inch-long finishing nails as a substitute. The screws will hold better over the years, but the nails will make the work go faster. The choice is yours.

The Finish

As always, the choice in finish depends on you and what's already sitting around your home. To set up that glamorous early French look, stick to ivory paint with gold added as an overcoat. Light blue or light olive green look classy too. You can even use tan as a base color.

If you want to make the table elegant and a bit showy, make sure that plenty evidence of a gold overcoat paint remains after you've done the final wiping. You can apply gold paint with an artist's brush to the center two laminates on the table edge, the middle groove in the apron, and the deepest part of every groove in the legs.

Natural-wood finishes seem to work best with darker stains. Walnut, dark oak, mahogany, and such are good choices. A deep treatment with maple looks elegant too.

To create a family heirloom, you could make the top surface

from hardwood plywood (see §5). Most big lumberyards stock a few varieties of 1/4-inch hardwood plywoods. The core layers are fir, but the surface layer is a veneer of real hardwood. It's more expensive than common fir plywood, of course, so use it only for the top of every laminated component.

One sheet of hardwood plywood is enough. Substitute the hardwood for the first sheet of plywood on Figure IV-13. Eliminate the two legs on the top inside and put two long apron pieces there instead. That arrangement will leave you with exactly enough pieces to enclose every laminated table component in hardwood.

For even more handmade elegance you can expand the patterns according to instructions given earlier until you have a table up to 8 feet long. The longer your table top, the wider it should be also. Keep the width at least half as big as the length until you reach 40 or 48 inches. Very few tables, no matter how long, need be much wider than that.

Once you push past the 60-inch (5 feet) mark, four legs can't give enough support. You need six. The two legs that go midway along the side should be made exactly like the corner legs except they should be flat on top instead of pointed. In other words, eliminate the dotted lines at the top of the leg patterns. Figure IV-11 in the last chapter shows how to reinforce your table's apron when you use six legs.

Painted, stained, or real hardwood, when this project is finished you'll not only have a real masterpiece to show off, you'll know you can tackle any piece of furniture alive today!

24.   Big, Square, Modern Table (Figure IV-21)

SKILLS:	Easy. Could be a good first project if you're confident.
TIME:	A weekend.
TOOLS:	Hammer, sandpaper, saw, drill, wrench or pliers.
ALSO READ:	§4; Chapters 3, 4

Figure IV-21

This promises to be a chapter long on pictures and short on words. It won't even take many pictures to make the point that this is a very flexible, sharp-looking modern table you can build in a flash.

Thanks to the little square tables which became the rage a few years back, this table looks most "in place" when the top is perfectly square. But if you want to make the top rectangular, go to it. As is, the plans on nearby pages will lead you to a 4-foot-square model.

Figure IV-22 shows how to lay out your parts onto 3/4-inch plywood (good 1 side). The 4-by-4-foot version fits onto a single sheet of plywood. For bigger tops you'll have to buy more than one full sheet. You can keep the legs 4 inches wide on each side for smaller tables and even for bigger tables until the top approaches 6 feet long. At this point, make your legs 6 inches on a side.

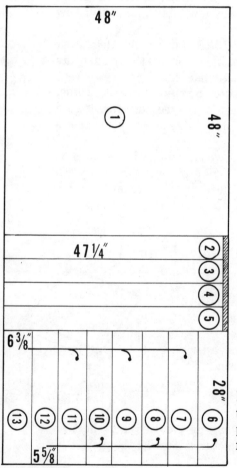

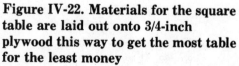

Figure IV-22. Materials for the square table are laid out onto 3/4-inch plywood this way to get the most table for the least money

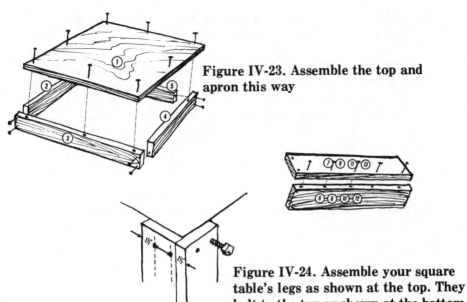

Figure IV-23. Assemble the top and apron this way

Figure IV-24. Assemble your square table's legs as shown at the top. They bolt to the top as shown at the bottom

Figure IV-23 shows how to assemble the top. Use glue plus 1-1/2-inch finishing nails, spaced 4 or 5 inches apart. If you plan to add Formica or vinyl plastic to the top, you don't have to countersink the nails with a nail set. Otherwise use a nail set and plug the holes later with Plastic Wood.

The legs are nailed together according to Figure IV-24. Again, use glue plus 1-1/2-inch finishing nails spaced 4 or 5 inches apart.

After your glue has dried, go over the joints with sandpaper or a SurForm tool. Each joint should be so smooth that the different pieces of wood blend in. After that, you can sandpaper the whole disassembled table, top—plus four leg pieces—according to §26.

In keeping with what fashion setters consider modern, this table deserves a high-gloss finish. Formica, vinyl, paint, or lacquer will do that for you. Look at the appropriate part of Chapter 4 for details on how to work with each method.

If you use Formica-type plastic, drill the holes after you've glued it onto your legs and top. Otherwise you can drill the holes any time after you've completed the rough sanding.

First drill the holes in each leg according to the dimensions given in Figure IV-24. The recommended hardware is a set of 3/8-inch stainless steel bolts 2 inches long. Try to buy bolts with square heads to match the square table top. You can buy a 3/8-inch drill which will fit into your 1/4-inch electric drill, or you can make a 1/4-inch hole and enlarge it with a file or SurForm tool. It's a lot less work to spend the dollar or two for a 3/8-inch drill bit.

After you've drilled holes into the legs, then set each leg in turn against one corner of the table top. Mark carefully where the holes are in the leg and drill matching holes in the top.

Ideally all of the holes in all four legs will be identically laid out. Don't be so idealistic, however, or you may end up with a wobbly table. Mark each leg #1, #2, #3, or #4. Then mark the corner of your table top likewise so your leg and top holes will match up almost exactly.

Put the shiny stainless steel nuts and bolts into the sixteen holes for them, tighten them up with wrench or pliers, and your table is on its own.

25. Quick Desks

SKILLS:	Very easy. Good first project.
TIME:	An evening or a weekend.
TOOLS:	Screwdriver, sandpaper. Drill is helpful but not required.
ALSO READ:	§'s 7, 13, 21; Chapters 4, 28.

Figure V-1

Anyone who needs a desk in a hurry will delight in these designs. For that matter, they're not bad for anyone else who wants a big, rugged, nice-looking desk. See Figure V-1.

The size of this desk is dictated only by how much room you need. This design will work for desk tops up to about 8 feet long and 3 feet wide. On the smaller size, a 2-foot-by-4-foot top is OK too.

You can choose three drawers or four. With a large enough top you can even stick in two sets of drawers, giving you a total of eight into which you can cram all the paraphernalia imaginable.

For a top on these desks, buy yourself a hollow-core door. They're cheap, lightweight, veneered with nice-looking hardwoods, and most lumberyards stock them in so many sizes and shapes that you can practically count on getting what you want. See §7 for more specifics.

You can buy ready-to-install legs at the same lumberyard where you buy the door. Several companies make easy-to-install, easy-to-look-at legs at a reasonable price. Some of the best legs are packaged individually. Although you need only two legs, you may have to buy a box of four if you decide on some of the simple, tapered, round legs. Don't worry about the extra two legs. You'll still be saving a lot of money.

Desk legs are typically about 28 inches long. If you like a higher desk you can shoot for 30 inches, although they're harder to find. If you're short or if you use a desk for typing, 24- or 22-inch legs might be better for you.

The third component in these desks is drawers. In order to keep this a one-evening project, buy a set of drawers at an unfinished furniture outlet. The price won't break you, and if you shop carefully for both quality and size, you'll get a set of three or four drawers fully compatible with your desk.

Chapter 28 shows you how to build a set of drawers which is just as strong and good-looking as ones you can buy at unfinished furniture stores.

If you decide to buy unfinished drawers, try to find a set that stands about as high as you want your desk to be, typically 28 inches. But there are plenty of ways to adjust a set of 28-inch legs to a set of 27- or 29-inch drawers.

For one, better legs have adjustable glides which add up to 1/2 inch to their length. Others come with supplementary glides you can nail in if you want them. If you need longer legs, nail in the glides to gain an extra 1/2-inch length for your legs. But if the legs are a bit too long, nail the glides onto the bottom of your drawers.

If your set of drawers is significantly shorter than 28 inches, you can add a small set of legs or finials to them. If you're building a permanent desk, fasten the legs only to the outside edge of your drawer set. If you like to move around a lot, maybe you

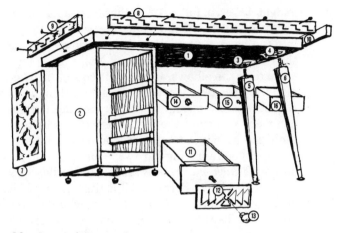

**Figure V-2. Assemble the various parts
for your quick desk in this fashion**

should support all four corners of the drawer set, which in turn
supports one side of your top.

Most desk drawers are 15 to 20 inches wide. You can go down
to 12 inches and up to 24 inches without encountering a lot of
problems either in construction or appearance.

Once you've acquired all the drawers, legs, and the top, assemble them as in Figure V-2. Unlike most other construction
projects in this book, you can't just nail or screw the parts together.

Hollow-core doors are little more than two pieces of thin veneer held in place by a central network of softwood or cardboard
cores. Consequently, you can't expect a nail or screw to hold onto
more than about 1/16 inch of veneer. Back in §13 you learned
about the Molly Screw, which expands inside walls or hollow-core
doors to give all the strength you need for a desk.

Lay each leg bracket into place on the bottom of your desk top.
Mark carefully where the four holes are located. Drill a hole at
each spot big enough to receive your Molly Screws. For the 1/8
S-size Molly recommended here, a 1/4-inch hole is fine. If you
don't own a drill it's easy enough simply to poke a nail hole in the
appropriate place and then to enlarge it with a file, a large screw,
or with the Molly itself.

Some hollow-core doors are more chintzy than others, so poke
your Molly Screws into their holes carefully. The unexpanded

gadget takes a full 1-1/2 inches. Cheaper doors may be a bit narrower than that, but don't despair. Shove your Molly Screw into the narrow door, grab the outside portion with a pliers, and then tighten the screw on your Molly. In doing so, you'll begin expanding the elbows, which will reduce the overall length of the Molly. By the time you've made eight or ten full turns, the gadget will be narrow enough that you can tap it into place with the hammer. You want the Molly Screw's barbs to grab firmly onto the wood so it won't twist around on you later.

When you're buying hardware for this project, invest in a few dozen *1/8-inch machine screws* 1-1/4 inches long. After you've twisted the Molly Screw until it fits within the confines of your hollow-core door, the screw itself may still be too long. Besides, after some hard turning, you may damage the slot so much that the screw is practically useless. So at some point along the way, replace the original Molly Screw with your own.

After both leg plates are held in place with the Molly Screws, screw in the legs just to make sure you've installed the plate where you like them. But don't stand the desk upright for good just yet.

Take all of the drawers out of your drawer set, and turn the outside cabinet upside down onto your door. Drill about six holes through the top of your drawer cabinet and into the bottom of your door. They don't have to be in any particular place. Just don't drill all of the holes in a straight line. Put Molly Screws into the door just as you did for the leg brackets. And then fasten the drawer set onto the top with the Molly Screws.

At this point, your desk is about ready to use. However, it needs finishing and you may want to decorate it a bit. In §24 you learned about dozens of ways to deal with the edges of furniture. Most of them apply here. If you glue and tack on some molded edge strips, you may want to put matching decorations on the drawer fronts too. You can buy some of the elaborate carvings described in §8, or build some of your own according to hints near the end of Chapter 28.

As you see in Figure V-2, the decorative carvings are simply glued onto the existing drawer fronts. The knob is installed through a hole. Sometimes you can shop around for big or elaborate knobs which will take care of fancying up your desk. If you really go all out, you can glue one or more of the molded carvings onto the side and front of your drawer set. There are other variations too.

You can buy a piece of 3/4-inch plywood as tall as your set of drawers but 6 inches narrower than your desk top. Buy three pieces of 3-inch *corner braces* and fasten them to your plywood as shown in Figure V-3. Fasten the corner braces in turn to your desk top. Use 3/4 × 8 screws into the plywood and Molly Screws into the hollow-core door. When you glue a carving over the plywood, you will have an impressive-looking pedestal to support your desk, and the carving will cover the hardware.

Figure V-3. Variation in the way you can assemble a desk. Instead of the traditional sort of legs, a pedestal, perhaps with carvings glued to it, supports one end of this desk

You can obtain the pedestal effect more cheaply if you plan ahead. Let's assume you want a desk close to 6 feet long or shorter. Buy your drawers in advance so you get the measurements. At the lumberyard, as you're shopping for a door, buy one long enough to give you not only a top but also a pedestal. Your lumberyard will cut the door into parts for you and, for an additional fee, will plug up the openings with solid wood.

Fasten 3-inch corner braces to your small piece, as shown in

Figure V-3. Then fasten the braces to your desk top with Molly Screws. If you turn the pedestal around from the way it's positioned in Figure V-3, the hardware will be hidden in the shadowy inner parts of your desk. In this way your pedestal can be finished with the same wood finish as the top.

Figure V-4 gives a couple more variations. On top you see how to use two sets of drawers in designing a desk. Attach each set just as you would in all of the desks we've already discussed.

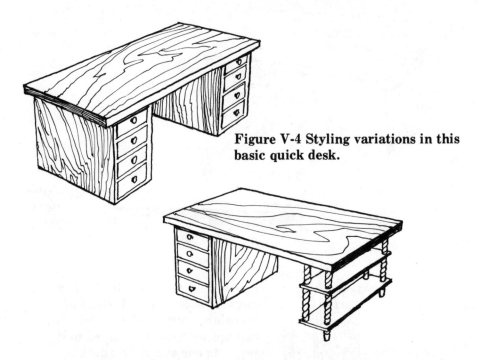

Figure V-4 Styling variations in this basic quick desk.

The bottom half of Figure V-4 shows how to use spindles in an attractive but space-saving desk design. Make sure that you fasten the tops of the outside spindles near the very edge of the desk top. That's where the solid wood is located, and you'll need some solid wood to hold the spindles in place. Choose spindles long enough to match the height of your drawer set.

Variations in Figure V-5 are more concerned with finish than design and construction. If your desk is going where the warmth of an upholstered look would be appreciated, you can do that in a jiffy. The simplest upholstering job of all is simply to use silicone adhesive to fasten a large strip of fabric over the top of your new

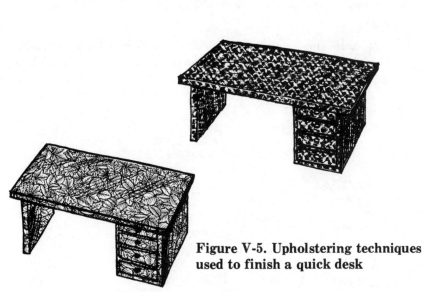

Figure V-5. Upholstering techniques used to finish a quick desk

desk, over its sides, and on all of the drawer fronts. Smaller areas can either be painted or fitted with smaller strips of cloth.

You can use a rough-textured cloth for this job, even though that might be hard to write on. No matter what kind of cloth you use, except for something like vinyl, you must put a protective coating of lacquer or varnish on the desk top. After enough coats of lacquer or varnish, even burlap takes on a smooth surface just right for writing on.

Your new desk can be treated to that padded upholstering look you saw in the headboard Chapter 9 and the coffee table Chapter 19. Glue foam rubber padding, either 1-inch or 2-inches thick, to all large surfaces such as the side of your desk's pedestal and the side of the drawer set. Stretch your fabric over the foam and tack it down about every 3 or 4 inches with fancy upholstery tacks.

Put fabric only—no padding—on the desk top. The drawer fronts are optional; padded or not, the desk will look good. Be sure to use upholstery tacks along the entire edge of the desk top. Space them at the same intervals you used in tacking down the padding and fabric. The bottom sketch in Figure V-5 shows what this kind of desk looks like when you're through with it.

There must be dozens of other variations you can apply to this basic quick desk style. If you leaf quickly through other portions of this book, or stroll through the furniture section of a large department store, you'll probably come away with some which tickle your personal fancy.

As with almost every piece of furniture you build yourself, your pocketbook and your imagination are your only limits. Especially your imagination.

26. Curvaceous Modern Desk

SKILLS: Easy.
TIME: A weekend.
TOOLS: Hammer or screw-
                  driver, sandpaper,
                  handsaw or sabre
                  saw.
ALSO READ: §'s 4, 7; Chapters 3,
                  4, 28.

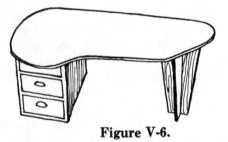

Figure V-6.

The morning after you start this project you could be writing on a stunning, curvy modern desk made of only half a sheet of 3/4-inch plywood and a set of unfinished drawers. See Figure V-6.

A three-way shaped leg supports one entire side of the desk, which contributes to the airy look. The other side of the top rests on the drawers. And the drawers in turn rest on short legs, further adding to airiness.

Use a three-drawer set so you keep plenty of air underneath all the parts of this desk. If you build the drawers according to Chapter 28's sliding comments, your set will be about 21 inches tall. If you buy a ready-made set of drawers, shoot for the shorter sizes so you can add legs to the bottom.

Drawings in this chapter show a 24-inch, three-way leg. That's a bit shorter than the usual big desks. It's an ideal height for typing, drawing, and for shorter people. You can extend the

Figure V-7. Material for the curvy desk is laid out onto 3/4-inch plywood this way, requiring only half a sheet

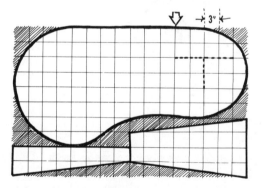

unique leg by adding several inches to the *top* of the two pieces that form the pedestal. Likewise, if you·want an even shorter desk, subtract a few inches from the top.

Be sure that you buy your drawers and legs before cutting out the parts for this desk's three-way leg. The length of that leg has to equal the total length of your drawer set, plus small legs. Figure V-7 shows how to lay out the shaped top and three-way leg parts. And Figure V-8 shows how to assemble the whole simple project.

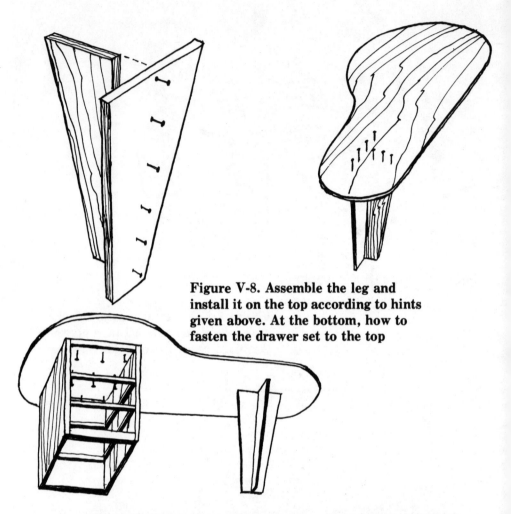

Figure V-8. Assemble the leg and install it on the top according to hints given above. At the bottom, how to fasten the drawer set to the top

When I built this, I used 3/4-inch plywood, good 1 side. The big curved top will only be seen on one side. True, the three-way leg is seen from all angles, and if you end up with a blemish there, you'll have to fill in a hole with Plastic Wood and sandpaper a little bit harder. I feel the savings is worth the slight risk of having to patch up a bad spot in the leg.

The layout drawing in Figure V-7 shows the entire project fitting onto a 30-inch-by-48-inch piece of plywood. That's for a 24-inch leg. If you want a longer one, you have to slide the smaller piece down a bit, which means you need a 36-by-48-inch piece of plywood.

If you use a keyhole saw or coping saw to cut out the top, you'll be at it for an hour easily. Most of the back requires no sawing at all if you lay out the pattern carefully as Figure V-7 shows. With a sabre saw, you should carve through the top in ten or fifteen minutes.

When you assemble the desk parts, first lay your top face down on a flat surface. Take out the drawers and lay the drawer cabinet upside down onto the top. Apply plenty of glue to the areas where drawer cabinet and desk top meet. Then nail or screw the top of the cabinet to your desk top.

Draw a straight line down the exact middle of your big part to the three-way leg. Start pounding 1-1/2-inch finishing nails into the back. Stop when their points just start to show through on the other side. Apply plenty of glue to the leg parts, and lay them carefully together, making sure their tops and bottoms line up well. Then hammer your nails in the rest of the way. Space nails about 2 to 3 inches apart.

The assembled three-way leg does not have to dry before you fasten it onto the top. But if you put it aside for a while and the glue starts to set, then you have to wait until the glue has set completely before disturbing it.

Draw a 12-inch line the long way on your desk top and a 6-inch perpendicular line. Figure V-7 shows how. Drive nails partway into the top, again pounding only until their points peek through. Put glue wherever the leg and top will meet. Line up the leg using the points of nails sticking out of the top as your guide. Make sure once and for all that the leg is well lined up, then hammer in all of your nails.

All of the finishing methods discussed in Chapter 4 will work on this desk. Even the upholstery method discussed at the end of Chapter 25 looks good.

Don't be afraid to apply Formica-type plastics to this desk top just because it's curvy. At first, disregard the curve. Simply contact-cement a 2-foot-by-4-foot piece of Formica to the top. When the contact cement is thoroughly set—probably the next day—cut around the curves with a fine-toothed saw such as a hacksaw, coping saw, or sabre saw with metal cutting blade. Sandpaper the edges smooth by holding medium-grade sandpaper in your hands instead of in a squared-off sanding block. Later you can use finer grades of sandpaper if you plan to paint or stain the edge. Otherwise, medium is fine enough. There are other ways of dealing with the edge discussed in §24.

As with almost every other project, there's plenty of room for you to add your own variations. In Figure V-7 there's an arrow showing where you can add an extra foot or two of plywood without seriously disrupting the design. That will leave you a desk 5 or 6 feet long instead of 4 feet.

You may like curves, but want lots of drawer space too. So make a 5- or 6-foot-long desk top and put two sets of drawers under it, as Figure V-9 shows. Although you can use most of the elaborate carvings (§8) to finish off the desk-drawer fronts or the do-it-yourself methods near the end of Chapter 28, the best-looking ornament for this project is the oval drawer front. You can carry that design over to the back of the drawer cabinet as well. Figure V-9 shows that effect too.

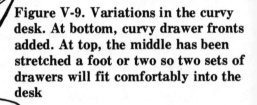

Figure V-9. Variations in the curvy desk. At bottom, curvy drawer fronts added. At top, the middle has been stretched a foot or two so two sets of drawers will fit comfortably into the desk

You can even flip back a few chapters to the coffee-table section and adapt some of the rounded tops there into tops for this desk. Once you really start to believe that building and designing furniture is easy, you'll see likely ideas everywhere.

27. Very Elaborate, Old-Fashioned Desk Done Simply (Figure V-10)

SKILLS: Complicated as a
whole, but individual
steps are easy.

TIME:	A month of Sundays.
TOOLS:	Hammer, srewdriver, saws. Although you *can* make this table with a handsaw, a sabre saw is recommended.
ALSO READ:	§'s 4, 7, 26, 28; Chapters 3, 23, 28.

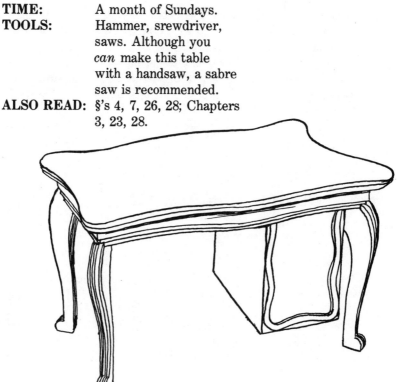

Figure V-10.

You've seen this project before, assuming you are reading page by page. It's nothing but the French Provincial (or something like that) table with a set of drawers added. Actually, the dimensions have been changed a bit. The desk is smaller than the table, since many people seem to put this kind of furniture where it should look petite. This one does.

After finishing this chapter, turn back to Chapter 23 about how to laminate the top, apron, and legs. This desk project adds only two pieces of wood over the number needed for the table—D1 and D2, which cover the otherwise plain backside of the drawer cabinet.

As for other desk projects, you can build your own drawers according to the ways presented in Chapter 28, or you can buy them according to the ways in Chapter 25 and §7.

For this 24-by-50-inch desk top, use the universal template back in Figure IV-14. Make your squares 3 inches apart the long

way and 2 inches apart the short way. Follow instructions in
Chapter 23 for cutting and assembling the four parts which become one beautiful desk top.

Chapter 23 also shows how to cut out and assemble the apron
which extends all the way around the top. The apron not only
beautifies your desk, but adds strength to the legs. Figure IV-19

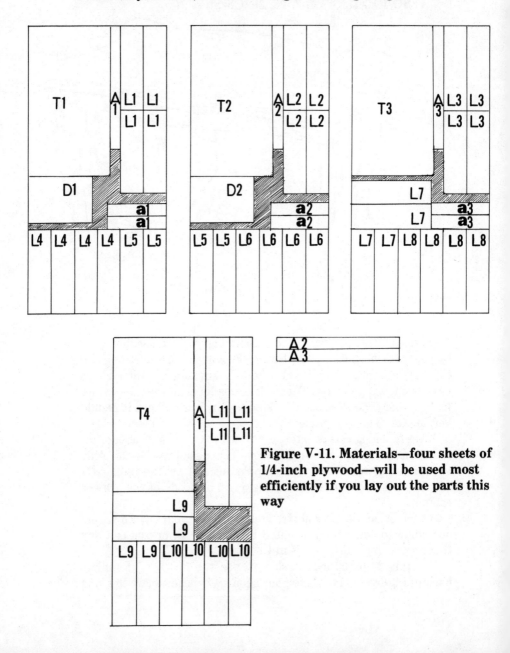

Figure V-11. Materials—four sheets of
1/4-inch plywood—will be used most
efficiently if you lay out the parts this
way

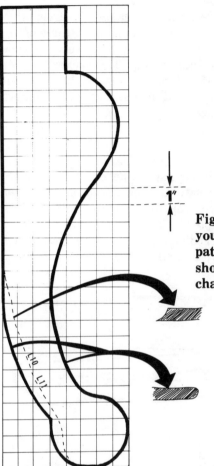

1"

**Figure V-12. Legs which attach to
your set of drawers are cut from this
pattern but assembled in the way
shown in the French Provincial table
chapter**

gives a pattern as well as a sketch showing how to assemble the
apron. For an apron to fit your desk, make the vertical spacing
1/2 inch, the same as in Chapter 23. For both the short and long
apron pieces, make the horizontal spacing for squares 1 inch.

Figure V-11 shows how to lay out your parts onto plywood to
get the most for your money. Use 1/4-inch plywood, good 1 side.

Make only two legs according to the dictates of Chapter 23.
Follow the pattern and assembly hints in Figures IV-17 and
IV-18. Those two legs will support the top at the end opposite the
drawers.

Make two more legs according to the pattern given in Figure
V-12. Assemble and finish these extra two legs the same way as
the ones from Chapter 23.

The two special desk legs differ in two major ways from other legs intended for the table version of this project. First of all, they're flat on the back so you can attach the drawer set to the legs. Secondly, they aren't pointed on top. That means the legs on the drawer side of this desk will not stick out at an angle, but will project at a right angle to your drawers. That gives strength and simplicity without detracting from the design.

Putting It All Together

First use glue and 2-inch finishing nails to fasten the desk top to the apron. But if you plan a natural-wood finish, better use an indirect way of attaching the top to the apron with 3/4-inch quarter-round molding. Chapter 23 covers that topic.

Next fasten the two freestanding legs to the apron and the top. Chapter 23, again, explains that well.

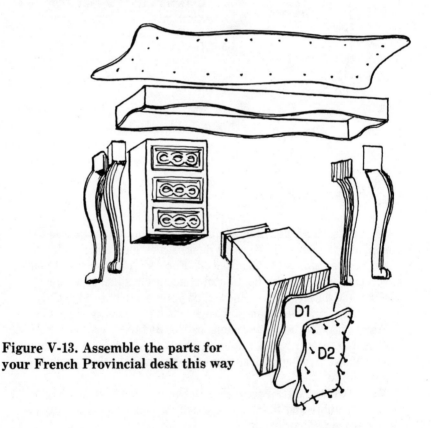

Figure V-13. Assemble the parts for your French Provincial desk this way

Overall, it would be easiest to attach the drawer cabinet to the legs and then attach the legs to the top and apron. If you feel your measurements are precise enough, that approach might be OK. If not, take a bit more time and go to the assembly indirectly.

First attach the two legs to the apron and top, just as you did with the earlier two legs. Then prop up the drawer cabinet on books until it's at the height you want. Make sure that the top drawer will open. Now you can drill pilot holes through the drawer cabinet and into the legs. You need half a dozen holes into each leg. Use 1-1/2 × 8 screws to fasten the drawer cabinet to the legs. Don't forget the glue too.

Those of you who make drawers according to the dictates of Chapter 28 should make the two side pieces longer. Instead of only 12 inches, as they would be in a normal three-drawer set, make them 25 inches. Let the extra length stick out at the top.

If you buy a ready-made set of drawers, you may have to construct a small box to fit as a false top. Depending on how tall the drawer set is, your box might have to be 3 or 4 inches deep. There's enough scrap lumber in these plans to allow for building such an improvised box.

The extra-long sides on drawer sets you build, or the false box on top of unfinished drawer sets you buy, serve several purposes. First, they give you a chance to hold up the drawers with more than the sides of two legs. This way you can nail through the top into the long sides or into the false top. Or you can fasten the drawer set to the top via quarter-round molding. In either case, you'll have a stronger desk.

What makes the construction of this desk different from others is that apron. Here's the mathematics of that element.

The apron is 4 inches deep. Therefore, the top 4 inches of your drawer set would be blocked off by the apron if you don't increase the room at the top of the drawer set. You wouldn't be able to open the top drawer, in other words. If you build or buy the recommended 21-inch-high drawer set, and extend the top by 4 inches, you'll have 3 inches left above the floor at the bottom. These legs are 28 inches high.

Finish

Finish the desk according to the hints given in Chapters 4 and 23 or according to your own taste and whims. Paying bills won't be any easier just because you're sitting at a desk you built. But the bill for making this desk will be about 10 percent of what buying a comparable one can cost you.

28. Cheap But Good Drawers You Can Build Yourself

SKILLS: Easy but requires some patience.

TIME: A weekend or two to three evenings.

TOOLS: Saw, hammer, square. Perhaps screwdriver, drill. SurForm tool.

ALSO READ: §'s 4, 10, 11, 14, 15, 16, 19.

Once upon a time, cabinetmakers had to saw or chisel elaborate and very precise grooved joints to hold their wooden drawer parts together. Now that chemists have improved the glues available even to amateurs, even many large furniture manufacturers have stopped making drawers with old-fashioned, elaborate joints. The glue is strong enough to hold even simple joints together for a lifetime or two.

Thanks to modern glues you can build your sets of drawers fully as rugged as what you can buy at most unfinished furniture outlets. For drawers up to 16 inches wide, use 3/8-inch plywood for all parts. From 16 inches to 30, use 1/2-inch plywood. Beyond 30 inches, especially for drawers which carry a heavy load, you may have to use 3/4-inch plywood for the drawer front and special reinforcement for the insides.

Use good 2 sides plywood for drawers if both the insides and outsides of the drawers will show. If you plan to line the drawers with fabric or Con-Tact vinyl, then good 1 side is OK.

A set of drawers can get awfully confusing. So think of it as a collection of parts.

- There may be three or four drawers, or even ten. Each drawer is simply made by nailing and gluing two sides onto a bottom piece, and two ends onto the sides and bottom. That's all.

- There's a drawer front. To decorate the otherwise plain drawer, you glue something fancy over the front piece of plywood. It can be Formica, Con-Tact, or another piece of plywood cut into an appropriate shape.

- There's a handle. Generally it goes onto the end of a long screw which fits through a hole you drill in the front of the drawer and in the fancy drawer front.

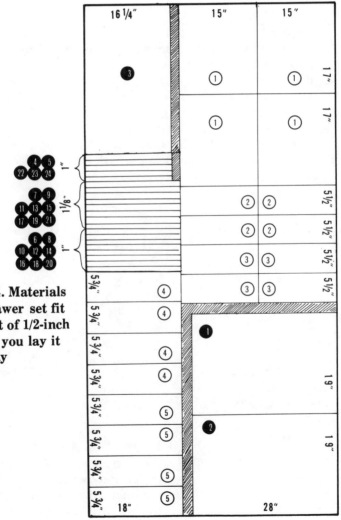

Figure V-14. Materials for your drawer set fit onto a sheet of 1/2-inch plywood if you lay it out this way

Fancier and bigger handles get two holes. So don't go drilling holes for your handle until you have bought the handles.

- There's a cabinet which holds all of the drawers you want in place. On many of the unfinished-furniture outlet drawer sets, the cabinet simply lets the drawer sit flat on a thin crosspiece. Your drawers have an arrangement which keeps the drawers straight as they're pulled out, assuming you build them according to the plans shown here.

Figure V-14 shows how to lay out the drawer and cabinet parts for a four-drawer set. Each drawer will measure 15 by 17 inches inside. Altogether, the set stands exactly 28 inches high, an ideal height for the projects in this book. if you scrap one drawer, you end up with a 21-inch-high, three-drawer set.

Figure V-15 shows how to glue and nail the individual drawers together. Since you're working with 1/2-inch plywood, use 1-inch brads for this job. Assemble the parts in the order shown. Part #1, the bottom, goes first. Then the back and front pieces, parts #2 and #3, go next. Finally the sides are glued and nailed on, parts #4 and #5.

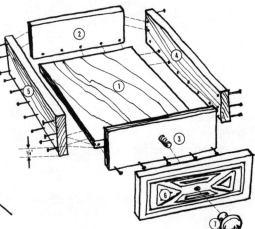

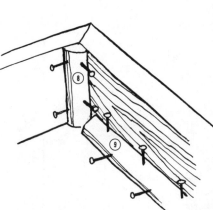

Figure V-15. Assemble the drawers this way. The small quarter-round molding shown in the bottom sketch is optional. But if you nail and glue it to the inside of your drawers, they will be substantially stronger

Unless you're particularly fastidious, you don't have to use a nail set. The nails are all concealed when the drawers are closed.

Notice that the two side pieces hang below the bottom of the drawer by 1/4 inch. That protruding 1/4 inch acts like a runner on a sled. Once you gently round off that runner, your drawer will move in and out smoothly. You can use a small SurForm tool to round off your runner (see §19).

The bottom half of Figure V-15 shows quarter-round molding being installed in the inside corners of a drawer. It's optional insurance. If you are in a hurry, if your drawers won't be subjected to heavy loads or abuse, they should stand up well without the molding. Buy the smallest quarter-round molding you can find, probably 1/4 or 3/8 inch. Use glue and 1/2-inch brads to attach the molding strips.

The Cabinet

Figure V-14 includes parts for the cabinet too. And Figure V-16 shows how to assemble the parts and in what order.

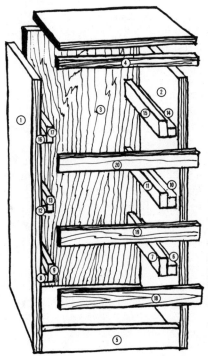

Figure V-16. Assemble the cabinet part of your drawer set this way. The piece at the very top is strictly optional. If you plan to put the drawer set into a piece of furniture where the top won't show—and that includes every piece of furniture in this book—you can dispense with the extraneous wood

There's a good reason why I've made a double strip to support each drawer. The piece glued and nailed next to the cabinet wall actually supports the weight of the drawer and its contents. Remember that when you're ready to measure and install it. Be sure that the top edge is just as smooth as your SurForm tool or medium sandpaper can make it.

That slightly larger piece, parts #13, #11, #9, and so forth, attaches to the support. It acts as a railing. When you pull out the drawer, the 1/4-inch drawer runner slides along the groove formed by the support and the railing. Without such an arrangement you could twist the drawer a bit and have trouble pulling it out. This is a feature you won't find on drawer sets from most unfinished-furniture outlets. Most completely finished desks don't even have that safety feature these days. But yours will!

Assemble the back and two sides of your cabinet first. Then tack the narrow dividers into place, parts #4 and #5. They give your cabinet enough strength so that your work on the supports and glides won't damage the outside of the cabinet. If you're working with 1/2-inch plywood, use 1-inch brads spaced 2 or 3 inches apart.

Measure carefully where each drawer support should go. The first ones, #6 and #14, should rest flush with the bottom. Apply plenty of glue and then nail it to the sides. Then put glue onto the support and onto the railing, part #7, and nail the railing into the support.

Measure carefully again. Always measure from the bottom, not from one drawer support to another. If you do that, you'll be multiplying any small errors each time you measure from support to support instead of from the bottom to each new support.

Assuming you stick with the drawer dimensions given here, 5-3/4 inches high, then the top of each new drawer support should be 6-3/4 inches farther away from the bottom than the one just before. The support itself takes up 1 inch. In other words, in the drawer set shown in drawings nearby, the top of each drawer support should be:

- 1 inch from the bottom
- 7-3/4 inches from the bottom
- 14-1/2 inches from the bottom
- 21-1/4 inches from the bottom

When building a cabinet for your drawers, the last step is to install the dividers, parts #22, 23, and 24. They're for cosmetic purposes only. They don't hold up anything, they just keep people from seeing the ugly lumber between drawers.

Figure V-16 shows an optional solid cover over the cabinet. It's not necessary if the drawers are going to be built into a desk or some other piece of furniture. But if you decide to build a set of drawers like those which will stand alone, then you'll probably want a solid top. Put the top in place of divider #4.

Decorating Drawer Fronts

The simplest, cheapest way to add sex appeal to the front of your drawer is with a simple wooden decoration. You can cut some out of 1/4-inch plywood, or buy hardwood for the occasion. Make the same decoration for each drawer.

You can leave the wood simple and unadorned, about 18 by 6-1/2 inches for the standard-sized drawers shown here. Or you can dig out the edging tool for your 1/4-inch drill and put a bevel or cove into the edges all around (see §20).

With coping saw or sabre saw, cut fancy curves into the drawer fronts if you like. Figure V-17 graphically illustrates that subject.

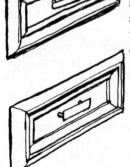

Figure V-17 Decorations for the drawer fronts are easy and inexpensive to make. All you have to do is follow these patterns or come up with similar ones of your own. You can even study how furniture downtown is decorated and figure out which basic materials went into the designs so you can duplicate the look on your own

Designing Your Own Drawer Sizes

Basically you can use the drawings here for any kind of drawer you want to make until you hit about 30 or 36 inches. If the drawer won't have to support a lot of weight, you can even expand the dimensions to 4 feet. However, both from the aspect of convenience and construction, most people do better with two 24-inch drawers than one 48-inch drawer.

Here's a 1-2-3 approach to coming up with workable drawer sizes of your own.

1. Decide how big you want the inside of each drawer to be. Make that set of dimensions the *bottom, part #1*.

2. Decide how high you want the space inside each drawer to be. You'll find that 4 to 6 inches is a convenient size for desks and similar furniture. Clothes drawers should be 6 to 8 inches deep. It is seldom practical to make a drawer deeper than 12 inches. Make this dimension the height of your end pieces, parts #2 and #3. The width of those pieces is equal to the width of your bottom.

3. To cut the sides for your drawers, parts #4, add 1/4 inch to the height of parts #2 and #3; make parts #4 that high. The length of parts #4 equals the length of your bottom, part #1, *plus* the thicknesses of two pieces of plywood. If you're working with 1/2-inch plywood, part #4 should be the length of your bottom part plus 1 inch.

4. Calculate how tall your cabinet should be by adding together the following: the height of all drawers together, *plus* 1 inch for the support of each drawer, *plus* as much space as you want above or below the drawer set. That total becomes the height of your cabinet side pieces and back.

5. The *width of cabinet side pieces* is not critical. They must be as wide as your drawers are long *plus* the thickness of plywood used for the dividers and the back. In the case of 1/2-inch plywood projects, you'd add at least 1 inch to the length of your drawers to use as the width of your side pieces. To be safe, you might want to add an extra 1/2 inch or so.

6. The *width of cabinet back piece and front divider pieces* is rather critical. If it is too big or too small, the drawer runners will not fit into the slots. The width of parts #3, 4, 5, 22, 23, and 24 should be the width of the drawer bottom *plus* the thickness of wood in the two side pieces (in the case of 1/2-inch plywood, 1 inch) *plus* a small extra amount to allow for clearance between the outside of each drawer and the inside of your cabinet. If you're sure you can work accurately, that extra need be no bigger than 1/8 inch. When in doubt, make it 1/4 inch.

7. The *length of drawer guides* should equal the length of drawers.

8. The *width of drawer glide pieces* remains pretty constant, regardless of other factors. Make the drawer support itself 1 inch thick. And make the railing 1-1/8 inch thick. Ideally you should make the support from 3/4-inch plywood so the 1/2-inch or 3/8-inch-thick runners will have some leeway in the groove. If you don't have excess pieces of 3/4-inch plywood lying around, and if you can't pick up some scrap at a lumberyard, you can make the support from the 1/2-inch plywood. When you put on the railing, however, test the drawer to make sure it will fit into the slot. If not, glue a 1-inch strip of cardboard between the rail and the support; test the drawer again to make sure that now there is enough room. If not, more cardboard. You don't want the weight of your drawers resting on cardboard, however. So if your measurements have missed the mark that badly, you may have to make a special effort to locate some 3/4-inch plywood or pine for supports.

After you have gone through the few mathematical steps required to plan your own set of drawers, pause before heading for the lumberyard. Take out a pencil, paper, and ruler to sketch how you can lay out the parts economically onto plywood.

Let each 1/16-inch mark on your ruler equal 1 inch in real life. So your 4-foot-by-8-foot (48 inches by 96 inches) sheet of plywood becomes, on paper, 3 inches (48/16) by 6 inches (96/16).

Starting with the bigger pieces and working down to the smaller ones, sketch every part onto your scale model. Try to make them all fit onto the least number of sheets of plywood possible. On a couple of really tricky layout problems, I actually cut out the scale-model pieces. Then I drew sheets of plywood onto other sheets of paper and tried to fit the paper parts together like a puzzle. It took almost an hour, but it saved a sheet or two of plywood every time.

After all of the shuffling and measuring is about over, if you have just a few parts left over which will have to go on a whole sheet of plywood, you may be able to economize by altering the dimensions just a bit. Sometimes by cutting off an inch or two in some direction there is suddenly enough room for all of the parts on one less sheet of plywood than before.

29. Shelves, Shelves, Shelves

SKILLS: Very easy. Good first
project.
TIME: An evening or a
weekend.
TOOLS: Handsaw, hammer,
sandpaper.
ALSO READ: Chapters 2, 3, 4.

A shelf is nothing but a piece of wood held up by something else—wood, metal, plastic, or a magic carpet. And if you keep in mind how humble a shelf really is, you can build all sorts of simple but intriguing bookcases, breakfronts, stylized wall units. . . .

You can even move your talents up to shelves covered with hinged doors or sliding doors. That kind of construction goes by fancier names such as medicine cabinet, kitchen cabinet, china closet, armoire, trophy cabinet, cupboard. . . .

There are two basic ways of holding up shelves. If you build them in a framework of their own, you've built a *freestanding* unit. It can be moved around at will. Various manufacturers are pushing another type of shelf, however—the *suspended* shelf units. They're screwed onto a wall and, although you can move individual shelves higher or lower, left or right, the set of shelves is permanently up against that wall.

No doubt you've seen the glossy ads for so-called easy-to-install suspended shelves. If you believe the ads, all you have to do is stick a few bits of hardware to any wall, and then shove some beautiful wood-grained shelves onto the hardware. Then stack your best china, records, books, or other personal effects onto the wood. Trouble is, the ads don't recite some of the statistics about records and books.

You can get between ten and twelve average-sized books onto 1 foot of bookshelf. The accumulation on that 1 foot weighs between 10 and 15 pounds. Bigger books, like art books and picture books, weigh considerably more.

You can stack about 75 records into 1 foot of shelf space. And that foot-long collection of LP's weighs almost 50 pounds!

Let's assume you plan to erect some of those shiny, expensive, advertised shelf units. You want three shelves for books, each 8 feet long, and one of the 8-foot-long shelves for hi-fi components and records. All together you will have to support about 600 pounds! You can't expect the plaster walls in your home or apartment to support that kind of weight for long.

If you insist on tacking ready-to-hang shelves onto your walls, it is very important that you screw their hardware into the wooden 2-by-4 supports behind the plaster. In most homes, it isn't hard to locate exactly where those 2-by-4 supports are hidden.

In general, 2-by-4 supports are spaced 16 inches apart. Doors, windows, vents, and the like are designed to fit *between* the 16-inch spaces. Therefore, start your search for 2 by 4's near one of those telltale points. And since the supports are so often doubled up by a door or window, start 4 inches away from the inside edge of a door or window close to where you want shelf supports to go. Then measure in multiples of 16 inches until you're in the area where shelves will conceal your mess. Measure and mark carefully.

Probe behind your plaster wall with a tiny drill or nail. The plaster is generally no more than an inch thick. If your drill hits something very solid beyond an inch, you've struck wood behind the plaster. However, the wood *could be* a thin lath which plasterers used in older houses. Stop the drill, if that's what you're using. Then push firmly against the drill or nail. If the wood underneath the plaster has a spongy feel to it, that's lath. You missed the 2-by-4 support.

If you missed, keep moving in one-inch increments until you find the first 2 by 4. Then carefully test exactly 16 inches to the right or left to make certain that your own 2-by-4 supports actually are spaced at 16-inch increments. If not, the most common alternate systems are 18 or 24 inches apart.

Those nail holes or drill holes can be concealed by the shelves you plan to install. But how about in years to come? Will you always want to have a set of shelves tacked permanently to a wall? If you ever decide to pull them down, the holes will take plenty of patching.

Another aspect of suspended shelving to consider is that the ready-to-hang shelves you buy in local novelty, hardware, and department stores are generally nothing but cheap chipboard covered with vinyl. You have to look hard and pay plenty to find real hardwood ready-to-hang shelving.

You can drive to a good lumberyard and buy real hardwood boards, cut them up yourself, sand them a bit, slap on a few coats of wood finish if you prefer, and enjoy real hardwood shelving for less money than what you often have to pay for the vinyl imitation. You can also make your own imitation hardwood shelving for about half what the store-bought imitations cost. And it will be stronger.

Common pine boards make dandy shelves. Sand them and stain them. They'll look every bit as good as most of the artificial ready-to-hangs. Don't even bother to sand them if you don't want to. Just wrap the pine boards up in Con-Tact vinyl. It'll take you only five or ten minutes per shelf. And your vinyl living room shelves will look just as good as the ready-mades—for less money.

There's one shortcoming with pine boards. Generally you can't find them in widths bigger than 12 inches. Hardwood generally comes in widths up to about 16 inches. But you can make the imitations in an infinite variety of sizes.

Invest in either a sheet of chipboard or a sheet of plywood sheathing. The cheap-grade plywood sheathing is very rough on both sides, designed to cover big areas on unfinished buildings. The chipboard is often cheaper and easier to cover with vinyl. But you can't nail or screw chipboard easily. Plywood is much stronger.

Saw your chipboard or plywood into appropriate sizes. Then wrap the ugly pieces in some beautiful self-adhesive vinyl, and your new shelves not only will be as good-looking as the Joneses', they'll be just as wide.

How Wide?

An 8-inch shelf is wide enough for average-sized books. Directories and other big books require at least a 10-inch shelf. Some even need 12 inches. LP records need shelves at least 13 inches wide unless you're content to have a little album hanging over the edge.

Most, but not all, hi-fi components fit on a 12-inch-wide shelf. Turntables in particular are often 15 inches deep.

If you love the appearance of books, if you want the varied colors of the books or records to become an integral part of whichever room you're designing shelves for, then keep the shelves as narrow as possible. That way the books will show through to the maximum.

However, if you'd just as soon tone down your image as an intellectual or music lover, aim for wider shelves which also give a more luxurious appearance. Freestanding units sold in stores downtown are generally about 16 inches wide. And that's a convenient size for you to work with too.

Nothing says that every shelf in any one set has to be the same width. You can start with one or two big 16-inch shelves at the bottom, for records and big picture books or turntables. You can make 12-inch shelves the rest of the way or you can make some 12-inch, some 10 and some 8. Go down to 6-inch shelves if you like.

Free-Standing Shelves (Figure VI-1)

The simplest set of shelves you can build is simply cut from 8-inch-wide pine boards. Using 8-foot lengths you could put the set together in an evening, and probably finish it too. It won't be elegant, but it won't look bad either. And it will hold your books or other belongings as well as any other bookcase.

To add the feel of elegance to even a simple set of shelves, simply vary some dimension in some way. If you're planning shelves to reach across a long wall, for instance, make several sets to cover the distance. For example, if the wall is 10 feet long, you could make two sets of 8-inch-deep shelves, each 4 feet across. Then put a 16-inch-deep set of shelves only 2 feet across between the wider sets. (See Figure VI-2.)

You can change the height of the middle set of shelves to add some class to an otherwise simple project. If your ceilings are 8 feet high, why not make two sets of shelves rise 6 feet? Then put a set between the 6-footers that stretches up 7 feet? That's all it takes, as Figure VI-3 shows.

With just a bit of careful measuring, you can make free-standing shelves look like built-in ones. That's a distinguished touch right out of the nineteenth century, but they are practical and lovely as can be. As much as possible, try to keep the indi-

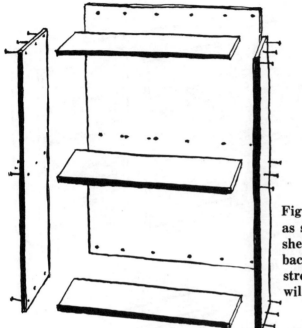

Figure VI-1. This is as simple
as shelves can be. Nail the
shelves from the side, add a
back for extra structural
strength, and your shelves
will stand up against any

vidual sets of shelves all the same size—width, depth, and of
course height. See Figure VI-4.

The built-in look is achieved by making the finished job seem to
be dug through the surface of an existing wall instead of just a set
of shelves propped up in front of the wall. Let your shelves be as
high as your ceilings. When the last set of shelves is shoved into
place, the entire space across one full wall should be covered.

You can't count on making your built-in shelves from
standard-sized lumber. You'll probably have to saw more boards
and waste a bit more lumber than with perfectly freestanding
ones. But there is also a way to save a lot of work and material.

On this type of built-in shelf, the plaster wall serves as the
back. Paint the shelves and the wall from the same can of paint,
and you're through. Let it dry and start stacking the books,
records, hi-fi components, and dust catchers into the set up.

Other systems of freestanding shelves need a wooden back,
and not just for the sake of appearances. The back strengthens
the shelves. In almost every simple furniture project the
weight-carrying elements are fastened or supported in three different directions. The triangle is a universal unit of design
strength.

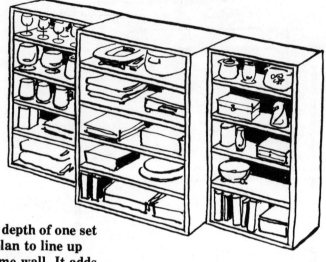

Figure VI-2. Vary the depth of one set of shelves when you plan to line up several against the same wall. It adds class to the arrangement

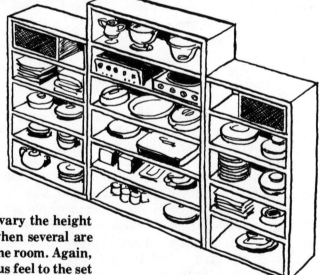

Figure VI-3. You can vary the height of one set of shelves when several are being built for use in one room. Again, it gives a more luxurious feel to the set of shelves

Before you tack a back onto your set of shelves, each shelf would be supported from the right and from the left. But that's not enough. If somebody ever leaned against the side of your shelves, the guest and your bookcase could topple over. Even a very thin back, 1/4-inch plywood or 1/8-inch Masonite, gives a

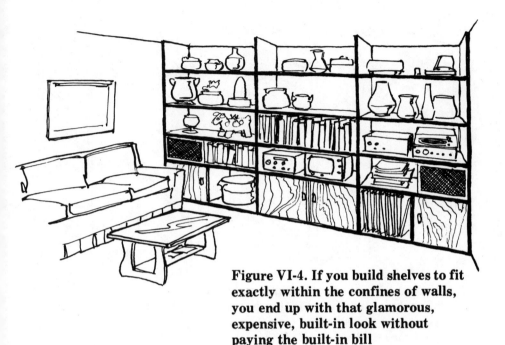

Figure VI-4. If you build shelves to fit exactly within the confines of walls, you end up with that glamorous, expensive, built-in look without paying the built-in bill

third point of support to every shelf when you nail it in place. And the addition of a back usually makes the bookcase or cabinet look better.

Getting Fancy

Almost all of the devices we've already discussed for decorating furniture in general apply to bookcases or other shelves too. Figure VI-5 shows four examples. The first three cases are identical except for their finish. To create a modern look, the edges are painted black. As an alternate, you can add gold, silver, or brightly colored tapes to the edges. Even wood-grained tape looks appropriate. Case A is best made 4 feet wide, but you can alter that to 3 feet or 5.

Case B comes up with a Colonial flavor, especially if you use maple stain or orange shellac as part of your finish. For economy, make this project 40 inches wide. That way you'll have 8 inches left after you cut the back out of 1/4-inch plywood, which is 48 inches wide. You can cut two pieces of 4-inch strips, using Figure VI-6 for your pattern. If you're daring, don't use a pattern at all. Genuine Colonial shapes were generally cut out by hand. You could pick up a saw and just cut curves freehand too.

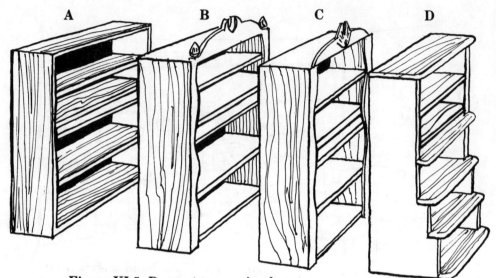

Figure VI-5. Decorate your simple set of shelves and end up with a period piece. (A) A modern or traditional bookcase or divider. (B) That distinctive Colonial look. (C) French Provincial. (D) Modern. For styles A and D, cut the shelf boards 46-1/2 inches wide so the resulting set will be 48 inches. In that way, your 48-inch-wide plywood or Masonite backing will fit without your having to saw it. In styles B and C, cut the shelves 39 inches long so you'll have an 8-inch-wide piece of plywood left over for the decorative effects. Find a pattern for the Colonial shelves in Chapter 31. Pattern for the French Provincial decoration comes from the doubled-up table-top pattern in Chapter 23

The top piece on case B is identical to the headboard pattern. Turn back to Figure II-17 in the Colonial-headboard chapter. Add three finials from some spindle department, and declare your independence from common shelves.

Case C simply adapts French Provincial styling. Proceed as with project B above, only turn to the French Provincial table for a pattern to use in cutting the side and top pieces. To really do it up grand, add some appropriate decoration to the top.

You'll have to look a bit harder to see that project D in Figure VI-5 is basically the same as the other bookcases. Like the others, the shelves are not all spaced identically. Reading from the bottom, the distances between successive shelves is 12, 12, 16, 8, 12, 12 inches. But the depth of shelves also varies in this very modern style.

Starting again from the bottom, here's a typical progression of board widths you can use: 12, 12, 10, 10, 8, 6, 10. Use 8-inch-wide boards for the two upright support boards. If you don't plan to put heavy weights on those big 12-inch shelves, they won't need any more support than what the 8-inch boards give them. But if you plan to stack books or records on the 12-inch shelves, give them an extra 2- or 3-inch-wide strip for support. Simply nail the strip onto the sides of the two 12-inch shelves so it seems part of the same piece which supports all of the other shelves. Figure VI-5 shows that extra piece in place.

Chapter 4, which tells you all you need to know for now about finishing furniture, tells plenty about finishing bookcases and other kinds of shelves too. Glance through that section and maybe through the finishing comments on other furniture projects which delighted you most. Then keep saying to yourself, "I'm not building a set of crummy shelves. I'm building a piece of furniture."

30.   3-D Mondrian Breakfront

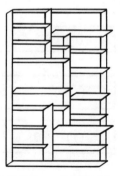

SKILLS:	Easy. A good first project if you're well motivated.
TIME:	A weekend or two.
TOOLS:	Saw, hammer, sandpaper.
ALSO READ:	§'s 1, 2, 10, 11, 12, 14, 15, 16; Chapter 4.

Not too many years ago a Dutch painter named Pieter Cornelis Mondrian made quite a name for himself painting geometric shapes. But Mondrian seemed interested only in squares and rectangles. Few of the lines in his simple paintings ever stretched all the way across his canvas.

Mondrian paintings are the sort of thing that highbrows sit and gaze at in museums for hours, looking always for hidden meaning. Personally, I think old Pieter just had fun painting.

Here's a tremendous breakfront which adds just one extra dimension to the Mondrian idea. Not only are none of the shelves built all the way across this piece of furniture, but the shelves come in varied widths as well. Don't ask me if Mondrian would have approved. If *you* approve, Figure VI-6 shows what lumber to purchase and how to cut it up so your 3-D Mondrian breakfront will look like mine. Figure VI-7 shows how to assemble the twenty-one pieces of pine board into one piece of furniture.

There is a subtle system beneath the seemingly random array of shelves and supports. The breakfront shown here is all of 5 feet wide and 8 feet high. If you want to reduce it to 4 feet wide, for instance, reduce all of the pieces which now are 2 feet long to only 1 foot. You can still get a lot on a shelf that long. Shelves to reduce include parts #9, 10, 15, 16, 17, 18, 20, and 21.

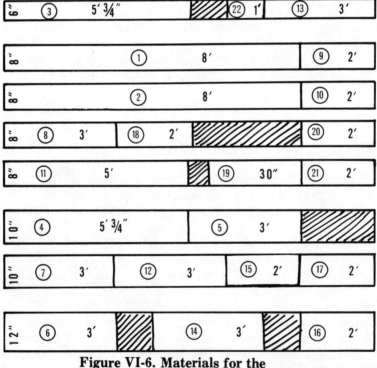

Figure VI-6. Materials for the
Mondrian shelves are displayed here

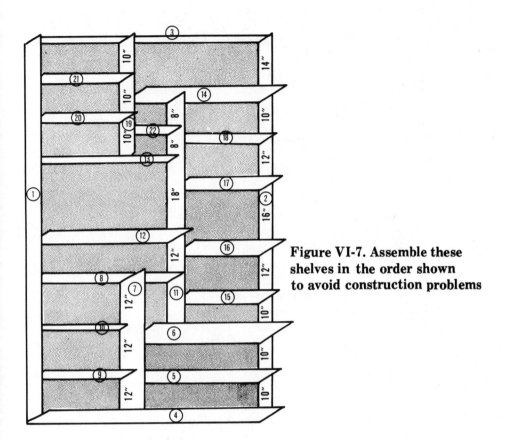

Figure VI-7. Assemble these shelves in the order shown to avoid construction problems

In order to take a foot off the height of this breakfront, reduce part #11 from its present 5 feet down to 4. Also get rid of parts #18 and #8.

You can use hardwood boards here if you wish. You'll have to nail them together more carefully, but your finished piece of furniture will be truly spectacular. If you'd like to add even one more dimension of variability to this project, you can buy *different* kinds of hardwood!

There is plenty of inherent strength in this design. You can use nails to construct it if you like; the work will go a lot faster than if you try using screws. And in the end it will probably be just as strong. But don't forget to use glue to strengthen the joints.

Use a sheet of thin hardboard or plywood for the back of this breakfront. Despite the shelves which seem to go in every direction, the strength of a backboard nailed to the uprights and most shelves is important.

Any of the traditional furniture-finishing methods works fine. You'll probably want to choose some stark color for the edges of the shelves and uprights to call attention to the fact that they come in sundry sizes. Black or gold vinyl tape stands out well. After all, once you've gone through the patient work of cutting out and assembling so many pieces, and keeping them straight, you'd like people to notice that you've built a breakfront inspired by old Pieter Mondrian.

31.   Colonial Corner Cabinet

SKILLS: Easy. Might be a
                good first project.
TIME: A weekend.
TOOLS: Handsaw, coping or
                keyhole saw, hammer,
                sandpaper.
ALSO READ: §'s 4, 8, 26, 27;
                Chapters 3, 8.

Figure VI-8. This is the Colonial corner cabinet. Lay out your materials according to the sketches here and next page. Use 1/2-inch plywood. Assemble the parts, following the numbers on the finished cabinet.

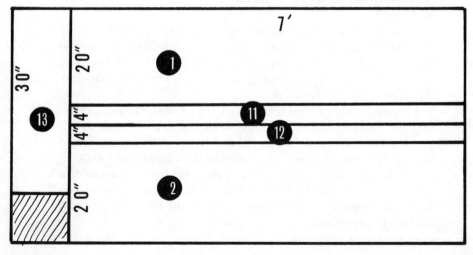

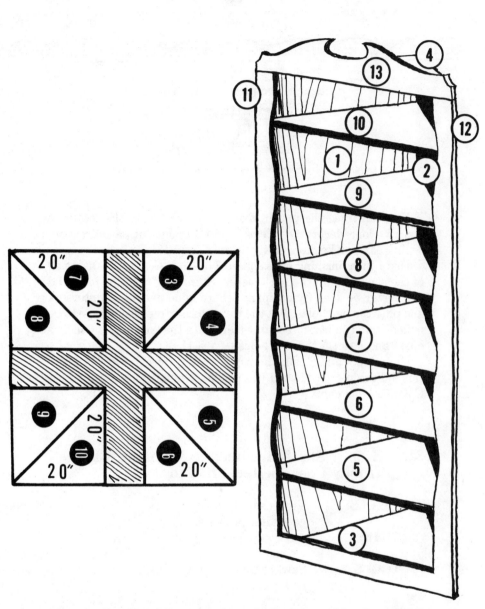

Folks in Colonial days must have had plenty of lumber. That famous, favorite old corner cabinet takes a lot of wood for a little bit of storage room. But if the style turns you on, the sheet and a half of plywood will be well worth it to you.

Figure VI-8 shows how the completed cabinet will look and how to lay out the various parts onto 1/2-inch plywood. For the full sheet, good 1 side is OK. But the half sheet should be good 2 sides.

Figure VI-9. Patterns for the
decorative pieces (1-inch squares)

You can trace the patterns of Figure VI-9 onto the top piece
and two long decorative strips. Cut them out with a sabre saw,
coping saw, or keyhole saw.

Use 1-inch finishing nails spaced 3 or 4 inches apart to fasten all
of the shelves onto the back pieces. Since they're in the back and
will never be seen by company, there is no need to countersink
and plug the nail holes. But the three decorative pieces have to be
nailed from the front. You'd better space the nails about 6 inches
apart and conceal the nail holes (see §11).

Chapters 4 and 8 talk about plenty of different ways to finish
this old cabinet. And then you can start putting away your best
Colonial bone china.

32. How a Shelf Becomes a Medicine Cabinet, Trophy Case, Settee, and More

SKILLS: Very easy. Can be
good first projects.
TIME: An evening or a
weekend.
TOOLS: Saw, hammer, coping
or keyhole saw,
sandpaper.
ALSO READ: §'s 4, 8; Chapters 3,
4, 29.

The idea of holding up several horizontal shelves with two vertical supports and a back works well for all kinds of furniture you
maybe never put into the "shelf" category. With or without
doors, hung on walls, mounted atop legs, or set squarely on the

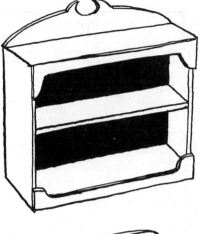

Figure VI-10. Here's what open shelves can look like

floor, a well-designed set of basic shelves can fulfill dozens of useful jobs (Figure VI-10).

Figure VI-11 shows how to lay out and assemble a basic shelf setup which stands about 2 feet high, 4 feet wide, and 1 foot deep. The back sticks up an extra foot for decoration, as a back rest on a settee or as a convenient place to mount the item to a wall with lag screws or Molly screws.

Use 1/2-inch plywood for the project, good 1 side, and 1-inch finishing nails. Don't forget the glue. The optional final pieces, parts #7 and 8, give the whole appearance a more united feel. And since they're easy to cut out, you'll probably want to include them. Space your nails about 2 inches apart when you install the shelves. Put nails every 3 or 4 inches for the back and decorative pieces.

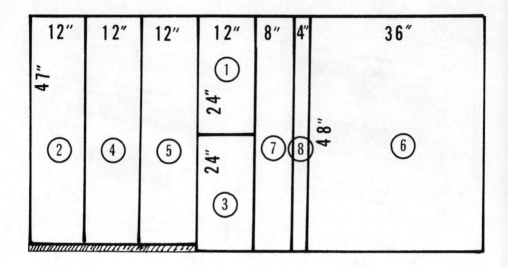

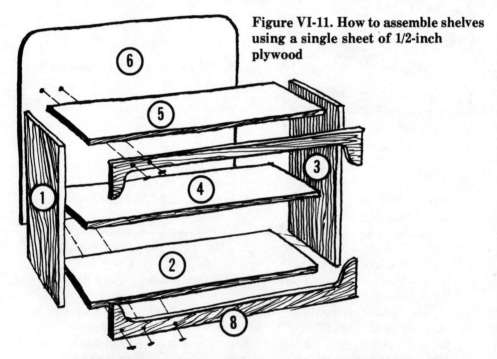

Figure VI-11. How to assemble shelves using a single sheet of 1/2-inch plywood

All of the finishing techniques in Chapter 4 work for your shelves. The third settee in Figure VI-10 has a department store cushion on top. The foam rubber pad covered with various fabrics come in so many sizes, shapes, and colors, you should find at least

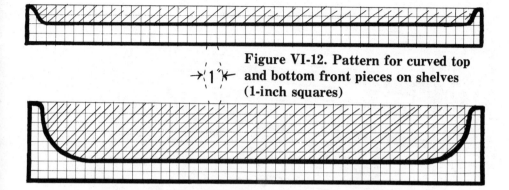

Figure VI-12. Pattern for curved top and bottom front pieces on shelves (1-inch squares)

one which fits your decorating scheme without having to look too long. See Figure VI-12 for pattern for top and bottom pieces.

The Colonial style in Figure VI-10 can be created by drawing the Colonial-headboard decorative top onto the top of your shelf back (see Figure II-17). It's exactly the right size, through no accident.

To go French Provincial, turn to Figure IV-14 in the table unit. Adapt the table-top pattern to the top of your shelf. Add some decorative carving or molding if you like. And finish with a French Provincial or other painted finish of your choice.

Sliding Doors

Every one of the shelf-inspired pieces of furniture already discussed can be enhanced with some kind of doors. If you want to emphasize the beauty of wood or the shine of your paint, solid doors are for you. But sliding-glass doors are easy to make, as are mirrored sliding doors.

Variations in the sliding-door idea can utilize the curved-front decorations. Without the decorative parts and the extended back piece, a simple, modern-looking piece of furniture results.

Basically, everything about the sliding-door furniture shown in Figure VI-13 is identical to the assembly and layout drawing in Figure VI-11 with two exceptions. First, the middle shelf is only 10 inches wide. You could get away with making it 10-1/2, maybe even 11 inches. If that extra space is important to you, don't install that middle shelf until *after* you've put in the sliding-door tracks and the doors themselves.

You can install the sliding doors in minutes with a set of sliding-door hardware available for very little money at hard-

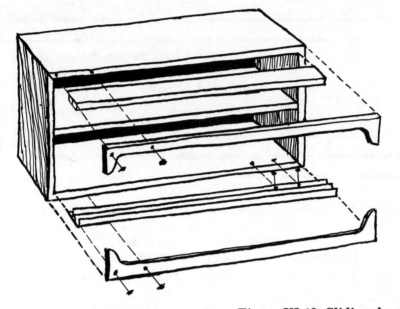

Figure VI-13. Sliding doors turn open shelves into exotic, useful cabinets. Here's how the sliding doors fit into your shelf and sliding door hardware

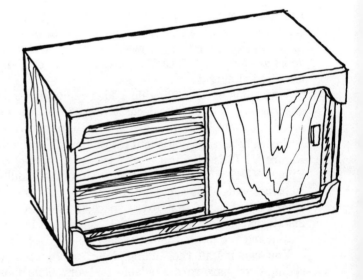

ware stores and lumberyards. Most of them are extruded from aluminum. The 4-foot-long set you need for the illustrated furniture is pretty common.

Sliding-door hardware is made to accommodate doors of varying thicknesses. Most common are 1/4, 3/8, 1/2, and 3/4 inch. For glass and mirror doors, the 1/4-inch size is generally best. There's no need to buy plywood any thicker than 1/4 inch for small doors like these, but if you get a good bargain in some other size, just make sure you buy a sliding-door kit to match.

Kits for sliding doors come with their own instructions. The top piece is thicker than the bottom. Both are installed with small nails or screws generally supplied in the kit.

The length of standard sliding-door kits seldom exactly matches the length of your shelves. Cut yours to size with a hacksaw or a coping saw with a metal-cutting blade. The soft aluminum parts cut almost like butter.

Doors which slip into the sliding-door hardware have to be cut with some care. Check your instructions, but most doors have to be 1/4 inch shorter than the height of your cabinet where the sliding-door hardware is attached. That 1/4 inch allows you to slip the doors in and out of the tracks as the need arises.

To insert a sliding door, slip the top of the door into the top strip. That's the bigger of the two. If you push the door up as far as it will go, the bottom should fit into the bottom track without using much force. Put a door into the inside track first. Then insert the outer door.

When you cut out doors to be used in a sliding-door mechanism, allow one door to overlap the other by at least 1/2 inch. In the sample shelves shown in Figures VI-11 and VI-14, the door opening is a total of 47 inches wide. So doors cut from a 48-inch-wide board will allow the left door to overlap the right by 1 inch.

Glass Sliding Doors

Glass doors are not as hard to work with as you might think. There are two ways to handle the matter simply. First, you can build the shelves, install the sliding-door hardware, and then make accurate measurements. Hand the measurements to a professional glass shop and ask them to cut some *double-thickness* glass to size for you. Never use ordinary window glass where people will handle it as much as they will your sliding doors.

A second economical way is to shop around for a piece of glass close to the size you want. If you find a glass shop with a piece of double-thickness scrap glass, you'll save a little money. Then you can adjust the size of your cabinet to the dimensions of your glass.

The top and bottom edges of your sliding glass doors are concealed by the hardware, but the four sides are not. You'll have to round those edges off to protect unwary fingers. Chapter 13, dealing with glass coffee-table tops, explains that art quickly.

You can use almost any kind of handles on your glass sliding doors. Flat pieces of molding 3 or 4 inches long work nicely. But you can invest in some more-orthodox handles at department or hardware stores. Fasten the handles to the glass with epoxy or silicone cement. Either tape the handles in place while the glue dries or lay the doors flat on a table overnight.

Sliding Mirror Doors

You'd go broke if you went to a glass or mirror store to buy a set of catchy-looking sliding doors cut to your exact dimensions. So the best way is to shop for a cheap, full-length mirror at a novelty store. There are a lot of them on sale for a song, generally in the 16- to 24-inch-wide bracket. They're about 4 or 5 feet tall.

Typically these dime-store mirrors are a thin mirror mounted to a piece of cardboard backing. It's a safe enough arrangement, but look for the word "shatterproof" just to be doubly protected. More than likely there will be a flimsy wooden or metal frame around your chosen mirror. Pull it off carefully when you get your purchase home. Measure how wide the mirror is, find out how much leeway your set of sliding-door hardware calls for, and those two figures, added together, become the up-and-down dimension of your medicine cabinet or other set of shelves.

You can let the length of your mirror dictate how long your set of shelves will be. Or you can make the shelves smaller and cut off some of the mirror. You have to cut the mirror in half anyway, so making the whole thing shorter involves only one extra cut. Although 1/2 inch is the minimum overlap you should have in sliding doors, you can have up to 6 inches in a long pair of doors.

You need a simple glass cutter to turn one floor-length mirror into a pair of sliding doors. It's a very inexpensive tool. Measure carefully where the one or two cuts should go. (You only get one chance with glass.) Lay a sturdy ruler or straight board along the line of cut and hold it firmly. See Figure VI-14.

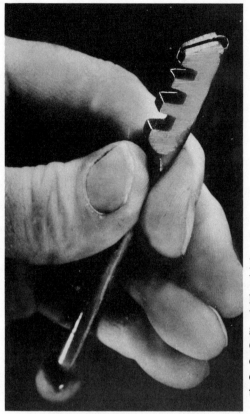

Figure VI-14. This is a glass cutter. Use it firmly to cut a scored line into a piece of glass or mirror, and you're well on your way to a successful glass-cutting job. The pointed wheel does the cutting. The heavy end opposite the wheel is useful for tapping on the scored line to make breaking the glass easier

Press very firmly on the glass cutter as you draw its cutting edge quickly along your line of cut. The round cutting edge has to make a deep scored line in the surface of the glass. Try to get the scored line uniform and bold the first time. If you have to pull the glass cutter down the same line a second or a third time, you're inviting trouble.

After the scored line is finished, slide the mirror to the edge of a flat table. Lay the scored line right at the edge so the table and the line of cut are parallel.

Lift up the end of the mirror which is hanging over the table edge and bring it back down with a quick snap. When the mirror hits the table, the glass should break neatly right along the scored line. If not, repeat the snapping procedure until it does.

If your mirror has a cardboard backing, you'll probably have to slice through it with a razor blade or knife after the mirror has been cut in two. You won't have to round off the hidden edges, but the surfaces where you cut are sharp. Again, check Chapter 13 for rounding off glass edges.

Sliding doors, since they're moving parts, require lubrication. A bit of talcum powder, powdered graphite, cornstarch, or silicone spray in the bottom track is ample. And the rest is smooth sliding for this basic set of shelves which can become a cornucopia of fine-looking furniture for the bathroom, den, living room, playroom, or kitchen.

33. How a Shelf Becomes a China Closet, Kitchen Cabinet, Bar, and More

SKILLS	Easy or demanding, depending upon how elaborate the design.
TIME:	A weekend to a month of Sundays.
TOOLS:	Saw, hammer, screwdriver, perhaps coping saw or keyhole saw, square, sandpaper.
ALSO READ:	Chapters 2, 3, 4, 29, 32.

Hinged doors make the difference between a set of open shelves and a cabinet. We went into great length about the construction of simple open shelves in Chapters 29 and 32, so now we need only spend a few minutes on how to make doors and work with hinges.

Before you can decide what kind of door to build, you have to decide what kind of hinge you're going to hang the door onto. Basically there are three ways to work with cabinet doors.

Flush-front cabinet doors fit within the outside boards of a piece of furniture. The front surface of the door is flush with the front surface of the cabinet outside boards. Figure VI-15 shows how this works.

Figure VI-15 also shows the two types of hinges used on flush-front cabinet doors. The common *cabinet hinge* is the least ex-

Figure VI-15. *Flush doors* and close-up
view of typical hinges used for
mounting them

pensive and least conspicuous. It gets mounted on the interior of
the frame and the inside edge of the door so only about 1/4 inch of
the hinge shows from the outside. *Ornamental flush hinges* are
priced according to how ornamental they are. You can get plated
ones cheaply. Solid brass hinges full of grooves and ridges cost
plenty. In either case, the ornamental hinges are built to show,
becoming an integral part of the furniture's design and decoration.

Flush-front doors have to be cut and fitted carefully. The
cabinet hinges have to be screwed into a slot which you chisel by
hand. If you miss the mark by 1/8 inch on a flush-front door, it
will probably show, especially on light-colored wood. Which is
why we're not going to talk about this style of cabinet door any
more.

Figure VI-16 shows the cabinet door most commonly used,
especially in kitchens—the *offset door*. It requires an offset
hinge, quite a reasonably priced item. The part of an offset hinge

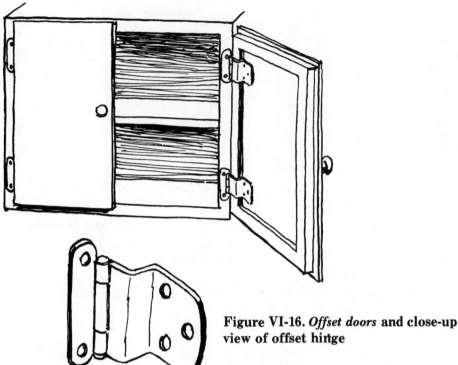

Figure VI-16. *Offset doors* **and close-up view of offset hinge**

which fastens to the cabinet remains visible, which is why this hinge comes in so many sizes and shapes. The part which fastens to the inside of your cabinet door is concealed until somebody opens the door.

Offset doors are called that because the back of the door is *offset* about 3/8 inch from the front. Commercial door manufacturers use an expensive wood shaper to cut a 3/8-inch groove into a 3/4-inch-thick piece of wood. If you'd rather not invest several hundred dollars in woodworking equipment, you can build offset doors by fastening together two pieces of 3/8-inch-thick wood and end up with the same kind of door.

Saving the best for last, the *door fronts* are becoming more and more popular. The theory behind this creation is simple—if you make the doors so big and hinge them properly, nobody will see any other part of the cabinet front *but* the doors. That way you can put your money into good-looking doors and make the rest of your cabinet out of solid but not-so-good-looking materials. Figure VI-17 gives a rough idea how this door works.

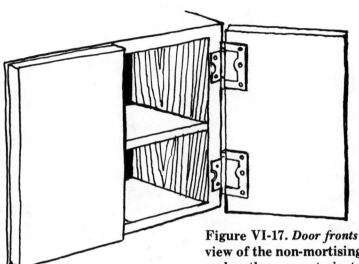

Figure VI-17. *Door fronts* and close-up view of the non-mortising hinge which makes them easy to install

Ordinary cabinet hinges can be used for this door style. You still have to chisel out a recessed space in the door and the cabinet for them. Otherwise your door will sit about 1/8 inch away from the front of the cabinet. Viewed from the right angle, that 1/8 inch or so looks mighty big. That chiseled-out space, by the way, is known in the trade as a *mortise*.

There's an item called the *nonmortising hinge* you should know about. It costs just a bit more than the standard cabinet hinge, but you don't have to chisel out space for it to fit in the door and cabinet. As Figure VI-17 shows, the two parts of the hinge fit inside each other when the door is closed. That way, the hinge forces the door to stand only 1/16 inch away from the cabinet, an acceptable gap.

Of the three door styles just described, the door-front system is the easiest for amateurs to master. The offset door is a bit more demanding than the door-front style. The flush front is too exacting for early furniture-building projects. There are a few other factors to consider before you settle firmly on your door style.

Decoration

Both the offset and the door-front system leave you with a large, flat, plain-looking front unless you decorate it in some way. If you're working with good wood, the fine wood grain and color is

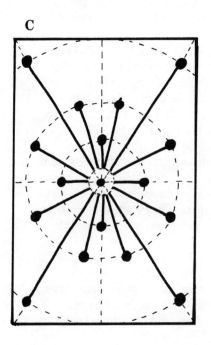

A

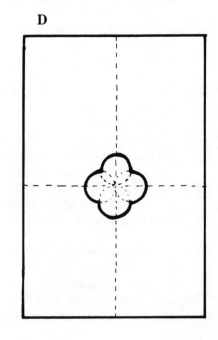

B

C

D

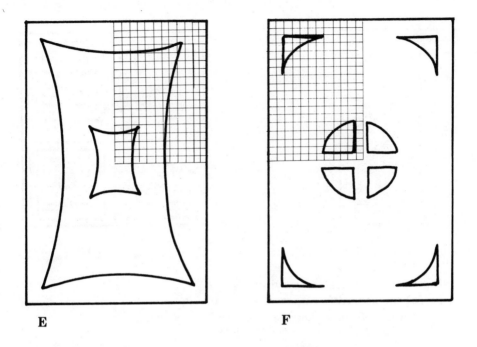

E   F

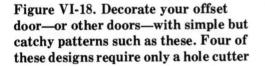

Figure VI-18. Decorate your offset door—or other doors—with simple but catchy patterns such as these. Four of these designs require only a hole cutter

all the decoration you need. In that case, the door-front system is probably your best bet.

When you work with less expensive woods—plywood, for example—the offset doors lend themselves to simple decorative tricks. Without spending a penny beyond the actual cost of the 3/8-inch plywood for the doors themselves, you can create several handsome designs on the doors. Then you can paint or stain the doors. This is a particularly good way of working on kitchen cabinets.

Figure VI-18 offers some simple decorations you can use on offset doors. They're laid out in such a way that you can use them for doors of almost any size or shape. The design is cut into the top piece of 3/8-inch plywood. When that top is glued and nailed onto the bottom piece of 3/8-inch plywood, people will think you

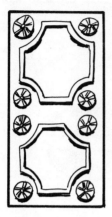 

Figure VI-19. Plastic "carvings" are useful for decorating doors. They can be used in unlimited combinations and will make even a door larger than the "carving" itself look attractive, elegant, and professional

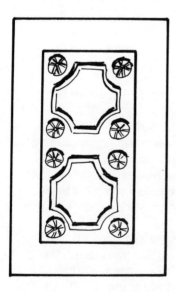 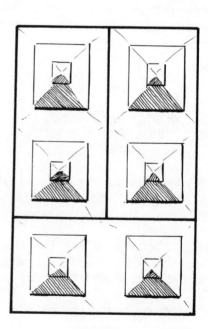

spent hours or days with elaborate tools to carve the three-dimensional design.

Both offset doors and the door fronts can be decorated with carvings or moldings which we covered in §'s 8 and 25. Figures I-57 and V-17 offer plenty of good ideas. Figure I-16 shows some of the typical carvings available for door fronts. Typical plastic "carvings" on the market are often sold specifically for use in decorating doors. Many of them are 1 foot by 2 feet, but they have a pattern which repeats in 1-foot squares. Therefore you can use the 1-by-2-foot size for doors of many sizes: 1 by 2, 2 by 2, 2 by 3 feet, and so forth.

Actually the 1-by-2-foot door decoration moldings don't look bad on even larger doors. Figure VI-19 shows one of them fastened to a door as big as 20 by 32 inches. The same idea goes for the more expensive, wooden, molded carvings. You can put a small one in the middle or slightly above the center of a fairly large door and still get the benefit of its charm.

You can also adapt some of the decorations in Figure VI-18 to a door-front system. The designs marked D, E, and F are especially useful, but A, B, and C will work too. After cutting out the pattern with circle cutter or saw, you should glue a piece of fabric to the back of the door so it will show through the cutout parts of the design. To make the whole project neat, cut the cloth to fit almost the entire inside of the door, not just the cutouts.

Measuring for Doors

Let's fit a set of doors on the shelves shown earlier in Figure VI-10. If you do away with the curved front pieces (parts #7 and #8, and don't extend the back piece 12 inches above the top of the shelves, there's enough left of the full sheet of 1/2-inch plywood to cut a set of door fronts.

The finished set of shelves will measure 2 feet high and 4 feet wide. With a door-front system you'll therefore need some doors which together measure 2 feet high and 4 feet wide. A 2-by-4-foot door can get pretty unwieldy to build and use. And four doors, each only a foot wide, would require twice as much cutting and fitting as only two doors each 2 feet square. Except on very small shelves, it's best to have two or more doors. So make two doors, each 2 by 2 feet.

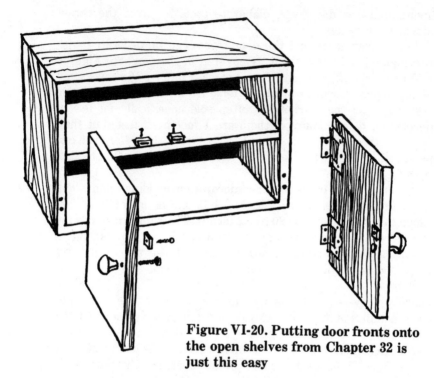

Figure VI-20. Putting door fronts onto the open shelves from Chapter 32 is just this easy

Figure VI-21. Another way of finishing and using a simple 3-foot-by-4-foot cabinet

Figure VI-20 shows the basic set of shelves you've worked with in chapters past. This time the door fronts are included.

After assembling the shelf part of this cabinet, fasten two nonmortising hinges to each door as you saw in Figure VI-17. Make sure the rough finishing work is completed before you attach the hinges. Then fasten each door by its hinges to the outside upright piece of the cabinet.

Offset Doors and a Big Cabinet or Bar

The 2-foot-by-4-foot cabinet with door fronts is convenient for all of those storage needs that seem to defy description. Catalogs can't find a name for such a creature, but every family seems to need more cabinets like that one. Toys, fruit jars, hobbies, hi-fi components and records, tools, sewing. . . .

Now let's talk about a type of cabinet which has a name—two or more names, in fact. Done with an appropriate finish, it'll be a dandy kitchen cabinet, what the trade calls a *base cabinet* since it stands on the floor. With a more living-room-type finish, it's a *hutch, bureau* or *credenza*.

Figure VI-21 shows the finished item with both offset doors in a kitchen style, and door fronts for the living room or den. The next two figures show how to lay out your materials economically and then how to put the few pieces together into a rugged but nice-looking piece of furniture.

As shown here, you'll end up with a set of offset doors. To make that version of the project, invest in a full sheet of 3/8-inch plywood (good 1 side) for the doors. For the shelves, cabinet, and top, buy a sheet and a half of 3/4-inch plywood (good 1 side).

Assemble the cabinet with glue and 2-inch finishing nails. Put six or seven nails into each shelf. If the sides of your cabinet will show, countersink the nails with a nail set and plug the holes with Plastic Wood.

If the cabinet did not have the 4-inch cutout at the bottom, people would be forever kicking it. That's why the bottom shelf is kept off the floor. Your shelves will be approximately 10 inches apart, which is plenty of space for kitchen needs. If you plan to put this piece of furniture elsewhere, you might want to think about different shelf arrangements.

One alternate shelf spacing is to make the first shelf 13 inches above the bottom. That's a good size for LP records. Make the second shelf perhaps 7 or 8 inches above the first. That leaves

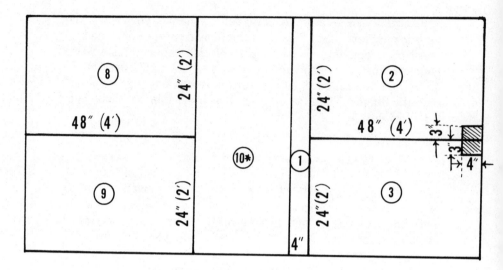

Figure VI-22. Material for your 3-by-4 cabinet with door fronts is laid out in this manner for economical use of the 3/4-inch plywood. Piece ten can be cut into two 6-inch pieces for use in mounting this cabinet against a wall. Or it can be used as an additional shelf

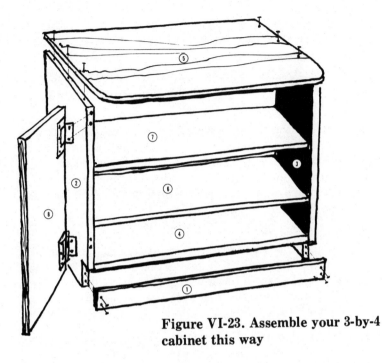

Figure VI-23. Assemble your 3-by-4 cabinet this way

close to 10 inches above the second shelf. The narrower shelf spaces are good for holding hi-fi components.

Another alternate spacing is accomplished by doing away with one shelf altogether. That way you'll have 16 inches above and 16 inches below the single shelf.

Now for the offset doors. In this project, the dimensions are already given. But if you had to design a set for yourself, here's how you'd tackle the mathematics.

- Measure the inside of the space which the door will cover In this project, 46-1/2 inches wide, 30-1/2 inches high.

- Decide how many doors you want to cover that distance. In this project, make two.

- Wherever two doors meet, it's practical and customary to put in a strip of wood. That way you don't have to make everything fit so precisely. If the doors don't meet—and they really shouldn't—the strip of wood down the middle hides what's inside the cabinet and looks attractive too. Since you have an extra piece of wood 1-1/2 inches wide at the bottom of the plywood which becomes shelves, make that center piece 1-1/2 inches. And that 1-1/2 inches has to be subtracted from the width of what the doors will cover, leaving 45 inches.

- Dividing the 45 inches by 2, since there will be two doors, you have 22-1/2 inches wide. The 30-1/2-inches-high figure stays. But you want to give yourself some leeway, so subtract 1/4 inch each way. Make the *inside pieces* for the offset doors 22-1/4 inches wide by 30-1/4 high.

- The *outside pieces* for offset doors have to be 3/8 inch bigger *all the way around*—3/8 at top, 3/8 at bottom; 3/8 at left, 3/8 at right. Therefore the dimensions for the outside pieces will be 33 inches wide by 31 inches high. It's this outside piece that gets any decoration you plan to give it (see Figure VI-18).

After you've sawed or drilled your decoration into the outside part of the offset doors, sandpaper any part of the decoration that needs it. Save the other finishing touches for later.

Since there's such a big area for the glue to grab onto, you shouldn't have to use many nails when you fasten the top onto the bottom, forming a complete offset door. I would, however, first draw a line around the back of the top piece so you know quite precisely where 3/8 inch is. Then apply plenty of glue. The liquid white vinyl glues generally work best for projects like this where you don't plan to use clamps or nails.

Set your bottom piece onto your top offset door piece accurately. Then pound in just enough 5/8-inch brads to keep the two pieces from slipping out of alignment. Maybe a dozen nails is all you need. When you've glued and nailed both doors together, set them on top of each other and pile as many books, cans, or other weights on them as you can find. Allow at least as much time for the glue to dry as the label recommends.

When the glue is dry, your own offset doors will be as fine as any turned out by cabinetmakers with expensive routers. And with some of the designs given in this book, you'll probably have spent less time on your doors than a cabinetmaker would have had to if he started with 3/4-inch boards!

It is easy to attach hinges to your doors and cabinets. Buy two pairs of 3/8-inch offset hinges that you think match your own décor. First attach the bent portion to the back of your door. Make sure that the zigzag in your hinge fits into the zigzag at the edge of your door. Then set the door into its designated opening and fasten the smaller part of the hinge to the cabinet.

Variations on this basic 4-foot-wide, 3-foot-high cabinet are practically infinite. Instead of making offset doors, for example, you could install simple door fronts. I'd dispense with the sheet of 3/8-inch plywood in such a project, and buy two full sheets of 3/4-inch plywood instead of only 1-1/2 sheets. Make the two door fronts out of that extra plywood, each of them 32 inches high and 32-1/2 inches wide. If you'd like to use the plastic "carvings" with such doors, there are at least two ways of laying out the 1-by-2-foot decorations. You could put two pieces on each door, one across the top and one across the bottom. A big, highly visible handle completes the design. For a quieter look, you can center one plastic "carving" or a molded wooden one on each door.

No back is needed on a cabinet if you plan to set the piece of furniture against a wall. But if you plan to use this creation as a room divider of some sort, put something attractive as the back. Thin plywood or Masonite is plenty strong, since the shelves will provide support. You can cover the plain-looking material with the plastic "carvings" if you used them on the doors. Otherwise finish the back in the same way you finish the rest.

The fastest way of all to put an attractive back on this free-standing cabinet is with a piece of wood paneling. It's exactly the right width. With surplus paneling you can cover the two sides.

Maybe you'd like a roll-around bar, or a small bar that doesn't roll around. With paneling as its back, or some other appropriate finish, this cabinet makes a delightful bar. No doubt you'll appreciate the convenience of wheels, so invest in a set of casters.

Unless you find some casters longer than 4 inches which you can simply screw to the recessed bottom of this cabinet-turned-bar, you have to cut a block of wood for each corner. There's enough scrap lumber in this project that you should find plenty for the blocks. Then fasten casters onto the blocks.

If you're anxious to build a whole set of new kitchen cabinets, you'll want more than just the glamorous and utilitarian base unit we've already talked about. No doubt you'll want a wall unit too,

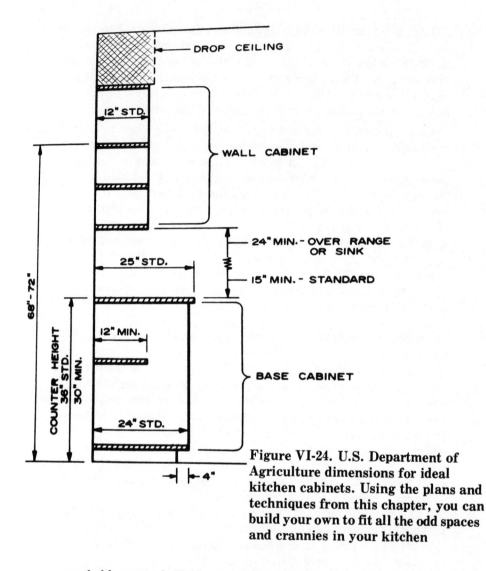

Figure VI-24. U.S. Department of Agriculture dimensions for ideal kitchen cabinets. Using the plans and techniques from this chapter, you can build your own to fit all the odd spaces and crannies in your kitchen

probably several. Unlike the base cabinets, wall units vary considerably in all dimensions but one: Their shelves are almost always 12 inches wide.

I'm going to let *you* create the measurements for your own wall units. Just a few pages ago we discussed how to measure doors so they'll fit cabinets of all sizes and shapes. And Figure VI-24 comes from the U.S. Department of Agriculture, which has studied kitchens pretty thoroughly. The drawing tells you how to calculate the size of your kitchen cabinets.

A typical height for wall units is 30 inches. But in older houses, or newer ones which include a drop ceiling for the cabinets, they may be almost 48 inches high.

Flip back to Figure VI-1 a few chapters back. That will show you how to assemble simple shelves out of 1-by-12-inch pine boards. Make only one important change. If you plan to install *offset doors*, ask your lumberyard to rip off 3/8 inch from the width of all the boards that will become shelves. Let the boards intended for the top, bottom, and sides remain full size. Inside shelves need that 3/8-inch clearance for the offset doors. And by the time you invest in a few boards for your project, most lumberyards will do that bit of sawing for you gratis.

Cabinet-Door Hardware and Handles

You can fasten a very professional-looking handle onto your doors with only one or two small bolts, depending on the type you choose. Figures VI-25 and VI-26 show just a few typical samples from the hundreds you can choose from. If you put on fancy hinges, no doubt the same company offers a fancy handle to match.

Since handles involve drilling a hole (or if you're without an electric drill, poking a hole through the door with a nail), you'd better decide where you want the handles before your final sanding. Don't put the handles on until the finishing is complete. Just have the hole ready.

Doors have a habit of slipping open if there's no hardware to keep them closed. There are two inexpensive ways of keeping your doors shut. One is a magnetic catch—a magnet in a plastic or metal frame is fastened to the cabinet, and a simple steel plate is fastened to the door. When your door closes, the magnet keeps it closed until somebody pulls gently to open the door. This system requires the least precise installation.

The second kind of door catch consists of a "nose" fastened via two small screws to the inside of your door. Somewhere on the cabinet or shelf a spring-steel pincer grabs hold of the "nose" whenever the door closes. For just a bit more money, you can buy this type of catch with soft plastic rollers included on the pincers. The plastic doesn't wear out as quickly, and works more

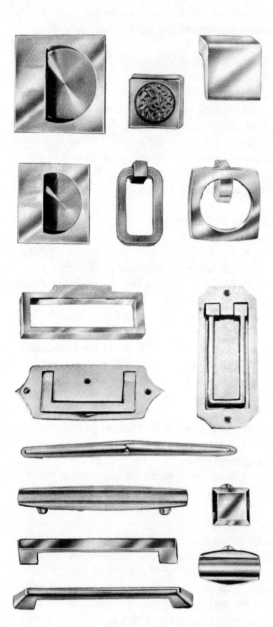

Figure VI-25. A tiny selection of the handles you can invest in. . .

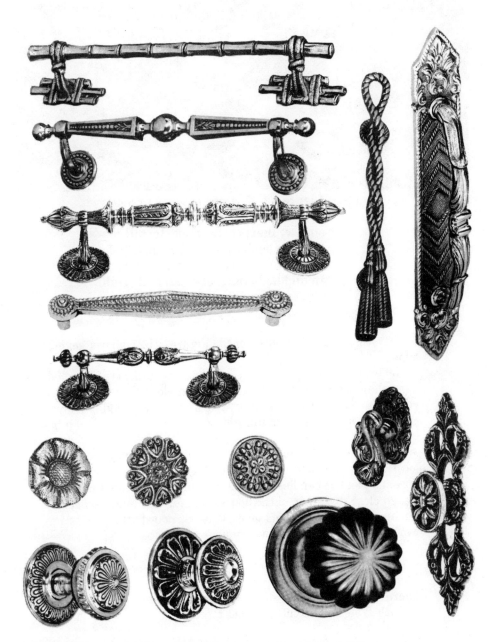

**Figure VI-26. . . . to dress up your own
furniture projects**

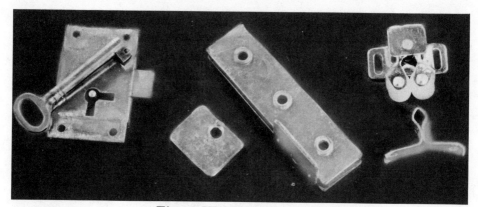

Figure VI-27. Door catches to keep
your cabinet doors closed. At left, a
simple, inexpensive lock. Install it
behind the door and drill small holes
for the key to reach the lock's keyhole.
In middle, a magnetic catch. At right,
pincers and nose

quietly than the all-steel catches. Figure VI-27 shows several
types.

Generally the best spot for a door catch as well as the handle is
near the vertical center of the door and close to its nonhinged
edge. You can put the catch on a shelf near the middle. Or you
can fasten it alongside an upright board that covers the gap between your two doors.

Sometimes you'll deliberately want to move away from ideal
locations for the handles and catches. On a kitchen floor cabinet,
for example, the handles are generally more convenient if they're
placed close to the top of the doors. And for wall units, especially
tall ones, the knobs should go close to the door bottoms. Catches
work best if they're somewhere near the knobs.

Finishing

There really is nothing different about finishing cabinets from
any other piece of furniture. That topic was discussed in Chapter
4.

If you enjoy fine woods, you can invest in 3/8-inch hardwood
plywood for a set of offset doors. For door fronts, use 1/2-inch or
3/4-inch hardwood plywood. Use the 1/2 inch for small doors, 3/4
for bigger ones.

The least expensive finishing touch is with paint or lacquer. That lets you use inexpensive materials, because they'll never show. However, small doors that have been stained look surprisingly warm and natural even in the cheapest of plywoods. You can give it a try without risking more than the price of a can of stain. Either way, you're going to have to sandpaper the wood, and if the stain doesn't come out the way you'd like, you can paint over it a day later! Done up right, your 3-by-4-foot cabinet can become a bar. With Formica on top and paneling on all sides, it's attractive and inexpensive.

Sometimes when the outside of a cabinet is finished, the builder just slams the door and walks away. But there's an inside too! At the very least, you should give the interior of your shelves a coat of wood sealer or varnish to protect them against spills and dirt.

On a piece of furniture that gets opened as often as a kitchen cabinet, the interior doors deserve almost as much attention as the exterior. If you painted the outside, why not paint the inside of at least the doors in the same color? Or paint it a contrasting color. It just might make putting away the dishes a bit more pleasant.

34. Chests with Drawers

SKILLS:	Complicated as a whole, but individual steps are easy.
TIME:	Several weekends.
TOOLS:	Saw, hammer, square, sandpaper, SurForm tool.
ALSO READ:	Chapters 2, 3, 4, 28, 33.

If you like making sandwiches, you'll love these double, triple, and even quadruple chests in your bedroom. All they are, in essence, is a set or two of drawers (covered in Chapter 28) plus a small cabinet or two with door fronts (covered in Chapter 33), sandwiched between a long, broad board on top and another on the bottom.

In order to keep the whole sandwich from resting on the floor, and to give it enough height for convenient clothes storage, you lift the bottom of the chest from 4 to 6 inches. A set of legs can give it a lift. Or you can build a small platform out of plywood or 1-by-4-inch lumber and fasten the chest on top of that. The platform has to be finished and perhaps decorated to match your choice of finish for the rest of the chest. The legs, therefore, require less time.

Many of these chests are very big. On any structure like this which is longer than 4 feet, you need more than the traditional four legs. You'll have to put two legs at each end and another two in the middle on the long chests. That's not an expensive undertaking and it contributes a bit to the long and leisurely appearance of the finished piece.

In general, use 3/4-inch plywood—either fir or hardwood plywood—for the top and bottom pieces. Often you can use the same material for the two outside pieces too. Throughout the rest of the chests, 1/2-inch plywood is plenty big enough.

For either a traditional or modern finish, you'll probably want to leave the door fronts and drawer fronts as simple as possible. You can get a beautiful wood grain by using hardwood plywood and finishing it natural. Or you can later add Formica or vinyl plastics. If you work carefully enough you can cover the edges of ordinary fir plywood with wood-grained tape and then stain the plywood. The best stains for that job are oak, maple, and walnut, as §27 points out.

The various old-fashioned styles call for some ornamentation. You can glue and nail strips of edge moldings to the top and bottom, maybe carrying through the same pattern in the door and drawer fronts. The platform, assuming you use that instead of legs, can also be done up with edge moldings.

As you get more and more fancy, the wooden or plastic carvings can go onto your drawer and door fronts. And a couple of designs, in the right bedroom décor, look splendid with the addition of spindles.

There's a very simple yet attractive way to finish the front and maybe the side too. Buy yourself a sheet of very good wood paneling that will go well with your existing bedroom furnishings. Make all of the door fronts and drawer fronts from the paneling. Be sure the grooved portions run vertically, as they would if you nailed the panel to a wall.

Lay out the door and drawer fronts so your finished chest looks like you glued one or two panels right over the front of your chest and then cut out the various openings. For example, in chest A (see Figure VI-28) you'd cut a piece from the upper left-hand part of your panel about 16 inches wide and 28 inches high. That becomes the door front.

Next you'd cut the four drawer fronts from the piece remaining at the top of the panel. In short, you use only the upper 28 inches of a panel in chest A. The remainder can be put on the sides and used as a back piece.

Chest B (Figure VI-31) requires about 58 inches of paneling. Most panels are 48 inches wide. Therefore, you cover the left-hand door and the drawers in the middle with the upper left and upper right parts of your panel. The right-hand door has to be cut from a lower portion.

One word of warning about the use of panels for finishing chests. There's a great temptation to use the panel on top of the chest too. It sounds like a great idea, but everybody I know who's tried it was sorry. It never looks as good as it sounds.

Speaking of good looks, let's begin a chest by examining construction details. If you and I had unlimited budgets, this wouldn't be necessary. I'd simply tell you to run out and buy half a dozen sheets of hardwood plywood 3/4-inch thick. To save some money, however, I've burned a lot of midnight oil to lay out the parts for each chest in the most economical fashion. The designs pictured nearby incorporate the inherent strengths of all of the materials used as well as the cheapest way of achieving that design.

CHEST A. A simple but nice-looking double chest. One side is drawers, the other some shelves. The addition of spindles at the side makes the piece of furniture look bigger and more elaborate than it really is.

Chest A

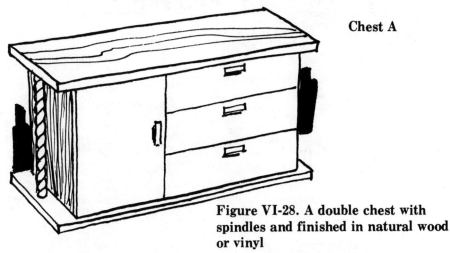

Figure VI-28. A double chest with spindles and finished in natural wood or vinyl

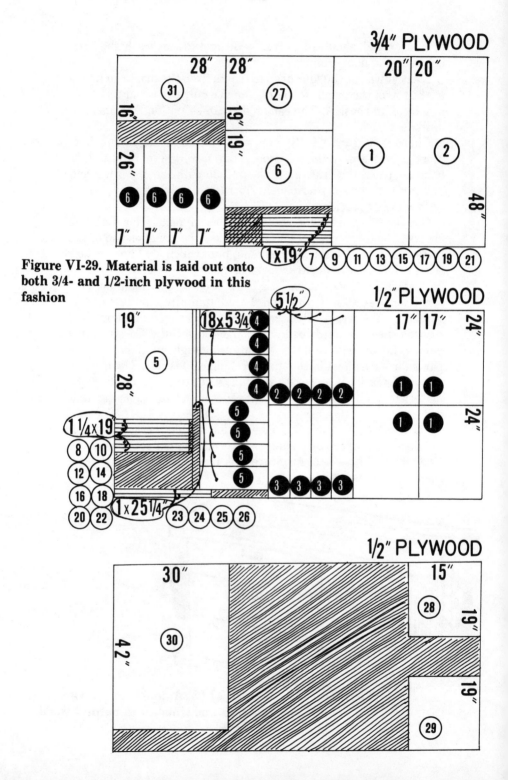

Figure VI-29. Material is laid out onto both 3/4- and 1/2-inch plywood in this fashion

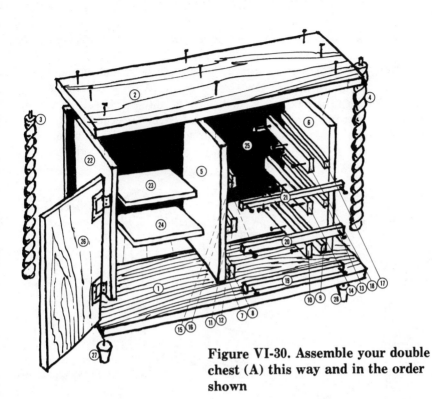

Figure VI-30. Assemble your double chest (A) this way and in the order shown

You can afford the extra top and bottom extensions for the spindles because standard plywood comes in 48-inch-wide sheets. To cover the bare necessities, we only need about 43 inches.

Use 3/4-inch plywood, maybe hardwood plywood for the top, bottom, and sides if you plan to give this chest a natural finish. The right-hand side becomes part of the chest for the drawers. The left-hand part of the chest for the drawer supports is made of the 1/2-inch plywood sheet. You need one sheet of 3/4-inch plywood (good 1 side) and one sheet of 1/2-inch plywood (good 1 side) to make this chest. There's enough 3/4-inch plywood to make all the door and drawer fronts.

Look back to Figure V-15 for details on how to assemble the individual drawers. The drawers back there were only 15 inches wide on the inside. These are 24 inches wide. But all of the other dimensions, and all of the construction details, are the same. Figure V-16 shows how to assemble the drawer supports. We're using some of the 3/4-inch plywood for the 1-inch drawer supports. But the 1-1/8-inch "railings" are still made of 1/2-inch plywood, just as in Chapter 28's tips on how to make all kinds of drawers.

CHEST B. This triple chest has a set of drawers and two sets of shelves. Again, due to the size of standard plywood sheets compared with the amount needed to cover only this chest, bare tops and bottoms, you have enough left over to economically include room for spindles. If you don't want spindles you can leave the extended sides or chop them off closer to the sides of the chest. See Figure VI-31.

Chest B

Figure VI-32. Material for chest B is laid out this way ➤

Figure VI-31. Triple chest, painted and decorated with a light, soft, antiqued paint to fit with French or Italian old-fashioned styles

As displayed in Figure VI-32, this chest is made from one sheet of 3/4-inch plywood for the top, bottom, and two sides. If you like the natural-wood look, you might want to invest in hardwood plywood. For the drawers and drawer fronts, also the back, you'll need two sheets of 1/2-inch plywood (good 1 side).

CHEST C. In order to pack two sets of drawers and one set of shelves into a chest, you need a full 68 inches. See Figure VI-34. That means it's not economical to extend the top and bottom pieces to include space for some spindles. Just as with Chest B above, the basic material list for this project calls for one sheet of 3/4-inch plywood and two sheets of 1/2-inch plywood (good 1 side). However, that doesn't include enough for door and drawer fronts or a back.

Figure VI-32.

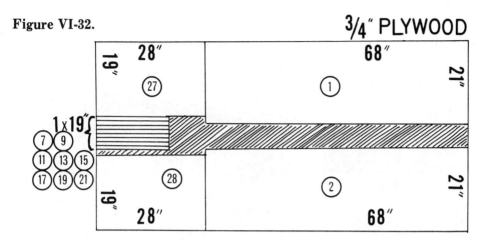

3/4" PLYWOOD

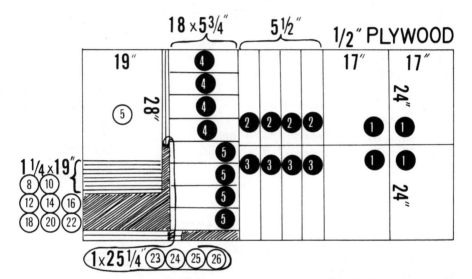

1/2" PLYWOOD

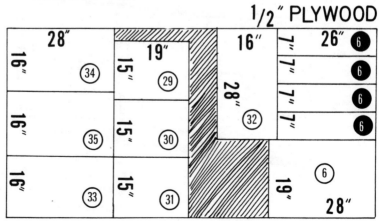

1/2" PLYWOOD

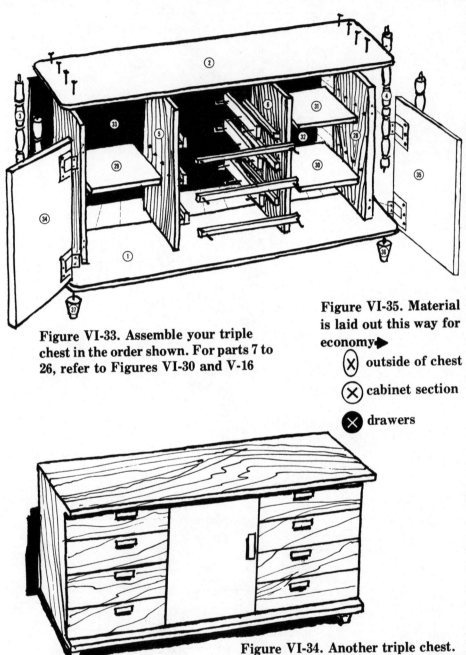

Figure VI-33. Assemble your triple chest in the order shown. For parts 7 to 26, refer to Figures VI-30 and V-16

Figure VI-35. Material is laid out this way for economy▶

ⓧ outside of chest

⊗ cabinet section

⊗ drawers

Figure VI-34. Another triple chest. This one (C) was finished with wood paneling, a fine choice to make this project economical

245

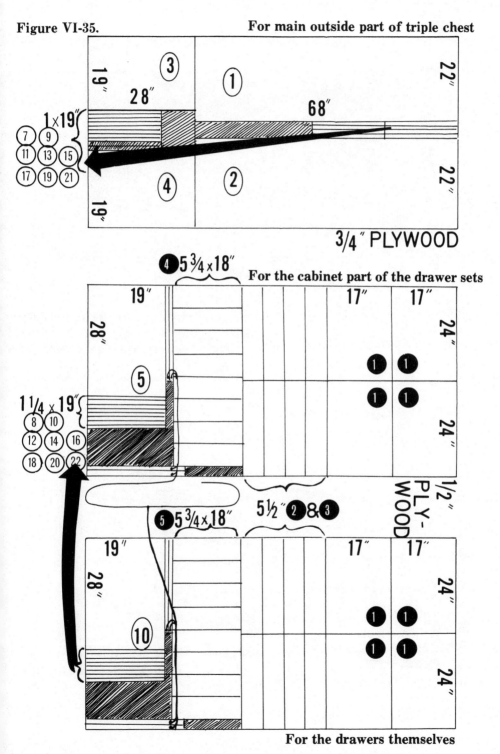

Figure VI-35.

For main outside part of triple chest

3/4" PLYWOOD

For the cabinet part of the drawer sets

1/2" PLY-WOOD

For the drawers themselves

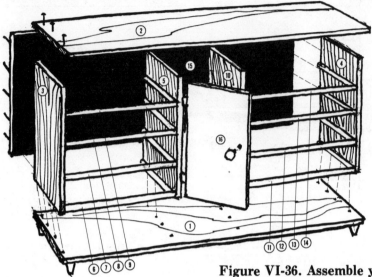

Figure VI-36. Assemble your triple chest (C) this way. Refer to earlier drawings for the drawer assembly techniques and preferred order

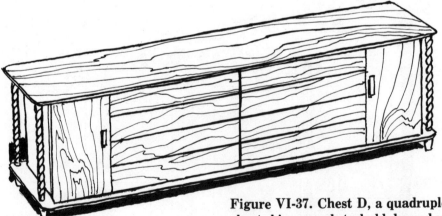

Figure VI-37. Chest D, a quadruple chest, big enough to hold darned near everything

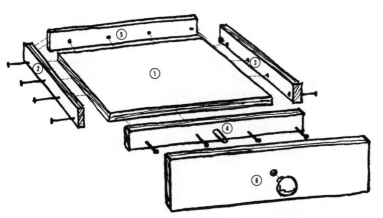

Figure VI-38. Drawers are assembled this way for all of the chests in this chapter

This might be a good chest on which to use wood panels as fronts. Otherwise you must buy another sheet of plywood or other material for the back, doors, and drawer fronts.

CHEST D. This quadruple chest doesn't look cumbersome just because it's big. See Figure VI-37. For one thing, we're showing smaller drawers. Instead of the 24-inch insides which other chests in this chapter used, the doors in nearby drawings are 15 inches wide. That's the same drawer covered in Chapter 28.

From one sheet of 3/4-inch plywood you can cut the top, back, and two sides. To make the drawers you need two sheets of 1/2-inch plywood. That doesn't give you material for door and drawer fronts or a back. Those items require another sheet of plywood. Probably 1/2-inch will meet your needs unless you plan to use a wood panel for the fronts. The surplus paneling will give you a suitable back too.

If you really want to let your imagination run wild, you can expand the dimensions of Chest D to a full 8 feet long! Instead of the 15-inch drawers, make 24-inch ones. The two sets of shelves and two sets of drawers reach out about 86 inches. Since plywood sheets are 96 inches long, you could cut a top and a bottom the long way on your plywood. That would give you about 5 inches overhang on each side. Spindles would go nicely into that 5 inches.

In case the 8-foot chest gets you kind of excited, think ahead a few years. Do you plan to stay put in the house you're in now? In case you ever move, there's a good chance the 8-foot-long and 2-1/2-foot-high chest will not fit through your doorways. (You may not be able to get it out of your work area either!) I once built an immense, beautiful solid mahogany armoire for our bedroom. What a work of art! Then we moved. No number of movers could coax that 100-plus pound armoire through any doorway. So I spent the rest of moving day taking it apart board by board. But it was worth it!

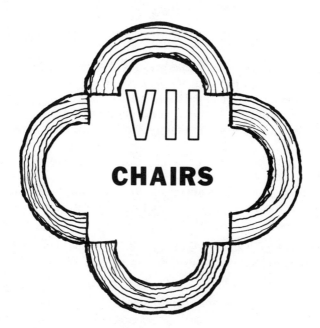

VII

CHAIRS

35. For a Frame, You Get the Chair

SKILLS:	Easy to demanding.
TIME:	An evening to a weekend.
TOOLS:	Saw, drill or brace and bit, hammer, sandpaper.
ALSO READ:	§'s 3, 4, 14, 15; Chapter 4.

If you've ever wondered why gentlemen used to stand up whenever ladies came into the room, here's the answer. Our chairs are so darned uncomfortable, who wants to sit?

At first I thought this book would reveal the secrets of building comfortable chairs. Alas, most of those designs involve either technology beyond the means of home craftspeople, or the appearances are so stark they fall into the ultramodern furniture categories.

But not including chairs at all wouldn't be fair either. If you like the traditional sort of easy chair, side chair, wing chair, or parlor dust catcher, I will reluctantly but cleverly show you how to make them.

Most of the chairs in use today are more similar than you'd think. That surprised me too! With a single frame pattern, six different seats, seven different backs, plus a couple of odds and ends, you can assemble darned near every popular chair on the floor today. Figure VII-1 shows a sampling of chairs you can assemble from the stock patterns in this chapter. The variations are close to endless. But as you decide what kind of chair you'd like to build, here are some factors to keep in mind:

- *Do you want arms or not?* If not, pick any back and any seat. If you do want arms, you have to decide on either wooden ones or a combination of arms and upholstered sides.

- *What back shape looks best?* Without exception, all of the backs can be upholstered. The narrow ones do best if you want natural wood on the back.

- *What shape do you want the seat to be?* If you want arms, pick a seat big enough to accommodate them. Beyond that, simply try to keep your back shape and seat shape compatible. A square back seldom looks good with a round seat. But the trapezoid-shaped back goes well with either a squared or rounded seat.

  Also, the very narrow backs, no matter if they're curvy or straight lined, can be used with seats of all shapes. Unless you include arms, however, these narrow backs have to be used with the smaller series of seats.

- *How much upholstery?* The more padding and cloth you tack onto your chair, the less wood can show. If you don't upholster most of your chair you will inevitably have to use hardwood for the visible parts. That's not a bad idea; the hardwood looks good. You have to decide which you prefer, cloth or wood. The next chapter gets into the upholstering procedures, but don't worry—it's easy!

- *High Seat or low?* You may never have noticed that chairs at the dinner table have a higher seat than the chairs you slouch in around the living room after dinner. Walk around your home with a ruler to see what I mean.

In the nearby sketches of chair styles, the caption tells whether a high seat or low seat is shown. In fact, it's the back frame which determines whether the seat will be situated high or low, and Figure VII-2 shows how to tackle that item.

Figure VII-1. Some of the chairs you can build yourself from the patterns for backs, seats, arms, legs, and frame in this chapter. Below is listed the back, seat, and other parts used for each chair, as well as approximately how much fabric is required to upholster the chair

STYLE	BACK	SEAT	FRAME SIZE	ARMS	WING	YARDS OF FABRIC
A	G	F	38″	—	—	1
B	D	E	38″	—	—	3 (back covered)
C	F	D	38″	—	—	½
D	G	E	38″	—	—	1
E	B	C	30″	C	—	6
F	B	C	30″	C	—	6
G	F	F	38″	B	—	1 (2 if back covered)
H	B	C	38″	A	—	2
I	B	C	30″	B	—	3
J	A	A	38″	B	—	3
K	A	B	30″	A	—	4
L	A	C	30″	C	W1	6
M	B	C	30″	C	W2	6
N	C	B	38″	A	—	3 (back covered)
O	C	B	30″	—	—	2 (back open)

A

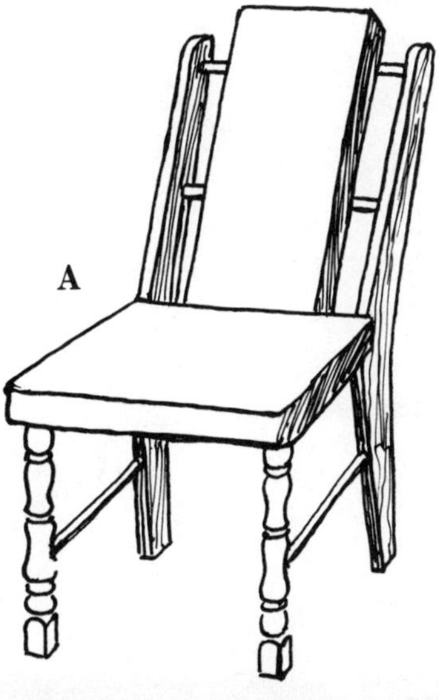

B

C

D

E

F

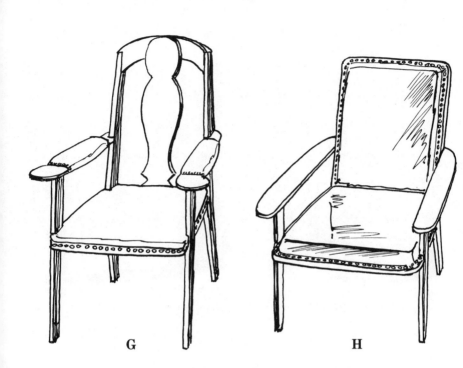

G

H

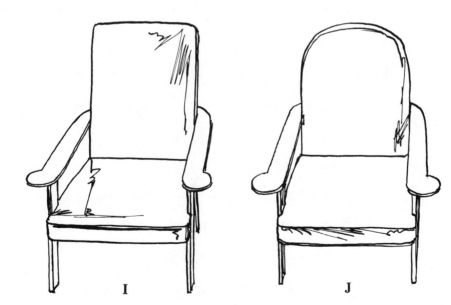

I

J

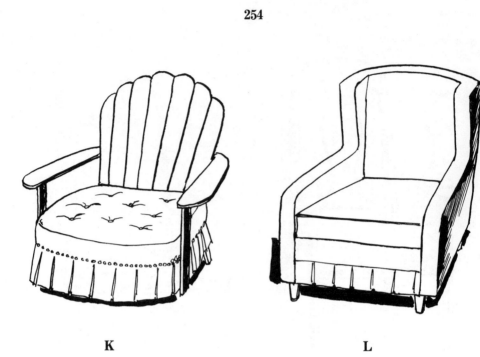

K

L

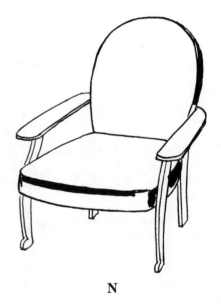

M

N

O

The Back Frame

This single contraption made of wood and dowels acts as the rear legs, the support for a back, and half the support for a seat. So you'd better make it strong.

If you want the back frame to show, make it out of hardwoods of your choice. With a modern décor you might be able to utilize 3/4-inch plywood (good 2 sides), even if most of it will show. If almost all of the back frame is going to be covered by upholstery, you might as well use 3/4-inch plywood, cheap hardwood boards, or any other material you think will be strong now and in years to come. Only the very best pine boards meet that requirement.

Figure VII-2 shows how to lay out the back-frame pattern for both the high- and low-seat chairs. For the low-seat models just cut it off on the dotted line.

Dowels hold the frame together. Buy 3/4-inch hardwood dowels or the closest to them you can find. With a brace and bit or an electric drill fitted with a 3/4-inch hole cutter or drill bit, drill holes according to the numbers given in Figure VII-2. Notice that the holes don't go all the way through the wooden uprights;

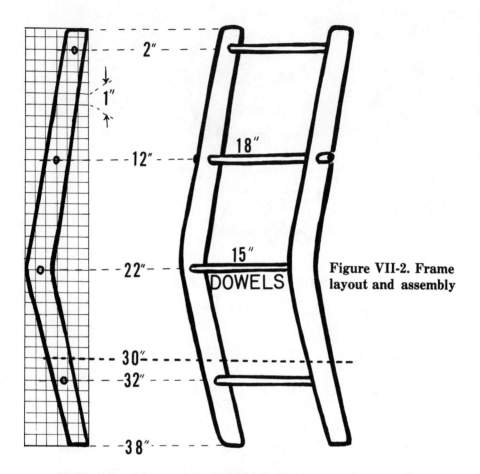

2"

1"

18"

− − − 12" − − −

15"

22"

DOWELS

Figure VII-2. Frame layout and assembly

30"
−32"

−38"

that increases their strength substantially. You can glue their ends as well as their sides that way.

If you're going to add arms to the chair, the dowel holding them to the back has to extend through the uprights. That particular dowel is 18 inches long when arms are involved. Otherwise it can be the same length as the other dowels, 15 inches.

When you assemble the back frame, use nails sparingly. If the upper parts *will not* show, you can drive a 2-inch nail through the uprights and into the dowels. I don't like to see nails used here unless very necessary. If the hole is drilled to the proper size —perhaps made a bit too small and then carefully expanded with rolled-up sandpaper—and plenty of glue is used, the resulting joint is very, very strong.

If you're really good at making the hole and dowel sizes match, you should have trouble shoving the dowel completely into the hole. Air gets trapped in the hole by the stick and glue. So use a knife, chisel, or other tool to make a small slot for the air to escape. Traditionally, woodworkers bought pegs with slots already in them. You'll probably prefer to make your slot in the wooden upright, since that piece of wood is easier to hold on to than a round dowel.

If all else fails, if the dowel wobbles a bit in the hole you've made for it, then pounding a nail is a darned better solution than watching your new chair wobble throughout its lifetime. For wood that shows, make sure you conceal the nail holes (§11 reveals how).

Let the back frame dry thoroughly before you fasten anything else on to it. But in the interim you can be making the back and seat.

Backs

Figure VII-3 shows how to cut your choice in backs out of 3/4-inch plywood or other material. Styles F and G are about the only ones you can make with natural wood unless you go to a good deal of trouble.

Styles A and B are often used in conjunction with "wings" attached to the top of the chair back. Two different wing styles are shown in W1 and W2. Look back to the finished sketches in VII-1 to see how the wings will look after your chair is completed.

If you choose style C for the back, make sure you notice the caption which says it's a wide one. In order to fasten arms on to style C you have to make the back frame wider. Use 19-inch-long dowels for all the connectors except the one which fastens on to the arms. Make that dowel 23 inches long. Tastes being what they are today, if you use back style C, you almost have to use a round seat. Seat style B or E will fit that requirement.

Back style F requires a little woodworking on your part. The top piece has to be cut carefully so that it fits snugly into the gap between uprights of the back frame. You fasten it to the uprights with glue and a nail or two driven from the inside. After the glue dries you have to sandpaper the joints carefully to smooth everything off. The curvy center board fastens on to the seat with glue and concealed nails, plus on to the cross piece, also with glue and concealed nails. Do almost all of your sanding on the center board *before* you install it. Figure VII-4 shows how to tackle chair back style F.

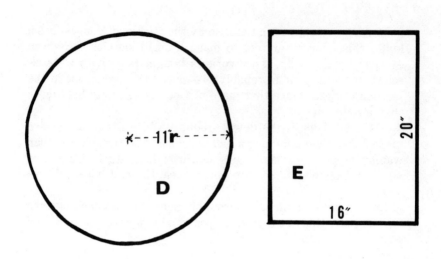

Figure VII-3. Back patterns. Back C requires a 20-inch-wide frame, so cut your dowels 20 inches long instead of 15 as in the standard frame

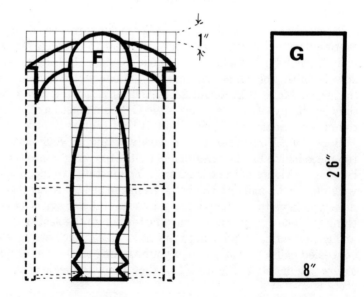

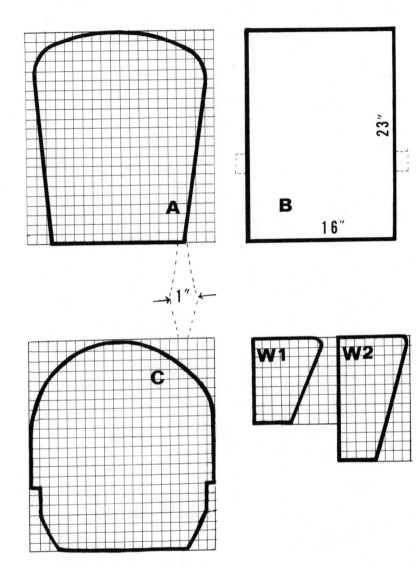

A

B

23″

16″

1″

C

W1   W2

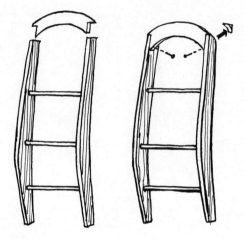

Figure VII-4. Assemble back style D this way

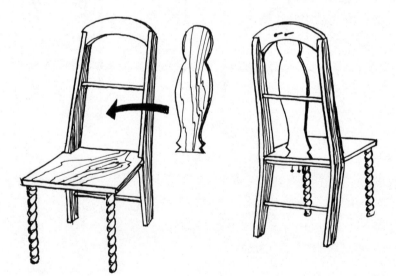

Back style G is attached first to the seat with glue and concealed nails or screws. Then you fasten the back to the two dowels, which keep it from slipping around. Since this connection doesn't support much weight, a single screw or nail through either dowel and into the back gives enough support.

The round back, style D, is a bit challenging to fasten on to the back frame. Easiest of all would be to glue and nail it to the back frame, then upholster it. Trouble is, unless you invested in some fine wood, you'll want to cover the back of that big circle with cloth too. Therefore, the best way of attaching back D to back frames is with screws. Drill a hole in each of the back-frame uprights. Then mark the appropriate two spots on the back of the chair back so you can drill small pilot holes there too. After you've upholstered the round back, screw it to the frame and then conceal the screw holes (see §11).

Other backs attach to the seat and frame easily. Since you'll be doing the upholstery after the attaching in most cases, all you have to do is carefully glue and then nail the back to the seat. And then glue and nail the back to the back frame. After that, you can start upholstering the project.

Seats

From Figure VII-5 you can pick out the seat you enjoy sitting on most. They're all upholstered, so plywood is the most economical choice of materials.

Styles A, B, and C call for arms. And the front arm supports incorporate legs too. If you like the easy-chair appearance with big padded arms which cover the whole side of your chair, only seat style C can be used.

On seats which do not have arms to support them, spindles and turned legs make a beautiful and sturdy set of front legs. They come with their own hardware, which you can attach to the seat in five minutes. The back frame, which forms the back two legs, has been designed to match the available sizes of ready-to-use legs. For a high seat, 16-inch legs are called for. On a low seat, use 10-inch legs.

Arms

For arms you must use hardwood unless you're willing to create a modern style with light, natural-wood finishes on plywood. On

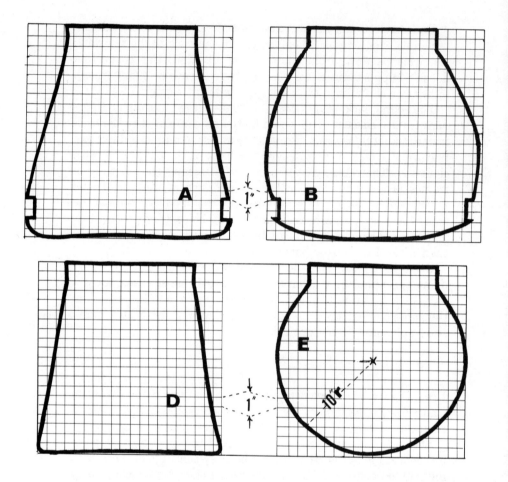

Figure VII-5. Seat patterns

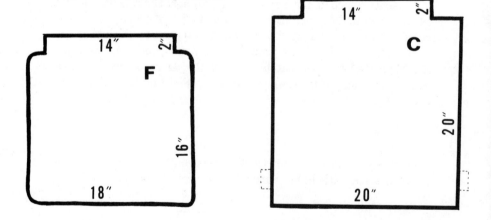

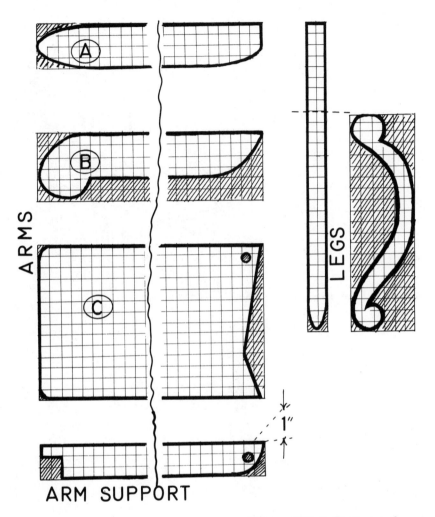

Figure VII-6. Patterns for arms and front legs

many of the chair styles shown in Figure VII-1 the arms are the most obvious aspect of the design, the first part of the chair most people will see. So you should execute them with loving care.

Figure VII-6 lays down patterns for you to use when you make arms. Style A is reserved pretty much for modern and traditional chairs. Style B works for some traditional chairs and the old-fashioned ones. That big side and arm labeled C is for that easy-chair design.

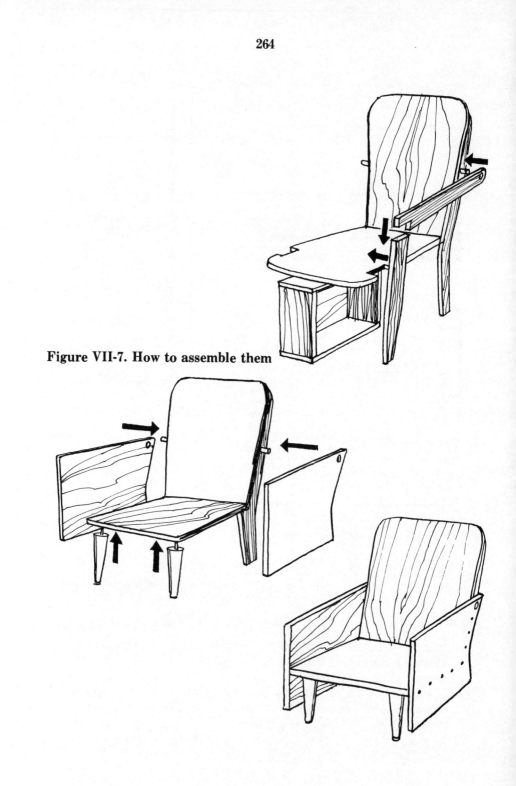

Figure VII-7. How to assemble them

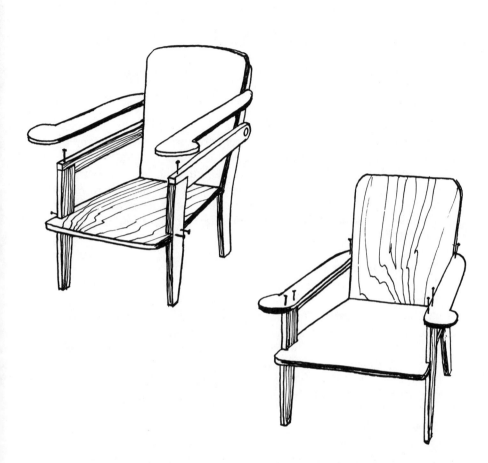

Figure VII-7 shows how to assemble some typical arms. Since anatomy was never my strongest subject, front legs are covered in the same drawings as the arms. Unlike people, they go together in chairs.

In order to integrate all of the comments about backs and seats and back frames and legs and such, a few typical assembly sketches will probably make more sense than more explanation. Figure VII-7 does that job too.

36. Upholstering Your Chair

SKILLS: Easy, maybe very easy.

TIME: An evening.

TOOLS: Hammer, scissors,
                 perhaps a knife.
ALSO READ: §'s 8, 24, 29.

The wooden parts you assembled in Chapter 35 make just the bare bones of a chair. Now you're going to add some muscle and a beautiful skin to form a finished chair.

Upholstering a chair is simple. It shouldn't take you more than an evening unless you want to perform some really fancy maneuvers. The fancy stuff isn't any harder, but it takes longer. Your first step is to go shopping for foam rubber padding and upholstery fabric.

Foam Rubber Padding

This material has become so popular that you can buy it from catalog "department stores," discount centers, dime stores, even some hardware stores. Actually very little real *foam rubber* is on the market these days, since it is heavier and more expensive than polyurethane foam and similar synthetic products. It's unlikely that your local stores are going to stock many different varieties of basic foamlike plastics, however, so take what you can get.

Only if a chair is going to receive plenty of hard use should you invest your money in the most expensive of the foam pads on sale. Even then, make sure your extra money is going for durability and not for some frills.

On the seat and the back, never use foam any thinner than 2 inches. Four inches is much more comfortable and 6 is not too thick for big chairs.

The seat and back patterns in Chapter 35 took into account the various standard sizes of foam pads available. Chances are good that you can walk into a store with the dimensions of your own seat and your own back, give them to the clerk, and minutes later walk away with an inexpensive package of foam pads.

One-inch-thick padding is used mainly for decorative effects where nobody will sit on it. If you plan to upholster the arms of your chair, as in style G in Figure VII-1, the big easy-chair arms are also given the 1-inch-thick padding before you cover them with fabric. The back side of many chair backs are also padded before fabric goes over the top. Used in that way, the

1-inch-thick padding helps to round off the otherwise square corners, but it also keeps the fabric from rubbing agianst edges which might wear through prematurely. And it feels so nice!

Before deciding on the outside dimensions of your seat or back pad, you first have to decide if you want the wooden back or seat completely covered over with fabric. If you used nice-looking wood and prefer the less modern styling, you can use upholstery tacks around the pad and fabric. Take a look back at Figure VII-1 to see the difference. Chairs such as D, G, and H use the tacks. Others on that same drawing completely cover the wooden support and pad with fabric. The choice is yours.

If you want to cover the pad and support completely, choose a pad at least as big as the wooden support. Ideally it should be about an inch longer and an inch wider than the wood.

For the tacked effect, choose a pad about 2 inches shorter and 2 inches narrower than the wooden support. And if you *really* want a lot of wood to show, choose a pad 4 inches smaller than both dimensions on the wooden support. This last style is best executed on the bigger backs and seats such as style O in Figure VII-1. By the time you subtract 4 inches from the size of a smaller seat or back, there's not much room left for padding!

It's seldom necessary to glue your foam pads to the wooden supports. Usually the fabric holds the pads in place very well. But if you have trouble making a pad stay in place while you're working with the upholstery fabric, silicone adhesives bond the pads to the wood very well. Several other adhesives on the market can be used—but there are also many which would ruin the pads. Rather than worrying about whether the glue you buy will eat holes in the polyurethane, you're better off sticking with the slightly more expensive silicone product. Besides, you're going to use the same glue to hold some of the fabric in place.

Fabric

Almost any heavy cloth makes a good chair cover. You can shop in the upholstery fabric department of your local stores or catalogs, or you can shop in any other place that sells heavyweight fabrics. I've found that most people make *appearance* their first criterion when shopping for cloth. *Durability* comes in a poor second. Anyway, if you'd like to buy upholstery material to last a while, here are a few of the more basic standards to watch for.

- *The more threads per inch, the stronger.* In other words, a coarsely woven cloth probably will not be as rugged as a finely woven one.

- *A smooth surface shows wear more than a rough surface.* One reason corduroy wears so well is that it surface is rough. Many mills now offer bright prints on corduroy, which makes it a fine choice for covering chairs.

- *Solid colors show wear more than patterns.* Plaids, checks, prints, and such can be counted on to look better longer than solid masses of one color. If the solids and prints are of the same fabric, the cloth itself will last equally long. But nobody will notice the wear so soon if the worn spots are camouflaged by a mixture of colors and patterns.

- *Blends of fibers often wear longer than unblended cloth.* If the textile mill blends fibers to select the best features of each, then the cloth will outwear its unblended counterparts. If the blending is done simply to cheat on the price, you're going to get stuck. About the only way to cope with this aspect of fabric selection is to buy at a store you know is reputable and from a salesperson who knows the business well.

- *Vinyl?* It's soft and cuddly in the winter time, sort of sticky during the hot summer months. Good vinyl fabrics wear well. Like other upholstery materials, a cheap product doesn't wear well enough to bother with. The other criteria for fabric durability—smooth versus rough surface, solid versus mixed colors—apply to vinyl too.

Here's an important rub to remember—in certain applications, vinyl is hard to work with. Forget about gluing the stuff. It's almost impossible. If you have a yen for vinyl furniture, read through the rest of this chapter to make certain that glue is not an important part of the finishing procedure for your chosen new chair design.

Sharp edges are more likely to poke through vinyl materials than cloth. So if you plan to cover a chair with vinyl, round off the corners and edges.

Buy *fabric-backed vinyl.* Even though the cloth bonded to the back of the shiny vinyl sheet is flimsy, it helps create a very strong upholstery material. The cloth backing has an additional benefit for you too. In case you absolutely must glue the vinyl into place, the glue will bond to the cloth even if it won't stick to the vinyl itself. In such a situation, use silicone adhesives.

When you tack or staple vinyl fabrics into place, don't stretch the material too much. Even with a fabric backing, vinyl can tear if you poke holes in it and apply too much tension all at once. The safest way to tack the ends of vinyl into place is by bending over the loose edges. Then you drive a tack through two thicknesses instead of only one.

The caption of Figure VII-1 includes approximately how much fabric you'll need to upholster a chair of each type. These estimates are approximate, first of all, and they're based on standard 54-inch-wide upholstery fabric. After you've finished reading this chapter, decide how you want to upholster your own chair and measure for yourself the size of the various pieces of cloth you'll need.

Before rushing out to buy cloth, experiment on paper with how best to lay out the required pieces. A single odd-shaped piece may take up more space on a bolt of cloth than several simple shapes.

In the assembly portions of this chapter, sketches will assist you in laying out your materials economically. But sometimes you'll want to capitalize on an intriguing pattern you've found. Then, if you have a creative whim, you may play around with a different sort of layout. That might require more cloth than the given estimate. But who knows—it might require *less*!

Getting To Work

The best way to learn is to do. So let's talk about doing up a chair with upholstery fabric. Style C in Figure VII-1 is the simplest, so we'll start with that.

Lay your foam rubber pad on top of the wooden seat support. Then spread your chosen fabric over the pad. Smooth out the wrinkles.

On both sides and on the front, the bottom of the seat support is pretty unobstructed. You can wrap the edges of your cloth around the edges of the seat without much trouble. Wrap the front first and hold it in place with a few staples or tacks.

Fold over the edges of your fabric just as if you were wrapping

Figure VII-8. Wrap your fabric around seat pads in chairs such as style C in this fashion

a package (see Figure VII-8). Then wrap the left side; tack it in place loosely. Finally wrap the right side, tacking it into place.

Now you can go after the back, which will be a bit rougher. Since the back is fastened onto the seat by this point of construction, cut two slits into the back flap of your piece of fabric for the seat. You have to tuck the center of the cloth under the seat cover so the back can stick through. Then you pull the outside two pieces down and tack them under the seat support just as you did on the other three sides. Figure VII-9 helps you figure out how.

Figure VII-9. Wrap your fabric around the back of chairs such as style C in this way

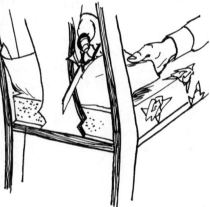

The technique you've just learned will work for the seat on chair style A in Figure VII-1, also for the back in chair A.

Chairs I and J in Figure VII-1 are *almost the same* as the ones just mentioned. The back goes all the way across the chair, however, so you can't just cut a slit into the back of your seat cover. Also, the back on these chairs should have padding at least 4 inches thick instead of the thinner material probably used on style A. So modify the upholstery technique for the seats on chairs such as I and J in just one aspect.

Start at the back of the seat. After you've made sure that the padding and fabric are the right size, lay your cloth on the back of the seat support as Figure VII-10 shows. Through the *back* of your fabric, tack the cloth to the wooden seat support. *Then* set your foam rubber pad on the support, cover the pad with your cloth, smooth out the wrinkles, and proceed to wrap the cloth around the pad and support as we did above.

The front wraps around just as the front did in style C above. But since chairs such as I and J have arms attached to the seat support, you *may* have to slit the cloth to make it fit around the upright arm pieces. If your fabric is pliable enough, it'll stretch around the arm supports. But if it isn't pliable, you'll have to look back at Figure VII-1 and cut the cloth, tuck under the bit near the arm, and proceed normally with the rest of the cushion.

Chair *backs* in styles I and J are done exactly like the *seats* in styles I and J. Start by tacking your fabric to the back support, then put the foam rubber pad into place, and finally wrap the cloth around the pad and wooden support. In the upholstery trade, by the way, this way of tacking something into place and then covering over the tacks with cloth or padding is called *blind tacking*. Or in the case of staples, *blind stapling*. Or *blind stitching*.

Don't let the irregular shape of the back in chair style J throw you. Proceed just as if it were perfectly square on all four sides. As your tacking moves near to the very rounded corners, you'll find that the fabric no longer pulls evenly into place. You may have to put a small fold or two into the corner areas. As long as you fold over the cloth yourself instead of leaving it to chance, and as long as you pull the folded material tight, you'll end up with a neat and professional-looking job. (The alternative to using a few easily concealed tucks like this is a horrible amount of work involving several hours of hand stitching.)

The backs on chair styles I and J need upholstering. What you

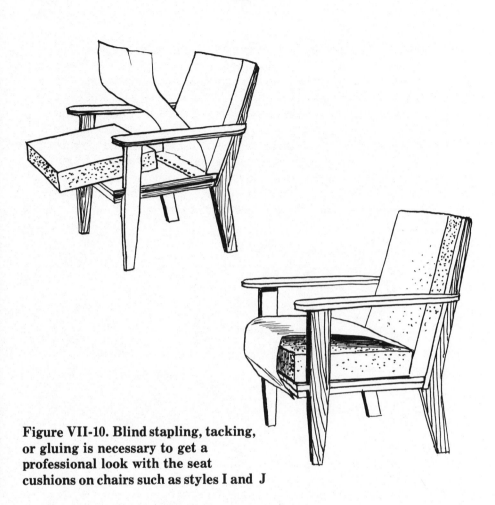

Figure VII-10. Blind stapling, tacking, or gluing is necessary to get a professional look with the seat cushions on chairs such as styles I and J

learn here will also apply to styles E, F, K, and N. You can accomplish this cover-up without foam padding, but the result looks bumpy.

Two-inch foam is about ideal for covering the backs of chairs like these. Figure VII-11 shows the general way to cut pieces of foam which will fit *between* the back frame uprights and on *both sides*. The method for installing foam padding on the back applies to chair styles L and M also; in chairs like that, however, the fabric covering over the back goes on differently than for the chairs we're discussing right now.

Unless you have an extra set of hands, you'd better glue the pads onto the back of your chair with silicone adhesive. Padding in the back has to be in place before you upholster the front. Cloth which you pull tight in the front and around the side has to cover over the edges of the foam on the back of your chair. In fastening the front and side covering to your chair back, silicone adhesive helps hold the cloth to the padding. But your major strength on that job of stretching the front's cloth around the side and to the back comes from tacks pounded into the back frame uprights. Keep that in mind when you buy fabric or cut the cloth. Allow enough so that your front piece can stretch as far as the back frame. It really doesn't take much extra.

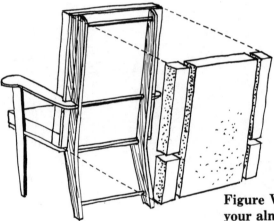

Figure VII-11. Foam for the back of your almost-finished chair

After you've cut the 2-inch-thick pads to fit into the spaces of your chair back—and after you've stretched your fabric from the front, over the sides, and to the back—then you have to cut a piece of cloth which covers the back. Make it an inch or two oversized in every direction.

For the quietest, most dignified-looking chair, glue the back cloth in place. With vinyl, of course, that's impossible because glue doesn't hold well enough to vinyl plastics. For that material you have to use upholstery tacks which either match the fabric color or deliberately contrast with it. You can use tacks on ordinary cloth, too. The tacks lend a flashier or a more old-fashioned appearance to a finished chair.

Even though the sketches show these chairs standing upright during construction, I lay them down to work on them. You should do likewise.

Smear silicone adhesive around the entire edge of your cloth's backside. Then fold over the edges, but don't crease the fold just yet. Using sewing terms, you're creating a *hem*, only with glue instead of thread. (If you're a sewing buff, you can make a stitched hem.)

Start at the top of your chair back. Lay the fabric into place and adjust the folded portions until they match the shape of the top of your chair back. But the edge of your backing material should be 1/4 to 1/2 inch away from the edge of the chair itself. Silicone adhesive holds the back in place.

After the top of the backing is in place, work on one of the sides in the same manner. Then tackle the other side. Keep smearing plenty of silicone adhesive in front of you. If excess glue oozes out, wipe it away promptly.

Finally you can tuck the bottom edge of your backing piece into place. Sometimes you'll notice an annoying bulge at the corners of your back piece. That comes from a surplus of fabric, which bunches up where you fold the side and the top or bottom into the same small area. Before your silicone adhesive dries, snip away much of that excess with a scissors, and smooth down the corners again.

Let your silicone adhesive dry thoroughly before you put the new chair into use. But in the meantime, you can be calling in the neighbors for a look!

Easy Chairs

Styles such as E and F, with big upholstered arms, are just a bit different from the chairs we've already discussed. First, assemble the wooden frame tentatively. Make sure all the parts fit together properly don't let any loose ends or sharp edges slip by to haunt you later, and check the back of your arms. The arms shown in the drawings in Chapter 35 were designed to be used on a chair given 2 inches of padding on the back. If you use less, you'll have to trim something off the back of each arm. If you use *more*, forget it; the excess padding will just round off the appearance.

After you're sure everything fits properly, assemble the seat and the back to the back frame. Put on the front legs. Then go through the whole upholstery procedure for the seat and for the

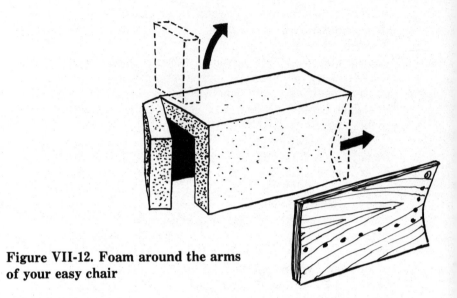

Figure VII-12. Foam around the arms of your easy chair

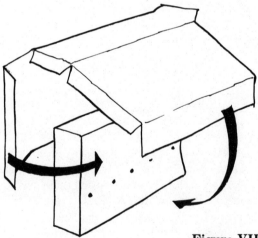

Figure VII-13. Wrap fabric this way around the foam-covered easy-chair arms

front of the back. But don't tackle the backside of the back just yet.

Start to upholster the arms before screwing them to the back. You can use nails, but screws are preferred. Glue 1-inch- or 2-inch-thick padding to the inside of the arms, and cut the rest of the padding so it fits around the arms. Figure VII-12 shows how it should fit when you're all finished.

Cut your fabric for the arm so it fits according to the suggestions in Figure VII-13. Fasten the bottom of the inside piece to each arm. As with the padding, let the rest hang loose until later.

You'll have to poke holes through the fabric and padding on the inside of each arm so that your screws can penetrate your arms' skin. Now install the arms to the rest of your almost-finished chair.

After the last screw through the arm into the seat support and back support is in place, glue the loose flaps of foam to the wooden arm support. And then you can glue the remaining flaps of fabric over the foam. On flaps which will be covered by other fabric, apply silicone adhesive both to the foam rubber side and to the fabric side of the flap.

Wherever they won't show, use ordinary upholstery or carpet tacks to fasten your fabric to wood members. When wrapping the arms in cloth, you'll find room for tacks underneath and in the back.

Once the arms are installed and covered, all you have to do is cover the back. You learned how to do that a page or so earlier in this chapter. Don't worry just yet about the fancy tufting which gives chair style F its distinctive up-and-down dimensionality. In just a few pages, the *Other Fancy Things* section tells how you do it.

Wing Chairs

In Figure VII-1, styles L and M are just like the easy chairs discussed in the section above, but they have "wings" added to them. It *is* possible to upholster these chairs in the same way you tackled the ones earlier, but you'd have a complicated bit of maneuvering to do with the padding and fabric on the sides. So I prefer an alternate plan.

Again, put the wooden pieces together tentatively to make the arms and wings fit together well with each other and with the rest of the chair parts. Then pull off the wings and arms for the time being, and pad and upholster the seat and back.

In earlier pages we talked about gluing, padding, and tacking fabric to the inside of the arms. Do the same here, but don't include enough padding and material to swing over and cover the outside of the arms too. Attach padding that is just big enough to cover the inside surface to the arms and to the wings. The single piece of fabric that you tack to the armpiece should be big enough to cover the inside of the arm and the inside of the wing. Leave enough surplus cloth attached so you can "hem" these inside pieces later on.

There is no need for you to run padding all the way to the bottom of the inside arm support. If you look at chair styles L and M in Figure VII-1, you'll see that only the very upper portions show. To cover all of the inside arms would be a waste of material. Besides, you'll need some bare wood to tack fabric for the outside of your arms.

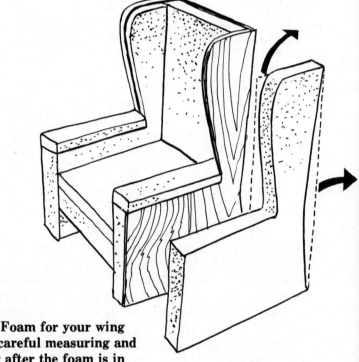

Figure VII-14. Foam for your wing chair requires careful measuring and some trimming after the foam is in place

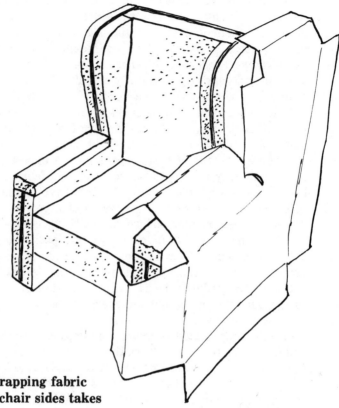

Figure VII-15. Wrapping fabric around the wing-chair sides takes patience

It's a good idea to tuck the front of your fabric around the front of your arm support *before* you screw the arms and wings into place. But if that proves cumbersome, you can always force the front flaps into place later and hold them there with plenty of silicone adhesive.

Now you can screw the partly padded arms and wings into place. If you can, pad the outside surface of each arm and wing set with a single piece of foam rubber. But if not, carefully glue one piece to the arm and another piece to the wing.

Extra padding from the outside or inside surface—or both —covers the edges of the arms and wings (see Figure VII-14). At this point of the installation you can glue the inside padding to the plywood. But don't glue the fabric into place just yet.

If you want the edges of your wing chair to be nicely squared, instead of pulling foam from the sides of your arms over to the edges, cut them off even with the edge of the plywood. Then cut another piece of foam, a long one equal to the width of your plywood plus the double thickness of foam rubber. Glue that onto the arm and wing edges. But if you'd like the edges rounded off, then bend the foam over to cover up those edge surfaces.

Each side of your new wing chair will be covered with a single piece of fabric. But cut the piece so big that there will be enough material to flip over the edges of the wings and arms and then still allow a couple of extra inches on the opposite side. Since there is no way to tack these side pieces of fabric except at the bottom and back, silicone adhesive will have to single-handedly hold them in place. So give your glue plenty of area to grip the surface of foam rubber underneath it. (Figure VII-15)

As you pull the side fabric firmly into position, apply liberal doses of silicone adhesive to foam rubber along the *edges* of the arms and wings. Also apply glue to the *inside* where the fabric will meet the padding. Don't use silicone adhesive to hold fabric to the padding on the outside areas of the arms and wings or you'll end up having troubles later on.

Here's a good schedule to use when you stretch the side fabric and fasten it into place: 1) Tack the bottom. 2) Glue the top region of the arm. 3) Glue and/or tack the front. 4) Glue the top of the wing. 5) Glue the front of the wing. 6) Tack the fabric to the back frame supports or glue it to the foam padding.

After all of the outside fabric on the wings and arms is fastened down, then tackle the loose pieces on the inside. "Hem" them with glue as you fit the cloth against the arms and wings. And then glue the cloth to both the foam and the ends of fabric hanging over from the outside cover. What you're doing inside your arms and wings is comparable to what you read about a few pages ago when covering the back of a chair like this.

The next step, of course, is covering the back. We discussed that earlier in this chapter, just before the subject of easy chairs was raised.

Round Seats and Backs

If you've read this far, you already know how to cover a round seat cushion or a round seat back. There are a few tips to keep in mind, however, if you want to keep your upholstering as simple as possible.

Buy the most flexible fabric possible. Wrapping cloth around padding is hard enough on square surfaces. Round ones make you fold over excess fabric more frequently, unless your chosen upholstery fabric can stretch at least a bit.

Try to stay away from big, bold patterns. If you have to fold over some cloth on the side of a round cushion, it will show up a lot if the fold interrupts a big, dark circle or line in the pattern. It will show up a bit in solid colors. It won't show up at all in a very delicate or busy pattern.

In a way, the chair in Figure VII-1, style O, is one of the easiest round chairs to make. Even if the color bunches up around the sides of the round back and round seat, the roughness fits right into the style. However, many people want something more genteel, like styles B or N. With them, proceed just as you would with a squared-off cushion.

Tack the front of the seat cover in place first, then the back of the seat cover. Move around the sides slowly. Tack then stretch, tack and stretch. Every time the cloth won't stretch evenly, make a fold. But make sure the openings in your folds all point backwards so they'll be less conspicuous.

When you're ready to glue a cover on the back of chairs such as styles B and N, you'll find that making a round "hem" can become tedious, especially with heavy fabric. If you find that fabric underneath your glued hem bunches up too much, keep snipping V-shaped notches into the material. The point of your V should be just barely turned under the hem, and the big part should be well toward the center of the back cover.

Rounded, Slanted, and Squared Cushion Shpaes

One way to cope with the complexities of covering a round cushion with stiff fabric is to alter its edge shape. Just because a foam rubber cushion starts out with squared-off edges, it doesn't have to end up that way.

If you pull the fabric covering a foam rubber pad just hard enough to get rid of wrinkles, but not hard enough to change the shape of the padding, you end up with a squared edge on the cushion. That's true no matter if the surface of the cushion is round, square, trapezoid, or rectangular. When you pull harder

on the fabric, the edges of the foam rubber are squeezed together. The effect is a rounding off on the side of your cushions.

To carry this effect even further, you can feather the edge of
your cushions. If you trim away a quarter or even a half of the
foam rubber near the outer edge of a cushion, when you pull the
fabric covering tight enough, the cushion slopes gently from a
high center to a low but rounded edge. Cut foam away from the
cushion where it will rest on the wood, not where the fabric
touches the foam. Figure VII-16 graphically shows the art of
changing the shape of pillows.

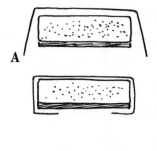

Figure VII-16. You can control the
shape of your seat and back cushions.
In style A, the fabric is pulled rather
loosely around the standard foam
cushion. In B, the fabric is stretched
tightly enough to round off corners.
Foam is trimmed from the *bottom* side
of the cushion, and the fabric is
stretched very tightly to achieve the
look in style C

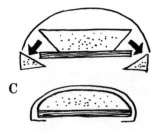

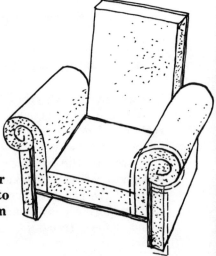

Figure VII-17. A rolled look on your
easy chair or wing chair arm is easy to
obtain. Simply *roll* some 2-inch foam
rubber. The dotted line shows how
fabric is glued

You can alter the shape of arms, backs, and other chair features by using the same techniques of pulling harder or softer. Try for uniformity, however—if you round off the back, round off the seat too. If you feather the seat, you should at least round off and preferably feather part of the back too.

You can change the shape of various parts of chairs even more drastically by using rolled-up foam rubber. Figure VII-17 shows a couple of places this jellyroll technique looks good—arms and backs in particular.

Nails

For a rugged appearance with durability to match, you can leave wood showing around the edge of upholstered cushions. In that case, nails—or to be more precise, fancy upholstery tacks—hold the fabric in place.

In Figure VII-1, styles D, G, and O make good use of the decorative upholstery tacks in conjunction with wood. A couple of other styles do use visible tacks, but the wood has been hidden. We'll tackle them in a few paragraphs.

To use nails in your new chair, pull your upholstery cushion covering to the edge of the wooden support, but not all the way around to the back. Decide in advance how much wood you want to show and draw a light pencil line at that point.

Since the fabric edges are unattractive, even if you fold them into a makeshift "hem," pros generally use the nailing technique along with *edging*, which you can buy at most curtain, upholstery, or sewing centers. It comes in different styles, sizes, and colors. Pick out a variety you think goes well with the fabric you've chosen.

Fold over the loose fabric at the front of your chair first, then lay the edging right at the very edge of the fold. Shove a fancy upholstery tack through the edging and the folded fabric. Then hammer the tack into the wood. Fold the fabric for another couple of inches, lay the edging into place, and drive home another tack.

On your first excursion around the edge of a chair cushion, space the tacks several inches apart. When the fabric, edging, and foam rubber pad are securely in place, then go back to put tacks in between and closer together. In general, the final nails are spaced about an inch apart, but you can put them closer together if you want. For a really flashy effect, the rims of the tack heads can almost touch each other.

Fancy upholstery tacks come in all kinds of colors as well as brass and silver. You can even find some with a hammered look or a leathery look. Pick out a style that appeals to you, calculate roughly how many tacks you're going to need, and stock up with at least the proper number of tacks in advance. If you run short in the middle of a project, you may have a devil of a time matching an unusual tack head.

Style K in Figure VII-1 shows another use for tacks. In that chair, no wood shows around the upholstering. The cushion cover is pulled down to the *side* of the plywood support. Instead of narrow edging, a wide flounce is placed on top of the upholstery fabric before tacks are driven into the wood.

You can buy ready-to-install flounces in sewing and upholstery stores. Or you can use tasseled edging. It's easy to make your own flounce from odd pieces of the material you're using to cover the rest of your new chair.

To make your own flounce—the best approach, in my mind —you must hem both top and bottom of the flounce. But that doesn't mean you have to *sew* a hem into it. You can buy a thin strip of iron-on hemming material, or a powder that glues the cloth into a hem after you run a hot iron over it. Both materials work well if you follow the directions on the package.

Figure VII-18 shows how to turn out a dandy flounce with the iron-on strip. If you like the appearance of your chosen strip, iron it to the *outside* of your flounce where it will show. But if you'd rather conceal the stuff, iron it to the inside. If you hide the iron-on strip, however, you'll then have to buy some narrow edging to give your chair a finished look. The upholstery fabric goes directly against the wood, your flounce comes next, then any edging you use, and finally the upholstery tacks.

The bottom of your flounce is given a small hem only to keep fibers there from unraveling, which sooner or later, would result in an ugly chair. In case you're working with a very heavy fabric, even an iron-on hemming material is tough to work with. You might want to use an alternate method. After the flounce is made, trim the bottom with a scissors until it looks neat. Then dip the very edge of the bottom in a diluted polyvinyl glue.

Dilute your Elmer's Glue-All with an equal part of water. After the diluted glue dries it will be colorless, but will hold the fibers in place so they can't unravel. The glue will also make the bottom of your flounce stiff, which is why you shouldn't apply the glue until after your flounce is folded and fastened for good.

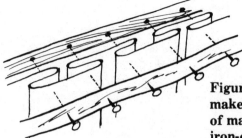

Figure VII-18. Flounces are easy to make, and they finish off the bottoms of many chairs. At left, how to use iron-on hemming tape if you like how the tape looks. You leave it showing that way. Below, how you tackle the same flounce, but conceal the iron-on tape which forms the flounce pattern

Other Fancy Things

Chairs L and M in Figure VII-1 show another kind of flounce. Since the arms extend lower than the seat support, a flounce fastened to the seat smooths out the chair bottom. The flounce you tack onto chairs L and M is handled exactly like the one discussed just above for chair K.

The two easy chairs, E and F in Figure VII-1, also have a piece fastened beneath the seat support to level out the looks of the chair bottom. You could just as well attach a flounce there if you like the appearance. The plain, fabric-covered piece shown in Figure VII-1 can be adapted to most chairs, lending a more luxurious feel and appearance.

Figure VII-19 shows how to create the padded inset for an easy chair. The best time to fasten it into place is just after the arms have been screwed to the rest of your chair. Padding is optional, but since legs and feet may rest against the inset, it's nice to include some foam rubber under the fabric.

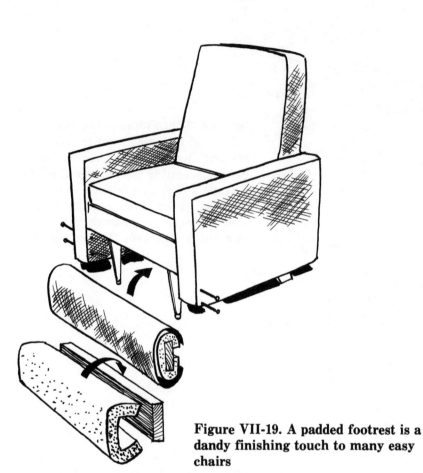

Figure VII-19. A padded footrest is a dandy finishing touch to many easy chairs

Tufting is a fairly complicated upholstery process, at least the way it's always been done until now. The desired result is that up-and-down look to a cushion; upholstered buttons at the bottom of the "down" areas; and an expensive, plush look to the finished chair. In Figure VII-1 chairs F, K, and M have used some tufting.

Personally, I'd say Chair F used too much tufting. K and L used just about the right amount. But you have to decide how much is right for you.

Ironically, the idea of tufting a chair dates back to days when loose cotton was stuffed into a chair as padding. It used to shift around and cause lumps, so upholsterers invented tufting buttons as a way to hold the cotton in place. Since foam rubber padding doesn't have such problems, all you have to do is mimic the tuft-ing effect with a minimum of labor.

Even before you cover a foam rubber pad with fabric, you have to plan for the tufting. First decide whether you want a square tufting pattern or a diamond-shaped one. The differences in ap-pearance are subtle at most.

Then sketch a pattern onto the surface of your foam pad. Start by putting a dot about every 6 inches starting at the very center of your pad. Test first to see whether you should put a dot on the center or whether two dots should straddle the center. If putting your first dot on the center brings your outside dots closer than 3 inches to the edge of your pad, then make your first dots straddle the very center.

Figure VII-20 shows how to create a pattern after your dots are marked. Draw lines between your dots, forming either a square or a diamond-shaped pattern. Then cut your foam with a razor blade or very sharp knife. Cut along the pattern lines until you come within an inch of the bottom of your foam.

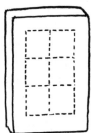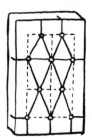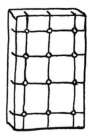

Figure VII-20. Tufting a seat back with either a square or diamond-shaped pattern

I prefer to do the tufting before the seat support or the back support is screwed into place on the chair. Lay your wooden support flat on a table or floor with the sliced side pointing up-ward.

Lay your fabric on top of the foam, smooth it out, and then grab a bunch of fancy upholstery tacks plus your hammer. In an intersection of two sliced lines near the middle of your pad, push a tack down through the fabric, through the foam and into the wood. Hammer it into place once you've made certain that it's in the correct place.

Select a second point where two sliced lines come together. Just before you poke a tack through the fabric and foam at that point, smooth out the cloth. Encourage the folds and excess fabric to fit into the sliced groove. That's why you put the slices there in the first place.

When nearby cloth looks neat, poke your second tack through the fabric and foam. Then hammer it into place.

Move slowly from the middle tufts toward the edges. As you go along, keep smoothing the excess cloth and folds into the slices. When the last tuft button is hammered into place, allow the edges to hang loose. Then fasten the back or seat support onto the frame of your chair and proceed with the rest of the upholstering according to advice given earlier in this chapter.

Chair style J in Figure VII-1 features channels on its back. You can make them in much the same way we just talked about making tufts.

Delicate chairs generally have delicate channels, about 4 inches apart. Bigger, heftier-looking chairs feature channels as big as 6 or even 8 inches apart. Chairs with a trapezoid-shaped back—as with style J—require channels bigger at the top than at the bottom.

Figure VII-21 shows how to cut a channel pattern into the back of chair style J. After drawing the pattern lines you slice through the foam to within an inch of the bottom. The top also has to be sliced an inch or two deep. Channels are pretty nearly always used on the back of chairs only.

Again, I prefer to work on channels while the wooden support, pad, and fabric are laid out on a flat table or floor. Spread your fabric over the support and pad, smooth it down, and then take up tacks and hammer.

Start with the center channel. Use your fingers to force the fabric right down to the very bottom of the channel. Then smooth it out carefully. Starting at the bottom, tack the cloth to the wooden support every 3 or 4 inches. Use tacks that match the color of your fabric closely, because you don't want them to be obvious when the job is finished. Unlike tufting, which is always done with tacks or buttons, channels have traditionally been created with blind stitching. To duplicate that appearance, therefore, your tacks have to remain inconspicuous.

After the first channel has been tacked down, force fabric into the next slice. As you do so, you have to pull the cloth tightly enough over the foam padding that it gets rounded off. Channels have to be round like a scallop, not squared like a razorback hog.

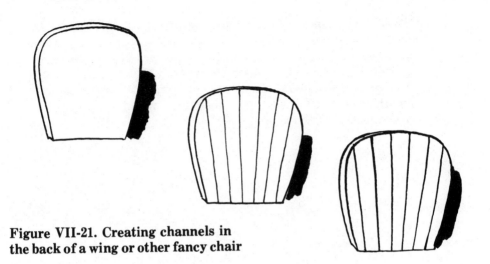

Figure VII-21. Creating channels in the back of a wing or other fancy chair

Once you've successfully pulled just the right amount of cloth into the slice, hold it there and tack the channel into place. Then move on to the next slice. Leave the ends hanging loose until you've mounted the wooden back support into the rest of your chair.

There are a couple of alternate ways to create channels. Both avoid the possibility that your tacks might be seen by some sharp-eyed neighbor. First of all, it's easy to shove a staple gun into the sliced opening after you've smoothed out the cloth. Staples do the job quickly and they're small enough to be easily hidden.

If you're handy with a needle and thread, you can stitch your channels into shape. Use a big needle and heavy thread.

Cut strips of corrugated cardboard about an inch wide and as long as your pad is high. Put a strip behind your pad every time you start to stitch a new channel. The cardboard will keep your thread from pulling right through the flimsy foam rubber.

Lay your foam pad on a table instead of the wooden support which will eventually go under it. Stuff fabric into the first slice and stitch it there. Be sure you use the cardboard backing strip.

Stuff fabric into the second channel, being sure you round off the foam while you pull on the cloth. Stitch that channel into place, again with a cardboard backing strip. When all of the channels are ready, glue your pad to the plywood backing. Then proceed with the rest of your chair upholstering in the way described earlier.

When you plan to channel your chair back, cut the back pad about 2 inches higher than the wooden back support. That way, when you stretch the fabric around to the back of your almost-finished chair, the curve of each channel can be extended all the way around to the back. That makes a very nice-looking chair, something every professional upholsterer would be proud to show off. And so will you!

VIII
THE
PLAYROOM

37. A Chair That Grows

SKILLS: Very easy. A great
             first project.
TIME: An evening.
TOOLS: Handsaw, hammer,
             sandpaper.
ALSO READ: §'s 1, 2, 10, 11, 16, 26,
             27, 28.

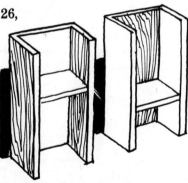

Figure VIII-1

When Junior or Sis are ready to act like big folks and sit down to play, they need a tiny chair. They get kind of attached to that first chair of theirs, however. They won't give it up even after they're so big their knees bump their chin whenever they sit in it.

Here's a homemade remedy. Build a first chair for each of your children. In its "early-days" position, the chair is just right for a 1- or 2-year-old, even some 3- or 4-year-olds (Figure VIII-1).

When the day arrives, however, all you do is flip the chair over and it's big enough to hold 6- and 7-year-olds comfortably. There's no magic to it. No hardware has to be switched around to make the little chair big.

The single board which acts as a seat is 8 inches from the top and 14 inches off the floor. Or you could turn it upside down and say the single board which acts as a seat is 14 inches from the top and 8 inches off the floor.

Whichever way you look at it, you can build this thing in an evening. In fact, you should be able to make three or four of them in an evening. They make great presents!

Buy yourself a 7-foot-long piece of 1-by-12-inch pine or hardwood. (Most lumberyards stock 8-foot lengths, so you'll have a foot left over for another project.) Make the four straight cuts shown in Figure VIII-2 with a handsaw. Round off and sandpaper all edges that will remain exposed. Then glue and nail the pieces together in the order shown in Figure VIII-3.

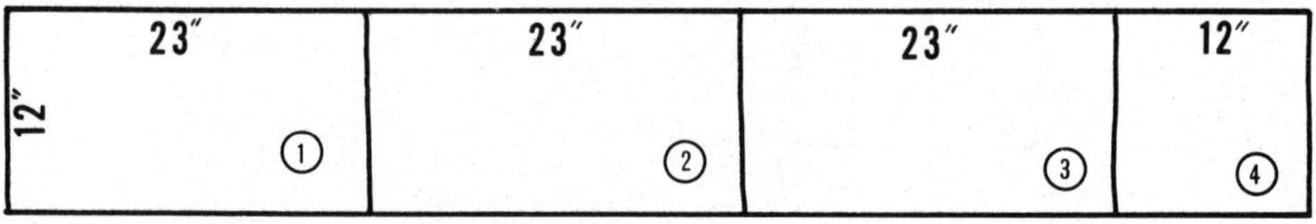

23″	23″	23″	12″
①	②	③	④

12″

Figure VIII-2. Material for your growing chair comes out of a single 1-by-12 board 7 feet long

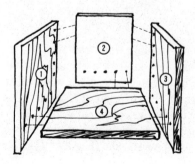

Figure VIII-3. Assemble the chair in this order

Give your assembled chair a good going-over with fine-grade sandpaper and then with extra fine. Paint the reversible chair, if you like, or give it one of the durable natural-wood finishes described in Chapter 4.

You'll want to give the chair extra finishing coats in evenings to come, of course. But by the morning after your first finishing coat, you can turn the chair over to its new owner for an exciting tryout.

38. Toy Chest

SKILLS:	Easy if you read and look at instructions well.
TIME:	A weekend.
TOOLS:	Saw, hammer, sandpaper.
ALSO READ:	§'s 4, 10, 11, 14, 15, 16, 26, 27, 28.

You've just stepped on the kids' skates for the last time! But what are you going to do? Buy one of those trunk-style toy chests which don't hold much and encourage kids just to toss everything into a big enclosed pile? Or invest in an upright toy chest with lots of little shelves and nooks, but which looks like it's built from cardboard and won't last beyond New Year's Day?

Here's your answer—an immense toy chest (Figure VIII-4) which has doors, shelves, and a big trunk-type compartment to boot. It's made entirely out of 1/2-inch plywood, making it so rugged you'll probably still have it when your grandchildren come to visit.

You need two sheets of 1/2-inch plywood. It helps if you buy good-2-sides grade. But if price is an object, buy the good-1-side grade and a small can of Plastic Wood to help you fix up the blemishes in the bad side. Your investment in plywood is about equal to the cost of one of those smaller, weaker toy chests on sale downtown.

Figure VIII-5 shows how to lay out all of the necessary pieces

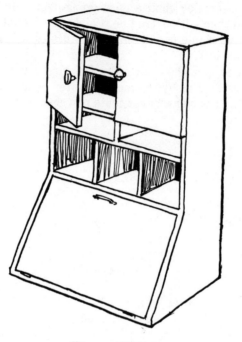

Figure VIII-4

on your plywood. That much material will give you a toy chest 4 feet high and over 3 feet wide.

Before you assemble all of the pieces into one big toy chest, sandpaper all of the edges that are going to show. By the time the four shelves and seven supports are in place, sanding will be a lot rougher.

The assembly drawings in Figures VIII-6, 7, 8, and 9 lead you through a four-step process. Don't let the four separate assembly drawings lead you to assume it's a tough job. It isn't.

Since most playrooms are small, it might be tough to assemble all the shelves outside the cabinet and then shove them into the completed cabinet. So I'm sharing with you, via the four assembly sketches, my own trial-and-error experience so you can find the easiest and strongest way to fasten the whole thing together on the first try—and in a minimum of floor space.

First build the cabinet part. After you've fastened the top and bottom to the two sides, the whole thing is pretty shaky. So lay it carefully on its front. Then lay the back piece (part #5) in place.

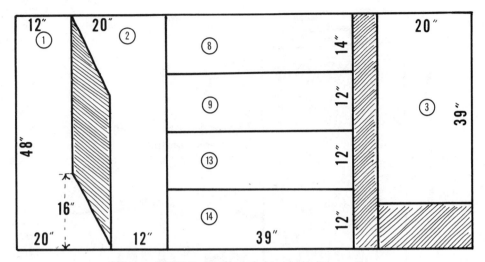

Figure VIII-5. Material for your toy chest should be laid out onto 1/2-inch plywood this way to get the most for the least cost

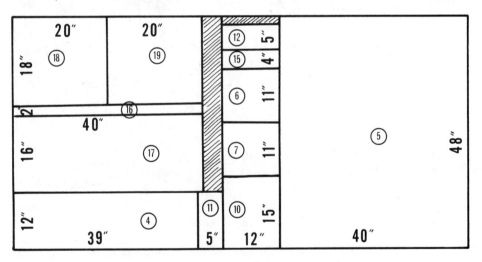

Look at Figure VIII-5 for a moment. Notice that the back piece (part #5) was deliberately laid out so that three of its four sides fall on the factory-cut edges of the plywood. That means three of the four sides on your back piece should be straight and

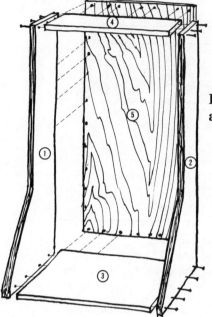

Figure VIII-6. Assemble the outside and back portions first

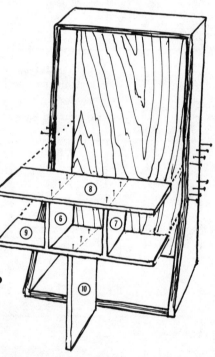

Figure VIII-7. Make the bottom two shelves with their supports next

square. Use those three factory-cut edges of the back to line up the rest of your cabinet. Then nail the back in place. Lay the cabinet on its back while you install shelves.

When the cabinet is done, assemble the bottom two shelves and their supports. Set that assembly into the cabinet, make sure it's flush against the back, and then nail the shelves into place from the sides only. Don't flip the cabinet over yet. You can nail the shelves from the back later.

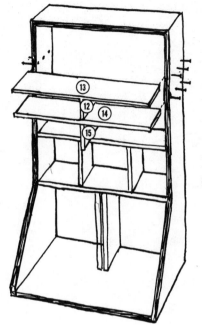

Figure VIII-8. The top two shelves and supports come after that

At this point you can assemble the top two shelves and their supports. Set that collection into place and nail it from the sides.

While the cabinet is still lying on its back, and only after all four shelves have been firmly nailed from the sides, then you can nail the two loose upright supports (parts #10 and 15) to the shelves beneath them. If you try to make that connection too soon you could bend some of the nails holding the shelves to the side of your cabinet.

After all of the shelves and supports have been glued and nailed into place, flip the chest over so you can nail the back onto all of the shelves and supports. Your job will be easier if you first draw the exact location of the various shelves and supports onto the back of your back piece (part #5).

Use 1-inch finishing nails throughout. Space the nails about 3 or 4 inches apart everywhere but on the back, where you can get away with 6-inch spacing.

Hinges for the three doors have to be rugged enough to withstand years of childish abuse. That's a tough order for hardware which can't be wider than the 1/2-inch plywood. So put three hinges on each of the doors instead of the traditional two.

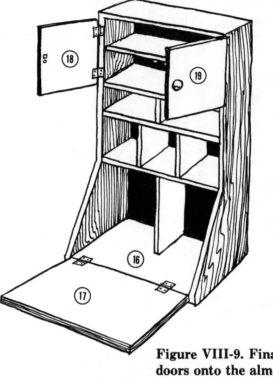

Figure VIII-9. Finally you can fit the doors onto the almost-finished toy chest

If you don't plan ahead, the big bottom door will probably get plenty of extra abuse. Kids will love to open it and use the door as a ramp for bicycles, trucks, and roller skates. Which doesn't help the door, hinges, or supports. You might think about putting your hinges on top to counteract that problem. But Junior or Sis then would have to lift it up to get at their toys, and a door that size is pretty heavy even for a 4- or 5-year-old to lift.

The best kind of hinge for the bottom is a *spring-loaded* one. If you put three big spring-loaded hinges on the bottom of the bottom door, after the kids take out what they want to play with, the door closes again. (This arrangement makes a lousy ramp, as your kids no doubt will soon tell you!)

If you're a real tyrant and want to put spring-loaded hinges on the two top doors as well, saw 2 inches off each door. Nail those 2-inch strips where the hinges will go. Make sure to nail it to the top, the upper two shelves, and to the side of your new toy chest.

With those 2-inch strips in place, you have plenty of room to screw some spring-loaded hinges there too. Chapter 33 presents plenty of open-and-shut advice about hinges and how to install them.

If you prefer bright colors, finish your toy chest with paint or lacquer. You can also give the plywood a natural-wood finish. Here's an ideal place to use the colored wood stain, the mixture of oil and enamel which leaves the grain showing through bright colors. Chapter 4 tells how.

If you really want to do this chest up proud, invest in hardwood-veneer plywood at the outset. If you do, you'll end up with a handsome family heirloom. The hardwood grain will match the appearance of all those expensive creative playthings like blocks and trucks and planes made from natural woods. But make sure you give your wood the hardest possible finish so the kids don't wreck your heirloom in just one generation.

39.   A Play Table That Grows

SKILLS:	Easy.
TIME:	A weekend.
TOOLS:	Saw, coping or keyhole saw, drill or brace and bit, wrench or pliers, sandpaper.
ALSO READ:	§'s 4, 7, 10, 12, 16, 17, 21; Chapter 4.

Every time a youngster gets bigger, it seems furniture for the playroom or bedroom has to get bigger too. If you're tired of that replacement grind, here's a workbench or desk you can build for a very modest investment of both money and time (Figure VIII-10). And it will never be outgrown.

This table starts out about 21 inches small, a nice size for little shavers just ready to start playing on a table. Call it a workbench then if you like, or a play table.

As your youngster's own legs get longer, the legs on his play table get longer too. First it gets boosted to 24-1/2 inches tall. Finally Pop or Mom can adjust the "table that grows" to have full-size, 28-inch legs. By then, you'd want to call it a desk.

A set of three drawers is simple enough to make, as Chapter 28

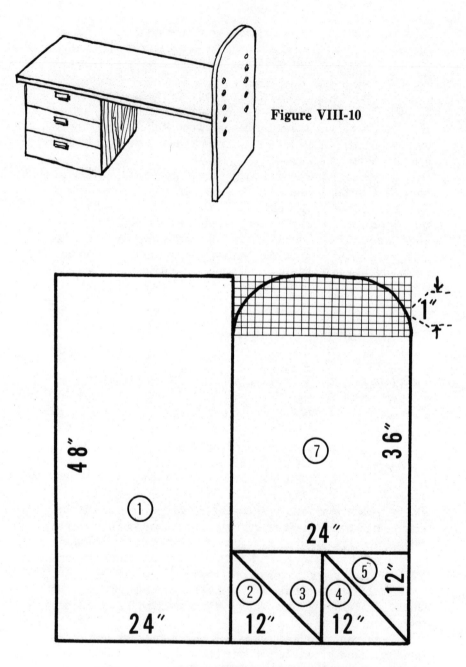

Figure VIII-10

Figure VIII-11. Materials for the table
are laid out this way

shows. You might want to buy a set of ready-made drawers at an unfinished furniture outlet. Going that route costs a little more, but will save you a couple evenings of work. Try to buy a set of drawers that measures close to 21 inches high.

From a half sheet of 3/4-inch plywood, cut the top, side, and braces shown in Figure VIII-11. You'll have four small triangular pieces when you're done cutting. Nail and glue them together into a pair of braces each 1-1/2 inches thick.

Figure VIII-12. Assemble the "table that grows" in this order

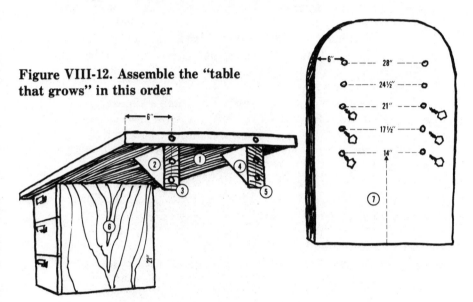

Glue and nail or screw each brace to the bottom of the table's top. The edge of each brace has to be right at the edge of the top. The center of each brace should be exactly 6 inches from the closest long edge of the table top. Figure VIII-12 shows the layout pictorially where it may make more sense to you.

Now you have to drill holes for the four big lag screws which will go through the side piece to hold up one side of the top. The set of drawers supports the other side of the top. If you made your own set of drawers and it came out to 21 inches high, then you can copy the dimensions given in this chapter. Draw two vertical lines on the side piece. Each line should be 6 inches from the edge to match the center of your braces.

Mark where the holes must go. From the bottom draw a mark at 14, 17-1/2, 21, 24-1/2, and 28 inches. Do the same for both lines.

Drill 1/4-inch holes at all the marks on your end piece. You'll drill five holes along each of the two lines, ten holes in all.

Next you have to drill pilot holes in the table top and braces. Make your first 1/8-inch pilot holes right in the middle of the 3/4-inch-plywood edge directly in line with the center of the brace. Glance at Figure VIII-12 for a picture of where the holes have to go. Drill additional pilot holes 3-1/2 inches and 7 inches below your first holes.

With your table top resting on the 21-inch-high set of drawers, you should be able to put screws through the bottom holes of the side piece and into the bottom holes of the brace. And you should be able to put other screws through the second and third holes in your side piece which will fit into the middle and top holes in your braces.

Don't use ordinary wood screws. Buy some stainless steel *lag screws*. They look like big screws with a square head instead of a slotted head. Buy 1/4" × 2" screws. You'll need six in all.

Fill up the unused four holes with bolts. Buy stainless steel machine bolts, 1/4" × 1-1/2". Make sure their heads match the heads on your lag screws. Put small washers under all of the screw heads, nuts, and bolts so you won't ruin the table's finish as you tighten up the hardware.

When this project is all finished, you'll have enough holes and hardware to adjust its height from 21 inches up to 28 inches. All you need is a pliers or wrench to loosen up the six lag screws which support the top. Then you loosen up the nuts and bolts which decorate the unused holes. Put the lag screws into the appropriate new position and fill up the unused holes with the nuts and bolts.

You adjust the height of your drawers which support one side of the top by adding inexpensive legs. To make the jump from 21 inches to 24-1/2 inches, buy a set of 4-inch legs. If you install them in an angled position, they raise the drawers about 3-1/2 inches. You can compensate for slight irregularities by putting a glide under the legs on the drawer side or under the side piece on the opposite end.

When you're ready to make the move up to a 28-inch-high table, invest in a cheap set of 8-inch legs. Installed at an angle, they raise the drawer set very close to 7 inches. Again, compensate for small amounts of unevenness by putting glides under one side or the other. Some legs, in fact, have adjustable glides built in.

In case you buy a set of ready-made drawers which is not 21 inches high, you have a bit of mathematics to perform. The spacing shown in Figure VIII-12 for the five holes in the side piece won't work for your drawers. Follow along, however, and the math will be relatively painless.

Let's call the height of your drawers D no matter whether it be 22 inches high, 25 inches, or any other size.

- Subtract the height of your drawers from twenty-eight. That's how far below the hole in your plywood top the hole in each brace piece should be, $28'' - D = X$

- Divide X by 2. That's how far apart the five holes in the support must be, $1/2X$

- Start with your first hole at $D - X$ inches. Then add $1/2X$ inches to locate your next hole. Add another $1/2X$ inches for the next hole. Continue that way until you've marked all five holes. The top hole should be 28 inches off the ground.

For example; let's go through the math for a set of 24-inch drawers. First you jot down $28'' - 24'' = 4''$. So $X = 4$ and $D = 24$.

According to point 3 above, the lowest hole on the side piece is drilled at $D - X$. And in our example, $D - X = 20''$. So you drill the first side-piece hole 20 inches off the ground.

Point 2 above says that each hole above the first is spaced at $1/2X$. And $1/2X = 2''$. Therefore, the next hole is drilled 22 inches off the ground. The remaining holes go at 24, 26, and finally 28 inches.

The pilot hole in the table top is always in the same position no matter how high or how low the drawers may be. But the two holes in your braces have to match the spacing of holes in the side piece. Therefore, pilot holes in the braces are spaced 2 inches and 4 inches below the pilot hole in the top.

Finish

Cover your "table that grows" with the toughest material you can afford. Formica-type plastics are none too strong for curious and active youngsters. If you go the Formica route, buy enough to cover not only the table top but *both sides* of the side piece too. In other words, you will need a 2-foot-wide piece of Formica, 10 feet long. Covering the three drawer fronts with Formica is also a good investment.

As an alternate, you can lacquer or paint this desk, or give it a natural-wood finish. If you think your kids are not the destructive kind, you might save a little labor with a natural-wood finish. It's almost ageless. Youngsters and oldsters go for it.

If you build this table for young kids, please don't use thin vinyls for a finish. Rough kids can finish it in weeks! And then you'll have to peel it all off before you can refinish the table with anything other than Formica. Even the heavier plastics such as MacTac are often torn apart by scissors, sharp trucks, and fertile imaginations.

If you use paint or lacquer in your family's formative years, you can add a more mature finish in later years. Con-Tact vinyl or MacTac will stand up to most high-school kids. Just as your table legs grow, the finish on your table can grow too.

Index